A Discourse-Centered Approach

Texas Linguistics Series

A Discourse-Centered Approach to Culture

Native South American Myths and Rituals

by Greg Urban

 University of Texas Press, Austin

First paperback printing, 1993

Requests for permission to reproduce material from this work
should be sent to Permissions, University of Texas Press,
Box 7819, Austin, Texas 78713-7819.

∞ The paper used in this publication meets the minimum
requirements of American National Standard for Information
Sciences—Permanence of Paper for Printed Library Materials,
ANSI Z39.48-1984.

Library of Congress Cataloging-in-Publication Data
Urban, Greg, 1949–
    A discourse-centered approach to culture : native South
American myths and rituals / by Greg P. Urban. — 1st ed.
        p.   cm.—(Texas linguistics series)
    Includes bibliographical references and index.
    ISBN 0-292-78526-7 (pbk. : alk. paper)
    1. Indians of South America—Religion and mythology.
2. Shokleng Indians—Religion and mythology.   3. Indians of
South America—Languages—Discourse analysis.   4. Language
and culture.   I. Title.   II. Series.
F2230.1.R3U73   1991
299'.88—dc20   90-19324
                                                              CIP

Contents

Figures

Tables

Map

Acknowledgments

*F*or her clarion insight into the clinical dimensions of acting out and talking out, and for whatever intuitions about unconscious motivation may have filtered into this book, I am indebted to my wife, Dr. Tricia Kent. My friends at the University of Texas at Austin—especially Steve Feld, Laura Graham, and Joel Sherzer, whose own research and collegiality have my admiration—helped to make this book possible. Warm thanks also to the Center for Psychosocial Studies in Chicago, and especially to Benjamin Lee and Bernard Weissbourd for their continuing support and intellectual companionship, as well as to other members of the path-finding group on "Text and Social Action" that met in Chicago from 1986 to 1987. Dennis Tedlock skillfully reconnoitered the tangled underbrush of an earlier draft, helping me to avoid numerous pitfalls; I thank him for it. A remarkable young man, Nanbla Gakran of the Ibirama Shokleng, worked with me for a year, transcribing and translating the words of his elders, which are reflected herein; to him and to other members of the community I am deeply grateful.

Portions of the present book were previously published in the *American Anthropologist,* the *Journal of American Folklore,* and *Native South American Discourse* (ed. J. Sherzer and G. Urban, Berlin: Mouton de Gruyter, 1986). I thank the respective organizations for the right to reuse these materials here in modified form. Field research in Brazil in 1974–1976 was funded in part by a Doherty Foundation grant. Further field research in 1981–1982 was assisted by a grant from the Joint Committee on Latin America and the Caribbean of the Social Science Research Council and the American Council of Learned Societies, by a grant from the University Research Institute of the University of Texas at Austin, and by a summer grant administered through the Institute of Latin American Studies of the University of Texas at Austin from funds granted by the Andrew W. Mellon Foundation. I gratefully acknowledge the help of these institutions.

If, in literature, the work of art as such
is the form of expression of an idea,
it is all the more so in folklore.

—Vladimir Propp (1976:281)

CHAPTER 1

An Approach to Culture and Language

*T*he discourse-centered approach to culture is founded on a single proposition: that culture is localized in concrete, publicly accessible signs, the most important of which are actually occurring instances of discourse.[1] While seemingly innocuous, that proposition opens up alternatives to the view of culture as an abstract system of meaning through which reality is apprehended and social order established. In the latter view (which came into prominence in the 1960s but has its roots in the linguistic structuralism of Ferdinand de Saussure and the sociological functionalism of Emile Durkheim), culture is assumed to be shared, even though it is not localized in concrete signs, and to exhibit continuity over time. In the approach reflected here, and in other discourse-centered work, the extent of sharing and continuity is opened to empirical investigation through the comparison of actual instances of discourse usage.

To view culture from the vantage point of socially circulating discourse is, simultaneously, to gain a new perspective on those objects that have so often fascinated anthropologists—myths and rituals. In the case of myths, a dominant paradigm of the 1970s was structuralism, associated with the work of Claude Lévi-Strauss and especially with his four-volume series (Les Mythologiques). Lévi-Strauss approached myths as narratives or stories in whose referential content one could glimpse the structuring logic of binary oppositions, such as the vertical space opposition (up : down or high : low) reflected in the "bird-nester" myths of central Brazilian Indians. A boy out searching for fledgling birds with one of his relatives climbs a tree or the side of a cliff, but is abandoned there by his male relative and is unable to descend until rescued by a jaguar. The vertical opposition intersects with the human : animal or culture : nature opposition in the guise of the (human, cultured) relatives versus the (animal, natural) jaguar.

From a discourse-centered point of view, however, the challenge is to see the myth not as a mental object, but rather as concrete, unfolding discourse. We do not lose sight of the boy in the bird nest, but, momentarily at least, we situate him inside the words carried along by sounds and then written down on paper and recopied and recirculated. How to see that the boy exists not in the world of the senses in a direct way, but rather in publicly accessible discourse, which in turn inhabits the sensible world; how to relocate him, giving him a place within the discursive community of which he is a part, rather than, or in addition to, the mythical village of which he seems to be a part; how to question his immorality or perdurance as a cultural symbol not on myth-internal grounds but on the grounds that, when the myth is told again, it is told differently—those are the challenges of an approach to culture from the perspective of discourse.

It is true that natives may essentialize myths by giving them names, although, as often as not, this is done by the ethnographer rather than by the native (as in "The Origin of Fire," "The Jaguar's Wife," or "The Monkey's Son-in-Law" from Lévi-Strauss's *The Raw and the Cooked*). The name lends to the myth the appearance of a thing, an object that transcends the instance of discourse in which it is momentarily trapped. The boy threatens to break out of his confinement in spoken or printed words and to assume an independent life in the mind, whether in the minds of the central Brazilian Indians or in those of the readers. But naming is itself a discourse practice, in this case, a metadiscursive practice, the name being about the discourse segment in question (as in "this is a story about . . .")—and metadiscursive practices, of which naming is one, require ethnographic investigation as part of the social circulation or life of discourse more generally. They provide no evidence for or against the existence of a Platonic form behind the shadowy occurrence of discourse. While there are two levels—the metadiscursive naming and the discourse instance, that is, the myth telling—and while one level seems to freeze the other, fixing it for all time, it remains for empirical investigation to determine precisely in what measure it does so. What are the relationships between one telling and another? Is there a myth that is told and retold or is each telling unique? To be sure, if we are dealing with culture that has been passed on across generations, the given instance is a copy of some earlier instance of discourse, but in what ways is it similar and in what ways different?

We have not yet brought into conceptual focus the boy in the nest, although we have established that he leads a double existence, a dual life. On the one hand, he wanders in a mythical world where jaguars speak, hunt with bow and arrow, and monopolize fire (leaving humans to warm their

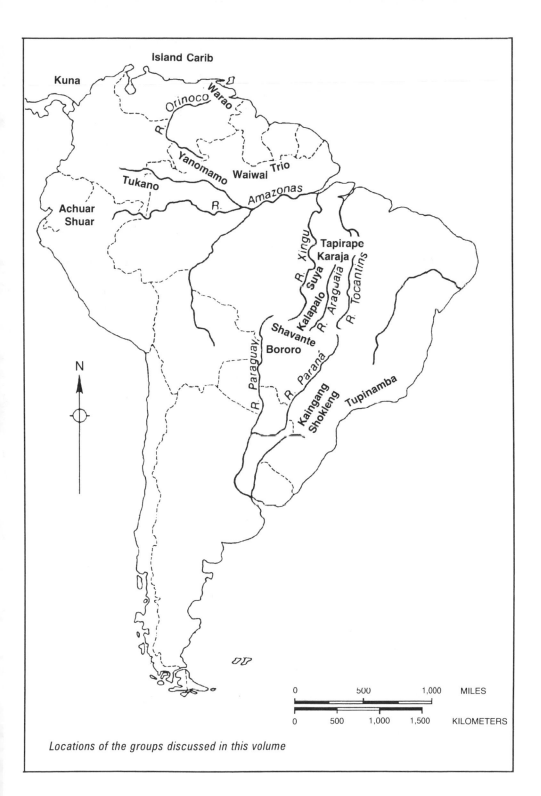

Locations of the groups discussed in this volume

meat by setting it out on rocks in the sun); on the other hand, he inhabits the sensible medium of speech or print, circulates within a discourse community in ways that remain to be ethnographically described, and changes and evolves over time, as the discourse in which he is embedded alters in the course of numerous replications and recontextualizations. But his life within the mythic world has not been linked to his life inside the moment of discourse; it is as if the two were unconnected, parallel lives—the discourse merely an indifferent vehicle for this other worldly object.

In fact, however, the other world is built up out of discourse itself, embedded in a social context; his life unfolds as part of a momentary, historically specific instance of speech, analyzable in terms of linguistically identifiable segments—phonemes, morphemes, lexemes, phrases, and clauses—as well as in terms of the parallel relationships between the constituents over the linear time of the text (cf. Hymes 1981), and, finally, in the case of spoken forms, in terms of pause, intonation, and voice quality (cf. Sherzer 1982; Tedlock 1983; Woodbury 1985). The discourse, as a concretely occurring sign vehicle, mediates the boy's dual life, for it is here that he is identified with microsegments of the longer discourse, segments that are decodable as lexemes or as anaphoric pronouns and that enter into syntactic relationships with other microsegments decodable as nouns and verbs or their substitutes; these relationships, spread out over the seconds or minutes of the myth narration or reading, produce his life. The transformations of structural analysis, which Lévi-Strauss identifies with the human mind, confronting sensuous, concrete experience, are recast from this angle as structures operating at the level of momentaneously unfolding discourse.

Lévi-Strauss's work—whose greatness is by no means diminished by its resituation from the point of view of contemporary discourse research— carefully elaborates, in almost painterly fashion, the social and natural world confronted by the mind in the course of myth production—down to the minutiae of central Brazilian flora and fauna and their habits. The shift in emphasis in the 1980s, however, questions whether it is the mind or discourse that confronts the sensuous world—or, alternatively, if it is the mind, then whether the mind should be equated with the brain or with the reservoir of discourse for which the community functions as a holding environment. There is an important difference: the mind as brain confronts experience from a purely intellectual standpoint; the mind as discourse, alternatively, includes the intellect, but it also includes more. If spoken or printed discourse is a vehicle for thought, it is also a tool for persuasion and manipulation, for commanding and coordinating actions, for kindling and expressing emotions, and for maintaining social relations. Rather than subvert the aims of structuralism, discourse research recontextualizes them, opening up for investigation the multiplicity of meanings that myths as utterances encode. Chapters 2–4 take up this problematic for Brazilian Indian myths, with special reference to the south Brazilian Shokleng. Chapters 5–7 extend the discussion from mythic discourse as ritualized to ritualized speech more generally.

In some respects, the bird-nester poses an inverse problem to the *mudyi* tree, the dominant symbol of *Nkang'a*—the girl's puberty ritual of the Ndembu studied by Victor Turner (1967). Whereas the boy analyzed by Lévi-Strauss resides in discourse, the *mudyi* of *Nkang'a* resides in the empirical world, a well-wooded plateau whose streams flow into the Zambezi River; and whereas the boy threatened to break out of his confinement in concrete speech or print, taking on an independent life in the mind, there can be no question about the concreteness and localization of the *mudyi* or milk tree (*Diplorrhyncus condylocarpon*). Its phenomenal reality is beyond doubt, from its visual to its tactile properties, including the milky substance extruded by its bark upon laceration. The sheer physicality of the milk tree, and of the ritual surrounding it, overwhelms the imaginary and intangible life of the bird-nester as a mental object.

However, the milk tree for the Ndembu is more than a physical object; it is a symbol possessing ideological meanings—human breast milk, the mother-child bond, and matriliny as the principle of Ndembu unity—and also contextual meanings, pertaining to social differentiations of women from men, daughter from mother, and own matriline from other matrilines. In his justly celebrated analysis, Turner (1967:20) distinguishes the types of data from which these meanings are inferred: "(1) external form and observable characteristics; (2) interpretations offered by specialists and by laymen; (3) significant contexts largely worked out by the anthropologist." The methodology permits the anthropologist access to the relationship between Ndembu and physical things, in a manner analogous to, albeit distinct from, the access Lévi-Strauss achieved through myths to the central Brazilian Indian mind as it confronted the physical and social world. The careful attention to naturalistic detail is important here: the milk tree exudes a milky sap, visually reminiscent of breast milk, which is associationally linked to the mother-child bond, which is in turn linked to the principle of matriliny. Informant testimony confirms that this path of associations is at work.

The physical object—the milk tree—like the bird-nester, leads a dual life: on the one side, it lives in the physical world accessible to the senses, presenting itself phenomenally through its visual, tactile, and perhaps also olfactory, gustatory, and even auditory properties (the rustle of its leaves, the sound made when it is struck); on the other side, it lives in discourse, where it is not the milk tree, but, for the Ndembu, the *mudyi*. As part of discourse it has a separate life, circulating in the community, undergoing transformations, taking on properties as a discourse entity situated with respect to other discourse. It is the *mukulumpi*, the "senior" tree of the ritual. Turner tapped into this circulation through the method of exegesis or elicitation from informants—a method that proves inadequate in central Brazil, for example, where there is no analogous circulating exegetical discourse—but for him the words provided access to the meanings possessed by the physical object or, rather, lodged in the relationship between the Ndembu and the physical object.

But other possibilities are opened up by the perspective from discourse. We see the meaning not as accessible through the spoken words, as if it were in some independent realm, but rather as residing in them. We see that the spoken words have in turn a public life that is both objective—as much so as the particular specimens of *Diplorrhyncus condylocarpon* Turner observed—and subjective; that it is not only the Ndembu as physical organisms but also the discourse reservoir of the Ndembu community that confronts the milk tree; and, finally, that the circulation of spoken words can be the subject of ethnographic investigation, alongside the investigation of physical objects and behaviors. We do not lose sight of the physical object, but we see that it has a double, an *alter* whose objective form is wholly distinct, consisting not of branches and leaves but of syllables and sounds. And we see that the environment of the latter is not only the deciduous forest of the Zambezi drainage, but also the adjacent sounds and syllables of actual instances of discourse, together with the historical residue of past instances.

Turner's clairvoyance in distinguishing exegetical from observational and contextual data cannot be overestimated; it presaged discourse research in the 1980s, which came to shatter the unity of exegesis with the physical object and to appreciate more and more the independent life of the former. At the same time, Turner continued with a model of meaning, at least ideological meaning—and, hence, culture—as abstract and shared, the same model that allowed Monica Wilson to "base her entire analysis of Nyakyusa ritual 'on the Nyakyusa translation or interpretation of the symbols'" (Turner 1967:26). These shared meanings were read through the exegesis. Moreover, despite his emphasis on exegesis, like so many of his colleagues, he paid little attention to the forms of discourse—such as songs and chants—that actually occur in the rituals themselves. There was a precedent within social anthropology for ethnographic research on linguistic usage, Malinowski's *Coral Gardens and Their Magic,* but the analysis of chants and songs was left by most social anthropologists to ethno-musicologists and later linguistic anthropologists, whose results were not until recently (Feld 1982; Seeger 1986, 1987) reincorporated. Culture continued to be ghostlike, suffusing the world with meanings but unanchored in an objectively circulating discourse.

It is curious that discourse was for so many of the social anthropologists—ignoring, for the moment, Malinowski and the recent work by Maurice Bloch and others—effectively invisible. It was not just a distrust for what natives had to tell one, a distrust that may be well-founded, as Lévi-Strauss's (1967) distinction between "conscious and unconscious models" suggests, and Turner's own work confirms. To comment upon discourse is also to produce discourse—metadiscourse, which is itself worthy of ethnographic description. What individuals say about what they say is not necessarily identical to what they in fact say. The dialectical tension between discourse and metadiscourse may well be central to the processes of culture and is, in any case, in need of empirical investigation, but the question of discourse invisibility goes deeper.

One issue here is ideological: the material world is regarded as fundamental or real, and the canonical form of the material is the visible—the white latex of the milk tree. Invisibility has to do in this sense with non-visibility, with the aural quality of discourse as part of social process in small-scale societies, with *mudyi* not as the printed word on the page, but rather as the sounds uttered in gesturing toward a specific tree. In societies like Ndembu, where evidence from overt behavior—the spatial arrangements of villages, subsistence habits such as hunting or herding, and the conduct of ritual involving visual displays—was noteworthy (or, in any case, where anthropologists wished to see it as noteworthy), the status of discourse could readily be downgraded to epiphenomenal. Under such an ideology, real cultural difference is phenomenal—even though the phenomena are suffused with ghostlike meanings—and to be phenomenal is to be visible. The formal speech styles discussed in chapters 5–7 present an intermediate case in this regard: while still invisible in this sense, they achieve greater objecthood by virtue of their saliency for both anthropologist and native.

If one uses one's own language to communicate with natives (or, if not, then once a foreign language is thoroughly mastered), discourse becomes invisible in another sense: it becomes transparent to the world. It carries meanings that are about the world, which, however, also presents itself to us visually, as shapes, outlines, colors, textures. Spoken words are in this sense for anthropology a window to the *invisible* visible world, allowing us to see what the native sees—to see not just a tree with leaves and bark and sap but also the matriline. There is a wonderful irony in all this: we need a window—or, better yet, glasses—to see what the native sees, yet we are not interested in the properties of those magical glasses. The visible world contains invisible meanings, which only become accessible when one is told what one is looking at. This is a curious form of visibility, reflecting an odd kind of materiality.

At the same time, however, technical discourse studies in the 1980s have themselves contributed to the problem. Trapped in fine-grained descriptions of linguistic detail, they are often unable to link these minutiae to the broader concerns that motivated social anthropology. So much effort goes into dissecting the textual tree—the *mudyi* rather than the milk tree—not just for its gross morphology but for the microarchitecture of its venation, for the configuration of its stamens into anthers and filaments, that the forest of social life in which it thrives cannot be glimpsed. The intention behind this book, which brings together some of my own research over the past decade, is to create the space for a dialogue within anthropology between these points of view, between the narrower concerns of fine-grained technical studies and the broader concerns addressed by social anthropology and structuralism. In calling attention to this locus of possible dialogue, the book is designed to encourage new thought about old problems and to direct attention to new areas for possible research.

*F*or linguistic structuralism, the lack of concern with discourse stemmed not from its transparency, but, in a certain sense, from its opposite— opacity. Whereas those concerned with culture saw through discourse to the meanings it carried, those concerned with language found the instance of discourse impenetrable or unintelligible without recourse to something that lay behind it or beneath it or that was carried along by it but could not be directly observed in it—namely, its meaning. A given fragment of discourse (". . . the boy got up to the nest . . .") has no significance as an isolated physical object, whether as lines drawn on the page or as sounds. From an objective point of view, we could describe the character of the lines and their arrangements; but no matter how thoroughly we did this, we would not arrive at its meaning. We would know nothing about the boy and the nest.

This problem—the problem of interpretability—is obvious to anthropologists who work in small-scale societies, where the languages have been very little studied. A given instance of discourse is for them literally meaningless. Despite painstaking efforts to describe the sound in all of its detail and daily work at reproducing it faithfully, the sound still means nothing.

A familiar prank trades on the distinction: encouraged by natives to re-produce some utterance, an obscenity, for example, without being told its meaning, the anthropologist does so—whereupon they all burst out laugh-ing. The anthropologist concludes that they know something he or she does not know: the meaning. Structuralism concurs, but it proposes in ad-dition that the meaning can be studied independently of the instances, that there are methods that can get us to language without going through dis-course. Moreover, language must be a capacity we have that is prior to and independent of discourse.

This is an argument that can be extended from discourse to any in-stance of behavior—a ritual behavior or mother-in-law avoidance, for instance—whose significance is at the outset unfathomable. It can be ex-tended even to the Ndembu milk tree. There appears to be an independent realm of meaning prior to discourse and prior to our encounters with physical experience more generally, of which discourse as physical object is only one example. And if that is true, is it not also the case that the meanings are shared within a community—by the individuals who are laughing around the anthropologist, for instance? An argument of this sort underlies linguistic structuralism and also the approach to culture as shared meanings. But the argument is vulnerable to the issue of publicness on the methodological front—how one studies language as an experience-prior system of meaning, as I will argue subsequently—and also in terms of its more sweeping claim for sharedness.

The isolated instance of discourse turns out to be an illusion, created by the observational stance of the anthropologist as outsider, for example, or by the reader reflecting upon the isolated written line. Within a discursive community, an instance of discourse arises only against the backdrop of a continuing history of such instances, in relationship to which it can be situated. The actual situating is done subjectively, but it is based upon a vast range of historical experience with other instances, which are also part of the public circulation of discourse in the ongoing life of a community. "The boy got up to the nest" is meaningless in itself as a physical object; but it is part of a reservoir of publicly accessible objects of a similar type, with which it can be compared, and comparison leads to recognition of similarities, differences, and contiguities. The constituent objects "b," "o," and "y" are familiar, traditional objects, as is the combination "boy." These are not novelties, presented here for the first time, but shapes that members of this discourse community have seen innumerable times. It is not that the meanings are necessarily shared, but that the collection of in-stances from which meanings are culled is publicly accessible. The collec-tion forms the basis for recognizing interconnections, but the interconnec-

tions that are recognized may vary from person to person, depending in
part on the degree and kind of access they have had to the overall community history. Recent discourse studies seem to be suggesting, therefore,
that shared meaning is a product of public accessibility rather than (or in
addition to being) a necessary precondition for it.

Another way of putting this is that linguistic structuralism creates the
appearance of abstract meanings by ignoring time. Saussure was explicit in
formulating his view of language as a synchronic system. Any given discourse entities, such as "x" and "y" in figure 1a, appear as abstract types,
which enter into two kinds of relationships: syntagmatic and paradigmatic.
But from the point of view of a community discourse history, those types
are actually built up from the recognition of similarities across historical
time, as in figure 1b. When physical marks on the page are observed, or
sounds heard, they have to be related to other ones that have come before
them in order for there to be public accessibility in the first place, on the
basis of which sharing becomes possible. The synchronic system is the result of an illusion, produced, so to speak, from looking down on a three-
dimensional array; the historically unfolding interconnections seem to be
present all at once.

But if this is an illusion, it is an illusion that corresponds to the subjective point of view on discourse. Much as myth essences are created by the
metadiscursive practice of naming ("this is the story about . . ."), so also
are linguistic types produced by metadiscursive acts ("this is a word that
means . . ."). The Saussurean scheme may be seen from this perspective
as reflecting specifically, in the first place, a subjective metadiscursive re-
flectionist point of view, which, in the second place, asks questions about
decontextualized (rather than contextualized) meanings: "What is the
meaning of . . . ?" "Is the following grammatical . . . ?" "Do these two
words mean the same thing . . . ?" It is a scheme that corresponds to what
can be, for members of the community, a subjective reality.

It would be a mistake to assume, however, that the meanings resulting
from this metadiscursive reflection must be shared within a community.
The matter calls for empirical investigation. An alternative proposition
might run as follows: all things being equal, two speakers will produce
similar metadiscursive reflections if and insofar as they have had equal access to publicly occurring discourse. If two speakers have the same kinds
of experiences with what is objectively describable as the same discourse,
then they will tend to produce, in their reflections on decontextualized
meanings, the same kinds of metadiscursive statements. The proposition
makes the meanings a function of accessibility, rather than the other way
around.

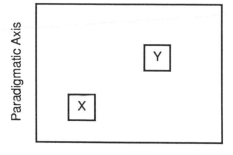

Fig. 1a. Synchronic model of structure

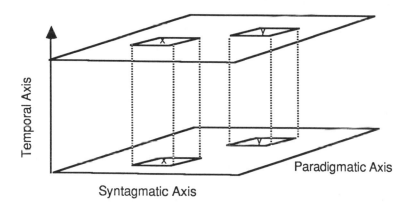

Fig. 1b. Discourse-centered model of cultural whole

There is in all this, however, a complicating factor: the metadiscursive reflections can themselves be articulated and thereby made to circulate publicly. A dictionary is a collection of metadiscursive statements that is also canonical. It says in effect: "this is how words are to be used as well as how they have been used." Grammars are also circulating metadiscursive formulations, which can be simultaneously descriptive and normative, as I will argue subsequently. But there are many other kinds of metadiscourse, some of them overt, such as publicly expressed evaluative judgments about a myth telling or song performance, and others subtle, such as poetic devices designed to call attention to the instance of discourse in question—Jakobson's (1960) poetic function. Interpretation—understood as

recognition of interconnections within the community discourse history—
is thus subject to manipulation and politicization through metadiscourse.
Two areas of metadiscursive politicization that are of special interest to
social anthropologists are authority, which rests on the metadiscursive
understanding of commands as linguistic devices (discussed in chapter 3),
and continuity (discussed in chapter 4), which rests upon the metadiscursive assertion that a given instance of discourse is continuous with previous ones.

It would be foolhardy to jettison the Saussurean framework from our
understanding of culture. Recent discourse-oriented research suggests not
that we dismantle language, but rather that we reposition it. A single self-
contained Saussurean system that is both complete and consistent, and
that is shared by a discourse community, is simply not a precondition for
public accessibility; at best, it is an ideal outcome of accessibility, an outcome that is never actually obtained. At the same time, the products of
metadiscursive reflection stand in a problematic, rather than transparent,
relationship to the processes by which speakers actually produce and interpret utterances. We cannot imagine that speakers encode or decode utterances metadiscursively, that is, by means of internal metacommentary
(saying to themselves: "a boy is a young male human being," "a nest is a
bird's bed"). Metadiscursive acts seem to freeze or fix the historical configuration of instances, giving it the appearance of general law, while normatively stipulating what it should be. In fact, the similarities over time
that form the basis for such metadiscursive acts are contingent and open-
ended, susceptible to reconfiguration (a new pronunciation that is suffi-
ciently similar to earlier ones to allow a recognition to take place, but
different enough to cause a reconfiguration). A focus on discourse thus
repositions language, making it appear to be the product of individual
metadiscursive reflections whose comparability across speakers is opened
for investigation. Primary emphasis, however, is placed on exploring community discourse histories and public circulation.

Another important shift has been in resituating Saussurean meanings or
sense relations within a broader view of the different types of meaning that
an instance may have. Sense is purely discourse-internal, that is, it has no
connection to the perceptible world, as the source of images, outside of the
sounds or visual shapes that are the sign vehicles of discourse. A given utterance—"but when the boy got up to the nest, he said that he could find
only two eggs" (Lévi-Strauss 1969b:66)—has a meaning that seems to be
disconnected from the immediate sensible environment in which it occurs.
Sense relations make a contribution to that meaning. We have a feel for the
distribution of the constituent sign vehicles with respect to others within

the overall community discourse. For example, we know that "the boy got up to the nest" has a meaning similar to but different from "the boy got up to the lair," which is in turn similar to but different from "the girl got up to the lair," which is in turn similar to but different from "the girl got down to the lair," and so forth. Sense relations allow us to move between discourse instances; sense is the meaning a fragment of discourse has by virtue of its position within a whole collection of comparable fragments.

But sense is devoid of imaginal content, that is, images drawn from a physical world of real boys and nests and birds. Nevertheless, readers or listeners may associate the words on the page with images. They do not have to do so in order to have a sense of the utterance, but they may do so. Such images, however, are based on a distinct kind of meaningfulness: associations grounded in the physical contiguity in space and time between some fraction of discourse, describable as a word or phrase or clause, and some sense perception. The association may be idiosyncratic, drawn from nests or pictures of nests one has seen in conjunction with the word "nest." But imaginal associations are ultimately grounded in public or community agreements about the relations between sounds or graphic symbols and sense perceptions (A: "Hey, look at that black cat" [pointing to a white cat with black spots]; B: "You call that a black cat?—that ain't what I call a black cat"),[2] even if the agreements are always also subject to contestation and renegotiation. By virtue of such agreements and renegotiations, the community discourse history adapts itself to a sensible world.

Associational relations are called in the semiotic literature—which is off-putting for many because of its forbidding terminology—indexical relations, in the framework of C. S. Peirce as transmitted through Silverstein (1976b), Jakobson (1980), Singer (1984), and Mertz and Parmentier (1985). A fragment of discourse understandable in terms of Saussurean sense, the word "nest," for instance, may also enter into an indexical relation with the world, as in the metadiscursive practice of ostensive definition: "that [pointing to a nest] is a nest." Not all fragments that have sense also enter into indexical relations; correspondingly, not all indexical relations in discourse involve fragments that are also segmentable in terms of Saussurean sense: the melodic intonation contour of singing, as a form of discourse, while nonsensical, may nevertheless have associational indexical value.

Nor does indexation necessarily involve metadiscursive reflection, so that, correspondingly, not all associational processes are intellectual. Indeed, intellectual reflection may not be even the primary basis for apprehending associational meanings—as if every experience were monitored through internal commentary. In the case of contiguities, interconnection is something that can be felt as well as commented upon; just as an internal comment can be made to circulate publicly as metadiscourse so, too, can an emotional awareness of interconnection be publicized in a gesture or facial expression. Felt interpretation of association is central to Steven Feld's (1982) path-breaking *Sound and Sentiment*, and also to Keith Basso's (1988) work on Western Apache place names, and to Ellen Basso's (1985) study of ritual and mythic transformations of grief among the central Brazilian Kalapalo.[3] Though scholars have been reluctant to recognize it, the interpretive role of affect is well established in American folk representations—for example, in the familiar scene from *Casablanca* where Dooley Wilson's "As Time Goes By" calls up in Humphrey Bogart the recollection of Ingrid Bergman, who has actually, as the audience knows, reappeared and signaled her presence by this means.

The other nonsensical (in the Saussurean meaning of sense) associational linkage recognized by semioticians is the icon, whose basis is physical similarity. Similarity is the objective relationship that makes possible talk about a discourse entity (for example, a word such as *mudyi*), as an "it" across distinct instances, although, as in the case of the myth name that essentializes interconnections among discourse instances, the "it" here performs the metadiscursive magic of fixing the relations among instances, whose character may also be investigated objectively. But similarity operates in many different ways in discourse: for example, in repetition or parallelism—studied in chapters 2–4—as in chanting the word *mudyi*, which makes the similarities palpable.

In his treatise *The Magic Art and the Evolution of Kings*, J. G. Frazier (1911:52–53) formulated the two great "principles of thought on which magic is based," which summarize the ethnographic underpinnings for similarity and contiguity as bases for forming interconnections—simultaneously giving anthropological precedent for semiotic usage. Frazer thought of the laws as capturing the magician's unarticulated but nevertheless apparently embodied reasoning about cause and effect. Under the "Law of Similarity," the magician reasoned that "like produces like, or that an effect resembles its cause"—as in the case of the voodoo doll, whose physical resemblance to the person affected—however remote—is the basis for its efficacy. Under the "Law of Contagion," the magician reasoned that "things which have once been in contact with each other continue to act on each other at a distance after the physical contact has been severed"—as when locks of hair, nail clippings, or pieces of clothing are secured and acted upon in order to affect the person from whom they were secured.

Later scholars proposed that magicians were not reasoning incorrectly about physical causality but rather correctly reasoning about psychological reality—the political figure burned in effigy not to kill physically but rather to kill psychologically, that is, to express rage. However one interprets the principles, their ubiquity also reveals something else: the importance of similarity and contiguity as forms of interconnection—and not just their importance intellectually, but also, and perhaps more to the point, their importance emotionally. If much of the semiotic discourse literature has emphasized these relationships, it is for good reason: the relations are culturally significant. They are fundamental to the formation of interconnections among discourse instances and, indeed, to the broad experiential backdrop within which public signs become meaningful. The Saussurean insight has overwhelmed this older one, which semiotic work justly tries to resuscitate.

At the same time, the Saussurean view rightly exposes the inadequacy of associations for an understanding of culture or language. A minimal addition necessary to make the framework function is the relation of difference—that two things are not the same. Saussure's (1966 [1915]) phrase has been repeated so many times that it is by now almost trivial, but no less, for that reason, true: "in language there is only difference." "Nest" is not the same as "bed," nor for that matter as "west" or "rest." But the addition of this relation changes everything. Whereas similarity and contiguity presuppose a sensible world prepackaged in discrete experiences that need to be pulled together—all of the spoken or printed instances of "nest"—difference presupposes a primal sameness that needs to be chopped up. Difference takes for granted sameness (that is, sufficient physical similarity or space-time proximity to require differentiating), whereas sameness (that is, the partial identities of similarity and contiguity) takes for granted difference. Whereas difference has as its point of departure the whole, similarity and contiguity have as theirs the part. The one tries to get from the whole to the unique instance; the other to work from the unique instance back toward the whole. The effort, in each case, is to read through from one to the other. From the perspective of public accessibility, as well as of recent discourse research, however, the two appear, on the one hand, resolutely irreconcilable but also, on the other, equally indispensable. They are discrete phases in the processes of culture: difference is part of the subjective (Saussurean metadiscursive) phase; similarity and contiguity parts of the objective (semiotic associational) phase.

The attention to discourse within culture resonates in the writings of early American cultural anthropologists, especially the work of Paul Radin. The title of Radin's 1949 monograph (*The Culture of the Winnebago: As Described by Themselves*) in light of its contents—a collection of myth texts—suggests an orientation to discourse akin to the discourse-centered work of the 1980s. He discusses the methods by which the texts were collected: standard informant elicitation, the writing down of myths in the Winnebago syllabary by the Winnebago themselves, especially by one man, Sam Blowsnake, and (surprisingly, in 1908) use of the old Edison phonograph to record elicited tales, from which transcriptions were made. While it is true that these texts were collected out of their normal cultural contexts of narration and are not the same, therefore, as the transcribed tape recordings of *in situ* discourse that have emerged as central during the 1980s, and while it is true that Radin paid no attention to the role of naturally occurring discourse within ongoing social life, the spirit of his work is nevertheless surprisingly contemporary. This is especially so with respect to the sense of historicity and contingency that he and other Americanists shared, which manifested itself in a concern for emergent cultural forms, such as the peyote cult studied by the "method of reconstruction from internal evidence" (Radin 1965 [1933]: 183–252), that is, through the discourse of native accounts, or the ghost dance religion described by James Mooney (1892–1893).

This is no surprise, since the lineage of the discourse approach begins with Boas and the Americanists and leads through the ethnography of speaking founded by Dell Hymes, who in fact proposed a four-level framework for the analysis of communicative events, beginning with the fine-grained analysis of discourse and leading out to the role of communicative processes in the ongoing adaptation of the culture (Hymes 1974a). The differing and continuing contributions of various scholars to this line of research are now too numerous to mention, but include the work of Dennis Tedlock (1983), who, unlike Hymes, began to make use of tape recodings, which allowed him to focus on pause structure and other pragmatic features of utterances; Richard Bauman (1986), who emphasized the performance characteristics of discourse events; and Joel Sherzer (1983, 1987a), who not only wrote the first full-scale ethnography of speaking, based on his research among Kuna of Panama, but first formulated the discourse-centered approach to the problematics of language, culture, and society. The Americanist roots are also evident in Silverstein (1976b), who was directly influenced by Hymes, but added to discourse research the semiotic framework of Peirce, handed down through Roman Jakobson.

The concern with discourse developed gradually out of the research on North American Indians by the Boasians, for whom language, in the form of texts, was seen as a vehicle for reading back in time to an older culture of which the present was a vestige. While the cultures of the southwestern United States were still flourishing, many of the early Americanists, especially Frank Speck and John R. Swanton, who were working on the Southeast, but also Boas himself in his Northwest Coast research, regarded the cultures they were studying as broken down, recoverable only through memories encoded in discourse. For them, discourse was a window to culture in a different sense; it was a portal through which one could peer back into time, seeing amid the debris of the present world customs that had vanished, a way of life that had been eclipsed by European culture. As one studies discourse today, discourse circulating in ongoing social life, it is all too easy to miss the important truth discovered by these early Americanists. Discourse is in fact the means by which the past is kept alive in the present, by means of which a culture is maintained. Without that splendid, nostalgia-filled image of the past, culture is reduced to little more than rote repetition. The truth that the Americanists found is that ancient times are alive in the present; they live in discourse.

Boas emphasized the collection of texts in the native language. Texts were critical empirical data for cultural anthropology, as one perusing publications of the Bureau of American Ethnology can attest. Because of their referential content, texts provided evidence about the past life of a culture, but they also gave to discourse a materiality or substantiality that was lacking in the ephemeral flow of the spoken form. Frozen visually in print, the Boasian text could become the object of empirical scrutiny and of the search for configuration or pattern. It is to the lasting credit of Dell Hymes (1981) that he made this breakthrough and began to focus attention on the primary vehicle of culture.

The success of discourse studies lies in their ability to challenge, through microanalysis, the transparency of discourse as a window to culture. The window is shown to have refracting properties—an internal configuration based upon parallelism that is attention-getting in its own right. Some of the fascination with culture appears upon closer inspection to be more properly a fascination with discourse. Moreover, the vast panorama of culture one imagines oneself to be glimpsing through discourse turns out to be at least partially an illusion induced by the medium—as if the medium had reflecting as well as refracting powers. Because of its ability to encode stories that only seem to be about the world, discourse can be a hall of mirrors, in relationship to which the apprehension of external reality appears at best problematic.

But at the same time these studies have generally failed to articulate with considerations of culture as a whole, despite the fact that culture provides the backdrop against which the specific instance of discourse becomes interpretable for the natives as well as for the anthropologist. Microresearch on discourse, as it has developed in the 1980s, is only beginning to engage with broader interpretations or hypotheses about the whole of culture, which provide the ground of meaningfulness or interpretability for the instance. This new line of inquiry recasts anthropological investigation in the form of a dialectical interplay between the microscopic study of discourse—with time scales ranging from fractions of a second to minutes—and hypotheses about culture—with time scales ranging from decades to centuries.

While a view of culture, conceptualized as a collection or history of discourse instances, is only beginning to emerge from recent work, some differences with respect to other approaches are already apparent. There is a resemblance to the early diffusionist view, in which, however, culture was an amalgam of disparate elements with little internal unity or consistency, each constituent myth motif or cultural trait having a unique history and dispersion. While a collection of discourse instances has something of this caldronlike quality, it is also the case that individuals, from their own vantage point, may see the collection as a configuration—indeed, must do so in some measure if they are to regard the instance of discourse as interpretable. Insofar as the perspectives converge on a single configuration, there is something resembling culture in the sense of a shared system of abstract meanings, the asymptotic limit of which is the monolithic whole, passed down from generation to generation.

That limit was made the point of departure for Durkheim and the social anthropologists. A. R. Radcliffe-Brown, indeed, viewed the social function of an element of culture as the contribution to the maintenance of the whole, where the whole was given reproductive primacy. From the point of view of discourse, it is possible that the collection of instances in some measure functions in this way, especially, for example, when there is a circulating metadiscursive ideology of continuity with the past, coupled with an ideology of sharing, making it appear as if the history of instances is a history of sameness and replication over time and space. Such discourse formations—discussed in chapters 6–8—are in fact to be found in central Brazil; but, while they may also be found elsewhere, they are by no means the universal type of culture. In adjacent areas in South America, north of the Amazon River, there is evidence for metadiscursive ideologies based not on similarity but on difference. For these cases, which are only elementary examples of how a metadiscursive ideology of difference may shape the understanding of discourse histories, the shared monolithic conception of culture is less adequate. In either type, however, it is important that, while a metadiscursive ideology may in some measure shape a discourse collection or history after its own image—so that, under an ideology of sharing and continuity, there may in fact be considerable sharing and continuity—there is bound to be slippage. No culture actually reaches the Radcliffe-Brownian limit.

What is the ontological status of that limit? Culture, as a collection or history of publicly accessible sign vehicles, the most important being instances of discourse, is—or so, anyway, I have been arguing—only half objective. Insofar as the instances are publicly accessible, that is, accessible to more than one individual, they have an existence as material things, however ephemeral. Speech can be tape-recorded and its sound characteristics studied and compared with those of other instances. The empirical similarities and differences can be demonstrated. These empirical characteristics of public discourse provide a check on the metadiscursive ideologies about the interconnections among instances, and they do so for both native and anthropologist. But the recognition of interconnectedness is simultaneously subjective, susceptible to influence from the metadiscursive ideology. The limit can be more readily approached from this side: it requires only sharing and continuity in the metadiscourse of continuity and sharing—all representing their discourse as the same as everyone else's and as continuous with the past—regardless of the realities. At the same time, however, if there is bound to be a slippage between metadiscourse and discourse—between the ideology of language use and its empirical characteristics—there is also likely to be a pressure on the two to align. A subjective feel for interconnectedness, based on continuity and sharing, coupled with a circulating metadiscourse of continuity and sharing, forces some measure of conformity as regards the objective discourse formation.

As the presupposition of continuity and sharing has undergone increasing challenge, especially in the 1980s, with a developing literature on resistance readings (Taussig 1980, 1987; Scott 1985), the opposite question comes into focus: what is the anti-Radcliffe-Brownian limit for a discourse formation? Is it coherent to speak of a discourse formation that exhibits no continuity and sharing? Here again the problem has both a subjective-objective dimension and a metadiscourse-discourse dimension. A metadiscourse of difference, as opposed to sameness and sharing, is, as just mentioned, found in the region north of the Amazon River in South America and is undoubtedly common in other parts of the world as well. The irony is that the ideology of difference in these cases is in fact shared. In empirical situations, such as those in the northwest Amazon described by Jean Jackson (1983) and Arthur Sorensen (1967), there appears to be considerable sharing beneath an ideology of differentiation. From a theoretical point of view, however, the minimum requirements are probably a byproduct of the notion of publicness, in terms of which culture is defined. When discourse instances are publicly accessible, when the members of a community, however broadly defined, are immersed in some discursive history or collection of instances, the interconnections they construe are constrained by the fact of that objective similarity. This is the inverse case to that of the convergence of meaning limit. If convergence is limited by the objective entropy of discourse, divergence is limited by whatever objective sameness is the precondition for publicness, regardless of how disparate the interpretations. The interpretations—that is, the tracing of interconnections within the discourse history—must be fashioned out of the same discourse instances, and this produces some shared meanings. True difference is possible, from this point of view, only when the discourse formation fragments into isolated publics between which there is no communication.

Faced with the problematic of publicness and the limits of sharing, one appealing alternative is the isolated world of the Cartesian monad, where a presocial serenity of biological givens and orderliness can seemingly be recovered from the chaotic multiple determinations of public life. This is nowhere more apparent than in Noam Chomsky's approach to language, which has been central to American linguistics for more than twenty years. Unlike Lévi-Strauss, for whom the study of brain structures required a comparative cultural approach, thereby casting anthropological research as philosophical method, Chomsky's (1984:6) proposal has been that "a great deal can be learned about UG [universal grammar] from the study of a single language."

Recent discourse research does not rule out the possibility of universals, but it does call up for scrutiny the Cartesian methods that are used to get at them. During its earlier history, American structural linguistics—which, unlike Chomsky's generative grammar or government and binding, stressed the comparison of diverse empirical languages—relied on two methods. There was, first of all, the method of elicitation of words, phrases, and sentences from informants. This typically involved, for native peoples, engaging in a new kind of discourse interaction, namely, taking fragments of their own language or discourse as topics of discussion, something the linguist had to train them to do. Second, it involved the analysis of texts, collected by the methods Radin (1949) has described in connection with his work on the Winnebago. Texts of the latter sort were also products of a new speech situation—teaching culture to an interested foreigner—but the line of linguistic research based on texts naturally gave rise to an interest in the discourse that circulates when the anthropologist is not there. What are myths like as actually told by natives to natives? What is discourse like when the anthropologist is not there eliciting it?

The first method, conversation about language or discourse fragments, in contrast, gave rise to an intuitionist approach. If it was possible to ask informants about their language, it was also possible to ask oneself about one's own language. The topicalization of language and discourse in informant elicitation was part of a new kind of social interaction for native peoples, but it was a discursively mediated social interaction. Language had a public existence, a social life, that still anchored it, methodologically, in the goings-on of a discourse community. Intuitionism seemed to cut its ties with the interactional sphere, allowing an isolated researcher to reflect upon what is grammatical and what ungrammatical. No social interaction was required to investigate language. Method and theory, in other words, here coincided, giving credence to the reality of a "prelinguistic universal grammar" the child has prior to any social interaction.

Studies of feral children, such as *The Wild Boy of Aveyron* (Itard 1932; Lane 1976), "Caspar Hauser" (Singh and Zingg 1942:277–365), and others (Singh and Zingg 1942; Curtiss 1977), seem to provide no firm ground for deciding, one way or another, whether a language might spontaneously grow in the absence of the discourse community as a holding environment for universal grammar. Correspondingly, the special languages occasionally developed by twins may tell us more about intensive social interaction than about innate capabilities. We cannot finally decide about the biological versus sociological basis of universal grammar, even if we are sure that discourse communities, and not genes, are the holding environments for empirical languages.

At the same time, the method of intuitionism, as used to discover preexperiential universal grammar, has a problematic relationship to public accessibility. It relies on normative judgments about grammaticality, whose correctness, however, is found in their social acceptance. While the test instances of discourse do not come from socially circulating discourse, but are instead thought up by the linguist in isolation—and for this reason have a cardboard feel: "the students want Bill to visit Paris," "the students want that Bill visit Paris" (Chomsky 1984:19)—they and the judgments about them are subjected to social circulation as the basis for their claim to validity. Publicness, in other words, has been reintroduced at the level of persuasion, and the persuasiveness rests, ironically, on the presumedly nonempirical status of the metadiscursive judgments themselves. There is an echo of the window transparency assumed by social anthropology, and, in a different way, by an earlier American cultural anthropology, but here language as discourse is transparent to itself. Metadiscursive judgments—discourse—are unproblematically related to the discourse they judge.

From the point of view of recent research on discourse, this method raises two questions. First, how do the object sentences, such as "the students want that Bill visit Paris,"[4] relate to discourse that socially circulates outside the linguistic literature? To be sure, that literature itself gives those instances a public life, as well as a special context, but what is the relationship between that public life and broader public discourse? Chomsky (1984 : 7–8) notes that "it is hardly to be expected that what are called 'languages' or 'dialects' or even 'idiolects' will conform precisely or perhaps even very closely to the systems determined by fixing the parameters of [universal grammar]." All the same, it is of interest that a micropublic (generative grammarians) has sprung up around agreements and disagreements about its own metadiscursive judgments, and this micropublic defines itself as embodying the judgments of ideal native speakers. Second, how can the linguists' judgments about the sentences they think up be checked? If grammaticality judgments are metadiscourse, which can itself socially circulate, a natural question concerns the social motivations scholars have for accepting the judgments. Is it because the judgments correspond to their own untutored intuitions, as if the metadiscourse were transparent to the object discourse? Or does the metadiscourse have a rhetorical persuasiveness that is at least partially independent of the object sentences judged? Is the theory, to use the terms employed to criticize traditional grammar, descriptive or prescriptive?

This is not to discount the great contributions of Chomsky and generative grammar or the research currently underway. As in the case of the metadiscourse of cultural continuity, if there is bound to be some entropic slippage between metadiscourse and discourse, there is also bound to be pressure for the two to align. The question again concerns asymptotic limits. At the same time, the asymptotic limit may already have been reached or breached—how would we know?—and, in any case, the stakes are high; it is healthy to be circumspect. The claim for the method is that it can produce knowledge of innately human linguistic capabilities, but there is no confirmatory procedure built in, no bumping into empirical considerations that might make it more difficult for a rhetorically persuasive metadiscourse to take on the illusion of validity.

The method can be contrasted with the elicitation procedures, enumerated above, that were employed in earlier field linguistics and continue to be used by researchers today. Words, sentences, and texts are produced by native speakers who are not trained linguists sharing in the researcher's metadiscourse. There is an encounter with publicness here, a check on the possibility that linguists might convince and perhaps even delude themselves about language in the absence of a struggle with the objective half of language. The procedure is itself a social interaction built around a metadiscursive ideology; as any fieldworker knows, one is too often training native speakers to give the response one wants or expects. But native speakers also resist; they are recalcitrant, supplying discourse in accord with principles that are in some measure independent. From this point of view, tape-recorded instances of socially circulating discourse exhibit an even greater recalcitrance, causing researcher and native speaker alike to reflect on the public life of language.

In calling for "A Discourse-Centered Approach to Language and Culture," Sherzer's (1987a) article stresses the need to make language research accountable to public discourse. If culture is localized in concrete, publicly occurring discourse, the same is true of languages, as part of the earth's empirical diversity, as opposed to language as an innate capacity, a point Chomsky (1984:7) effectively concedes when he notes that "experience . . . serves to fix the parameters of [universal grammar], providing a core grammar." This is not to flatten or compress languages or, for that matter, cultures, into the objective characteristics of sound or visual shapes, since discourse, as mentioned earlier, is only half objective. But it is important that it *is* half objective—like the proverbial glass. If sound or visual shape does not determine linguistic segmentation, neither can linguistic segmentation be arbitrarily imposed on that shape. The two exist in a state of tension, attracted to one another by the pressure to produce a perfect communication, a perfect form of publicness, and repelled by entropic forces, creativity, and subjective systematization.

It seems true that, for an instance of discourse to be interpreted, individuals require a presupposed sense of linguistic interconnections—of meanings as sense relations. Looked at through public discourse, however, the sense relations are individual and virtual, the degree of sharing within a discourse community becoming an investigable question. The projection of a language onto a community—a projection made by natives and anthropologists alike—is subject to reconfiguration with new instances, which are part of the public life of discourse. Some of the instances may languish as uninterpreted or misinterpreted or partially interpreted, but others may cause realignments within the sets of interconnections recognized by individuals and may correspondingly affect the character of future discourse within the community.

The notion of creativity, which Emmon Bach (1974:24) in his textbook on generative grammar glosses as "the ability to invent and understand novel utterances and to use them appropriately," has been central to modern arguments about the character of language as a system. But the argument needs tempering through a study of the actual life of discourse within communities. An alternative point of view might stress discourse as traditional rather than novel. For example, using the genetic code as an analogy, a past instance might function as a template for replication. The replica would not necessarily be identical to the template—indeed, would rarely be so, if entropy were at work, even where speakers exerted themselves to produce faithful copies—but would involve low-level lexical and morphological substitutions. An individual might make use of a finite, albeit perhaps large, number of such templates, the relationships among which were themselves not perfectly systematized. The notion is similar to that of surface—as opposed to deep—grammar, which has been common in the literature, with the difference that in recent discourse-centered work there would be no assumption of a single shared set of such templates for the entire community.

From this point of view, novelty would take its chances against tradition. A new utterance—one not transparently a replica of some template stored in the discourse history of the community—might be incomprehensible or contextually inappropriate. Every new piece of discourse runs a chance of failure. But there is also a chance that it will succeed, that it will become a new fashion, a new template for the construction of other instances. Looked at from the point of view of tradition, innovation is not an argument for the rule-governed character of discourse, which makes it appear as if the element of chance had never been there. It is rather an argument for the lack of self-containment of the system, for the ever-present possibility that something new will emerge that might cause the system to reconfigure.

*I*n spite of what Barbara Herrnstein Smith (1978 : 168) refers to as Stanley Fish's "saturation bombing of stylistics"—a characterization that Fish (1980 : 247) himself adopts in subsequent ruminations on the subject—it does not seem especially dangerous to devote a portion (chapters 5–8) of the present book to the phenomenon of style or to deal in the remainder with the related problem of parallelism. After all, literary criticism and anthropology occupy different territories; a bombing in one need not be noted—except, perhaps, as interesting news—in the other. But the two territories share a common border, and some anthropologists have established squatter settlements in the literary area, just as a few migrants from the other side have drifted into this territory. There are also general regional trends that sweep across borders—the culture concept, for instance. Indeed, Fish's standpoint, the interpretive community, sounds remarkably like the anthropological concept of culture. Especially because he draws inspiration from a primal dyad of interpretation and text, however, as opposed to the complex distinctions within the semiotic discourse area, it is important to note some architectural differences between his camp and that within linguistic anthropology, at least as mapped out here.

The anthropological approach to style (cf. Hymes 1974b; Urban 1985; Feld 1988) has to do with ways of speaking rather than of writing, as in the ritual wailing and ceremonial dialogue discussed in chapters 5–8. A style consists in a recognizable set of features, as in literary criticism, but the features are not only or even primarily or importantly the grammatical forms of Saussurean sense relations—not, in other words, the products of introspective (metadiscursive) reflections on meaning. They are instead such non-Saussurean forms as intonation contours, voice qualities, and participant role alternations—accessible to the senses, much the way the milk tree (as specimens of *Diplorrhyncus condylocarpon*) is. Knowing nothing of the language or culture, one can pick out of the soundscape an occurrence of Shokleng ceremonial dialogue. This is the palpable, objective life of discourse. But ceremonial dialogue also leads a subjective life, like the milk tree whose *alter* is *mudyi:* it is also *wãñēklèn*, sensical in Saussurean terms, circulating socially independently of the objective form, and usable metadiscursively in ostensive reference ("that is *wãñēklèn*" [said while pointing to two men engaged in a performance of ceremonial dialogue]). Style is in this sense a discourse object; it is both sensible and intelligible, and it exists independently of a Saussurean textual interpretation. The notion is akin to that of musical style.

What is its relationship to style in literary stylistics? Most importantly, style there is a function of Saussurean meanings, not of sound properties, and it is typically a characteristic of a single text—an idiosyncrasy with respect to other texts that is internally regular in the text in question. In M. A. K. Halliday's analysis of William Golding's *The Inheritors*, discussed by Fish (1980:80–84), a key issue is the predominance of intransitive clauses in the first nine-tenths of the novel—"even such normally transitive verbs as *grab* occur intransitively" (Halliday 1971, cited in Fish 1980:81)—followed by a heightened transitivity in the final tenth. This is the formal stylistic pattern, and it is said to correlate with the subject matter: the story of two tribes, one of which (the "new people") supplants the other. The correlation is that the fuller transitivity patterns reflect the "higher stage of development" of the supplanting tribe. Fish criticizes Halliday for attributing independent meanings to the grammatical patterns, when in fact the meanings have been derived from an interpretation of the text and then read back into the forms. This criticism subsequently mushrooms into an all-out condemnation of literary stylistics: "my thesis is that formal patterns are themselves the products of interpretation and that therefore there is no such thing as a formal pattern, at least in the sense necessary for the practice of stylistics" (Fish 1980:267).

If taken in its proper literary theoretical context, the argument is convincing, if not wholly irrefutable. If taken out of context, however—for example, if interpreted as meaning that all public sign vehicles have only the meaning that is given to them by interpretation, in other words, that interpretation is imposed on sign vehicles without in any way coming from them—the argument is debilitating. And it is too easy to hear in it an echo of the old culture-as-shared-meaning concept. Our squatters, dazzled by the sights in this foreign land, fail to notice that the buildings are adapted to a specific climate. What makes the argument successful across the border is the peculiar nature of the literary critical task: interpreting texts whose patent meanings are accessible to any normally literate reader. The interpretation must supplement the patent meanings, embed them within an encompassing understanding. This is a metadiscursive task within a discourse community that also already includes the discursive activity of reading. Fish's critique is convincing within literary land for this reason. His argument is that metadiscourse is not transparent to discourse—the same argument that was applied earlier to the problem of grammaticality judgments—and it is solid enough. The error is to extend it to discourse, and thereby to reproduce the Saussurean fallacy, namely, that, because the isolated utterance seems to have a meaning that is independent of it, there exists a realm of shared meanings independent of the objective life of discourse. When removed from its literary context, the thesis that "formal patterns are themselves the products of interpretation" can be read this way, but the conclusion is false: shared meanings presuppose public accessibility, which leads us back to the life and circulation of discourse.

The distinctiveness of the anthropological approach resides in its ability to play off two perspectives: the objective perspective of the researcher entering the community, for whom nothing (at least initially) is meaningful, and the subjective perspective of the native, for whom everything is. The two are denied to the literary critic, whose problematic is built up within a single discourse community. It is this playing off that allows anthropologists access to unconscious (associational, grounded in similarity and contiguity) as well as conscious (metadiscursive reflectional, grounded in sense relations) meanings; that allows us to hold in mind two equally unreachable goals: differentiating the presupposed whole to reach the infinitely rich part and building up from the parts to the complete and consistent whole; that allows us to view creativity as risky—subject to failure but also potentially transformative—rather than mechanical; and that allows us to grasp the simultaneously presupposed and emergent nature of culture.

To go back to the case of Halliday and *The Inheritors*, Fish is correct: the specific meaning Halliday attributes to fuller transitivity, namely, the "higher stage of development" of the supplanting tribe, can only be read back into the stylistic pattern from a broader understanding of the text. The discourse (Golding's *The Inheritors*) does not uniquely specify the metadiscourse (Halliday's Darwinian reading); literary critics are in no danger of being put out of work. But from this nonuniqueness proposition, one cannot conclude either that the metadiscourse is perfectly free with respect to the discourse. As in the Radcliffe-Brownian limit, if there is slippage between metadiscourse and discourse, there is also a pressure on the two to align. The transitivity issue, which is really a question of parallelism,[5] as shown in the following chapters, may not be resolvable in terms of the unique meaning necessary for a specific reading of *The Inheritors*, but that does not mean that stylistic patterns do not constrain the class of possible readings. Persistent intransitivity may provide an inchoate feeling of some sort—a sense of lack of control by agents over patients, for instance—especially when contrasted syntagmatically with heightened transitivity. The feeling may be characterizable across distinct instances of discourse and may constrain, without determining, the acceptable range of metadiscourses. This is a matter for investigation. It cannot be resolved by fiat.

So while the dynamic duo of interpretation and text works in literary criticism, and may be a healthy corrective to transparent readings of the text, it cannot work for us in anthropology, if we are to maintain the problematic of public accessibility. Saturation bombing is just too indiscriminate. In the rubble we find not only the target, but also the remains of collapsed distinctions, which are, alas, our only fortification against a naïveté emboldened by rhetorical flourish. We want to maintain that interpretation is not just one undifferentiated activity, for anthropologists or for natives; that there are more and less consciously accessible interpretations; that metadiscourses are publicly accessible in their own right and have to be held accountable in some measure to their object discourses; and that there is therefore some measure of public constraint that serves to set limits on the centrifugality of subjective meaning, which, if unconstrained, would, finally, represent a denial of culture as socially shared or transmitted altogether. Fish is right to guard against a crude scientism, but we do not want either to wander off into a land of chicanery and illusion. Anthropology should instead be the site of an encounter between objectivity and subjectivity, between unconscious and conscious meanings, between discourse and metadiscourse, between sensibility and intelligibility, an encounter that is, after all, the life force of discourse and of culture.

CHAPTER 2

Grammatical Parallelism and Thought

*I*n *The Savage Mind* (1966), Lévi-Strauss uses the phrase "logic of the concrete" to characterize thought operating in the sensuous realm of animals, plants, physical space, time, taste, and smell, realizing itself through the structured organizations of worldly experience. Concrete logic contrasts with the abstract thought that is presumed to be characteristic of the West. The type case for the latter is propositional logic or formal axiomatic theory, characterized by symbolically encoded propositions, organized in deductive fashion with a set of privileged propositions and relations of inference or entailment. At least insofar as the dominant values of modern western European and American culture are concerned, Lévi-Strauss is right: scientific rationality and deductive reasoning are valued over and above concrete logic and mythological thought, although the latter may be the most pervasive in society at large, the former but a "thin veneer" covering the teeming reality of contemporary public life.

Between sensuous concreteness and deductively organized abstraction, however, lies the realm of discourse, and it is to discourse that one can turn to understand thought as it is displayed in the public life of culture. Discourse is simultaneously concrete, residing in actually occurring instances, and abstract, dependent upon networks of interconnection for its interpretation. In fact, when Lévi-Strauss subsequently traces the structures of concrete thought, he follows them into myth and hence into the realm of discourse; but, as discussed earlier, he looks through myth— understood as a collection of sign vehicles in its own right—to the concrete world that it seems to encode. Myths are treated not as discourse but rather as structures of experience, characterized by binary oppositions (such as high:low, nature:culture, raw:cooked). Important as this analysis is, it takes no account of the organization of the way actually occurring discourse publicly embodies collective "thought."

It is possible, in fact, to look at myths from the point of view of their internal organization; in keeping with much recent research, what comes into focus is parallelism. The purpose of this chapter is to take the analysis of parallelism into the realm of thought, to show that the public display of thought in myth obeys not only concrete logic, but the discourse logic of similarity or parallelism as well. It is not that concrete logic is absent from the myths investigated here, but rather that it is not *all* that is present; what supplements concreteness is not the propositional logic of entailment or consequence or inference, but the simultaneously sensuous and intellectual logic of unfolding iconicity between propositions encoded in discourse segments (i.e., parallelism).

The specific focus here is on grammatical parallelism and, in particular, parallelism in the participant role of nouns within transitive clauses as agents (subjects of transitive clauses) or patients (objects of transitive clauses). While such parallelism occurs concretely in discourse—as unfolding similarities in the formal devices that encode transitive relations— it simultaneously pertains to the abstract quasi-philosophical level of orientation to agency and objecthood or "patiency." In what measure does the world emerge through agents performing deeds, and in what measure through luminous objects, which are affected and given shape by events but are not themselves especially agentive?

Simultaneously, one appreciates that the concrete logic of myth, viewed in terms of its linguistic manifestations, tends to be a logic of nouns and adjectives, the relationship, for example, between the "raw" and the "cooked" or between "high" and "low." Concrete logical analysis leaves out of the picture the linguistic relations characteristic of grammar, which, though logically abstract, are concretized in actually occurring discourse instances. Mythological discourse may be understood not just as an array of nouns and adjectives, but also as a structure of grammatical relations.

To look at it in this way, however, is already to invoke a hypothesis about discourse history—namely, that some discourse fragments are characterizable in terms of a shared linguistic segmentation. The hypothesis may be modified during subsequent investigation; but, temporarily at least, it calls up the subjective side of discourse, and the side of culture as shared meaning. Discourse as sound is entextualized into a clause, characterizable in terms of phonemic segments, word boundaries, and grammatical relations, as in the following example from a Shokleng myth from southern Brazil, as tape-recorded in 1975.

glũ	wũ	pètï
trans. subj.	nom. marker	verb

When we talk about a shared linguistic segmentation at this level, we are talking specifically about distributional relations internal to the discourse history: that the /g/ phoneme entextualizing the initial sound representable as [ŋ], for example, is identifiable with similar sounds that are or were present in the public discourse of the community; that the combination of sounds transcribable phonemically as /glū/ encodes a noun that is nominatively marked as a transitive subject; and so forth.

At another level, the clause also encodes a proposition, which may be translated as "(the) toucan pierced (or pecked at) (it)." Here the discourse seems to enter into contact with the nondiscursive world populated by real toucans and acts of pecking or piercing. Insofar as the discourse is connected to the world, however, the connections are based upon private indexical associations (as discussed earlier), which are publicly correctable. The image that one individual associates with *glū*, "toucan," need not be identical with that of another individual, though the conflict can be brought into metadiscursive focus if necessary (*tòg tē glū hā wā*, "that is a toucan" [said while pointing toward a colorful, large-beaked bird]), as in fact happened in the course of my field research among the Shokleng.

For purposes of simplification, it is possible to omit the clauses that are descriptions of situations and states, making up the background and contributing to the concrete richness of an actual myth, along with the numerous rhetorical devices. Within this simplified model, the propositions may be thought of, with respect to imaginal content, as encoding events. The mythic discourse juxtaposes events or goings-on, encoded in clauses, in which the states of persons and things are affected and typically modified.

An event, in turn, can be conceptualized as having an internal structure, generally involving three, though often more or fewer, components: (1) the "action" or what takes place (symbolized in figure 2 by an arrow); action in this sense is a conception narrower in scope than Propp's (1968) "function," which includes a built-in reference to the actors involved even if only as variables; (2) the "agent" (Ag), or the doer who brings about the action; and (3) the "patient" (Pa), or person or thing affected by the action.[1] From this perspective, it is possible to define three basic event "types," which are schematized in figure 2. These correspond roughly to "transitive clauses" (type A), "intransitive clauses" wherein subject is agent (type B), and intransitive clauses wherein subject is patient (type C).

Interpretive work, involving the subjective sense of interconnections, takes place at the clause level and below. This is the aspect of discourse that is intelligible. But discourse is also sensible, and the parallelism of grammatical relations or events takes place simultaneously in this perceptible realm, with the physical juxtaposition in space and time of the sound

Fig. 2. Basic event types

fragments encoding the clauses understood as propositions. Grammatical parallelism involves the awareness that proximal portions of the sound (or writing) are similar in terms of their intelligible characteristics.

One aspect of this similarity—linked to what in the linguistic literature is known as cohesion (Halliday and Hasan 1976)—is that the proximal clauses making up an extended stretch of mythic discourse typically have a primary topic/person/thing or what might be termed a "center"—to emphasize the conceptual centering at the quasi-philosophical plane—that functions as a connection linking the various narrative events and episodes and forms the principal basis of continuity of the narrative discourse.[2] The topic or center is thus agent or patient in some portion of the individual events constituting total sequence. It is entirely possible for the center to be distributed randomly as agent and patient in successive events— indeed, this is in some measure what one finds in actual myth tellings. However, there is a tendency or bias in a given myth instance for the center to distribute in a nonrandom way with respect to agency and patiency. The bias may be actually characteristic of a given culture as a whole. It is the product of grammatical parallelism at the discourse level and a function simultaneously of the intelligibility of clauses and of their sensible contiguity.

This empirical claim suggests a parameter for the comparative study of myth, a parameter whose endpoints may be labeled "agent-centric" (center is predominantly an agent) and "patient-centric" (center is predominantly a patient), respectively. An ideal or perfect agent-centric discourse has a structure as in figure 3. One and the same agent appears throughout the sequence, the events differing only in regard to the patient and the action. Correspondingly, an ideal or perfect patient-centric myth has a structure as in figure 4. It is possible, in either schema, for the action type itself to be held constant in some measure, action-type distribution giving rise to a "thematic" structure, but my concern here is with the noun phrases encoding agents and patients.

The general proposition—that a given stretch of mythic discourse will show a bias toward agent- or patient-centricity—is stated crudely, and I suspect that more complex and interesting structures of parallelism at this grammatical plane will be demonstrated in the future. In an oral response

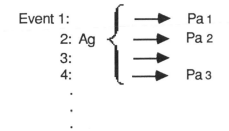

Fig. 3. Ideal agent-centric discourse

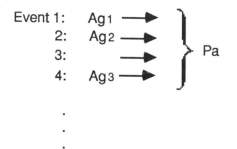

Fig. 4. Ideal patient-centric discourse

to an earlier version of the ideas presented here,[3] Terence Turner has proposed that some myths, at least, tend to show a structure in which the center moves, over the discourse, from patient to agent. In fact, subsequent investigation shows that this is sometimes the case; and one can envision yet more elaborate and intricate patterns of parallelism. The simplifying hypothesis of a contrast between agent- and patient-centricity is maintained here only for heuristic purposes.

The opening segment of an instance of myth narration recorded in 1975 among the Shokleng Indians of southern Brazil illustrates this. The myth concerns the discovery of honey by the birds and details the events surrounding this first encounter. The myth fragment as represented here is segmented into lines with side-by-side format in Shokleng and English, so that the parallelism of the actually occurring forms can be observed.

Fragment of the Origin of Honey (Shokleng, 1975)[4]

1. kũ cagõñ tẽ wũ wãñmõ tõ kòzï ki wũ
2. mõg tẽ mõg tõ kòzï ki nẽ

1. And the birds, something inside of rock,
2. The honey, the honey lay (encased) in rock,

3. we kũ òg wũ pètï gèke mũ

4. ē ya tõ òg wũ pètï gèke mũ

5. ñãglò tã to òg ya tē to mlòñ gèke ñã

6. glũ wũ pètï
7. ti ya tē to mlòñ ke mũ
8. kũ wũ culag wũ ti pèzïn man mũ

9. ti ya tē to mlòñ ke man mũ

10. kagñē wũ wèl pèzïn man mũ

11. ti ya tē to mlòñ ke
12. caklēguy pèzïn mũ
13. ti ya tē to mlòñ ke
14. kinkïm pèzïn

15. ti ya tē to mlòñ ke mũ
16. kũ ciklè wũ
17. cãgõñ tē òg tõ pètï mũ
18. ñãglò òg ya tē to mlòñ gèke

3. And then they would (try to) pierce (it),

4. With their beaks they would pierce (it),

5. but their beaks would break against (it).

6. The toucan pierced (it).
7. His beak broke against (it).
8. And the *culag* pierced it again.

9. His beak broke again against (it).

10. The *kagñē* really pierced (it) again.

11. His beak broke against (it).
12. The woodpecker pierced (it).
13. His beak broke against (it).
14. (Another) woodpecker pierced (it).

15. His beak broke against (it).
16. The *ciklè* pierced (it).
17. All of the birds pierced (it).
18. However, their beaks would break against (it).

The internal parallel structure of this portion of the longer discourse is built upon pairs of clauses (6 and 7, 8 and 9, 10 and 11, 12 and 13, 14 and 15), in which the first clause formulates the act of endeavoring to pierce a beehive, which is encased in stone, and the second clause indicates the failure: the bird's beak breaks. The principal parallels are between clauses 6, 8, 10, 12, and 14, on the one hand, and 7, 9, 11, 13, and 15, on the other. In each case, the parallels are grounded in close formal similarities between the clauses in question. The verb in the first group is "to pierce" (*pètï* or *pèzïn*), which in Shokleng designates the act of piercing (or pecking) as well as its result. The object of the clause in each case is "hive" (*mõg* = "honey" or "hive" or "bee"), although except for clause 8 (where it is present as the anaphoric pronoun *ti*) it is present only through the zero form because of a process of anaphoric deletion in co-reference. What varies between these clauses is the transitive subject noun phrase: the bird that is doing the piercing. The second group of clauses similarly shows close formal parallelism based upon the verb "to break" (*mlòñ*), the postpositional particle "against" (*to*), and the anaphorically deleted postpositional object "hive." What varies is again the subject noun phrase, which is marked by a pronoun indicating its identity with the subject noun phrase of the preceding clause.

The parallelism also extends to the clause pairs 4 (together with 3) and 5 as well as 17 and 18. Instead of reference to specific birds here, there is a generic reference to the group of "all birds" (*cãgõñ tẽ òg*). The dangling clause 16 lacks its complement, but still fits the overall parallel structure. There are thus in total seven parallel units, each *mutatis mutandis* consisting of two clauses; the parallelism lies not just in the morphemes and lexemes and their syntactic array, but also in the intonational contours and pause structures. In the first clause of each pair the intonation falls, and in the second it rises. The parallelism is simultaneously in the concrete sensuous realm of sound and in the patterns of interconnection linked to the linguistic analysis of that sound.

As isolated parallel units, this discourse fragment does not pertain to a coherent thought; at best it encodes a series of artistically organized images. What turns the otherwise disparate parallel units into a continuous thought is the presence of a single topic or center—the beehive. From the point of view of grammatical relations, the beehive is in each case in objective position, whether as the grammatical transitive or postpositional object. It never appears as subject.

If we think of parallelism not at the linguistic plane of clauses, coded in the sensible material of discourse, but rather at the more abstract plane of events, this myth fragment embodies, perhaps as perfectly as is possible, the ideal of patient-centricity. In terms of public thought, the parallelism makes the object (the beehive) stand out, turns it into something salient that can be beheld and whose properties as an entity emerge through the repeated (and in this case unsuccessful) efforts of different agents to affect it. There is no concern in this fragment with developing the properties or capabilities of a salient or powerful agent. Public thought, in other words, as encoded here, is turned toward thinghood and toward what affects thinghood.

The opposite tendency toward the agent-centric structuring of similarity is found in nearly perfect form in another myth fragment, which was also recorded among the Shokleng in 1975. This fragment occurs late in the course of the larger discourse of which it is a part, which is concerned with the origin of irreversible death and with the "giant falcons" that are said to have once terrorized the world. I will examine it from another point of view more thoroughly in the next chapter. In the portion represented below, the main character has just encountered a group of giant falcons, which he is about to destroy by shattering them. From the pieces of these giant birds emerge the numerous types of falcon we see today.

Fragment of the Giant Falcon (Shokleng, 1975)

1. kũ yi tã yugug tẽ mẽ òg nẽkukèg	1. And it is said that he destroyed the falcons.
2. kò tõ yi tã òg pènũ ge kũ	2. He threw a stick at them and said:
3. wãcõ mã yè kòkàg	3. "You will become a *kòkàg*[5]
4. kũ mã peñ ko we kè	4. and you will eat the *jacutinga* [Portuguese] bird."
5. ũ pènũ kũ yi tã	5. He hit another, it is said, and he said:
6. wãcõ mã yè yugug màg	6. "You will become a *yugug màg*
7. kũ mã põn ko we kèke	7. and you will eat snakes."
8. ũ pènũ kũ tã	8. He hit another, and said:
9. wãcõ mã yè tàtà	9. "You will become a *tàtà*
10. kũ mã cãgõñ ko we kèke	10. and you will eat little birds."
11. ũ tã kò tõ pènũ kũ tã	11. He hit another with a stick and he said:
12. wãcõ mã yè yatàñ	12. "You will become a buzzard
13. kũ mã nèn kukrè ko we kèke	13. and you will eat rotten flesh."
14. ũ pènũ man kũ yi tã	14. He hit another again, and, it is said, he said:
15. wãcõ mã yè kòkàg	15. "You will become a *kòkàg*
16. kũ mã kòñãl ko we kèke	16. and you will eat monkeys."
17. tã mẽ òg pin kan mũ	17. He finished hitting them.

The basic unit of parallelism here is a triplet of clauses. There are five of them (2-3-4, 5-6-7, 8-9-10, 11-12-13, 14-15-16). In each case, the first clause details the act of throwing a piece of wood and hitting one of the giant falcons. The next two lines are clauses of quoted speech, the first commanding the falcon in question to become a particular kind of falcon, such as one sees in the world today, and the second commanding it to eat a particular kind of food. The parallelism is grounded in numerous overt lexical, morphological, and syntactic similarities. There is, for example, the verb *pènũ*, usually meaning "to shoot and hit," but here meaning "to throw at and hit," which appears in the first line of each triplet. The command "you will become" (*wãcõ mã yè*) occurs in the second line of each triplet, and the verb *ko*, "to eat," in each third line.

As in the case of the first fragment examined above, these parallels would be merely artistic without the presence of a noun phrase tying them together and converting them into a continuous thought. Unlike the previous fragment, however, the grammatical role of the linking topic or center is not that of the transitive object; rather, it is that of subject. In each of the fully transitive clauses (1, 2, 5, 8, 11, 14, 17), the topic or center—here present in the form of a pronoun *tã*, whose co-referent noun phrase must be traced back to the very first few lines of the larger discourse in which this fragment is embedded—is the transitive subject.

The analysis is complicated by the presence of quoted speech, a topic discussed in chapter 3. From the perspective of agency, we can examine the role of the topic as speaker or hearer of the reported utterance. In fact, in each of the instances in question, the topic or center is the speaker, a grammatical role that is arguably more agentive than that of hearer. In addition there are the reported clauses themselves. In the fragment transcribed above, the quoted speech in each case is a command, and the topic occupies the role of command issuer, again, a role arguably more agentive than that of command receiver. In any event, in no case does the topic occupy the role of transitive object. Transitive object instead varies: the object of the actual throwing is in each case a different giant falcon; the object of the verb "to eat" is in each case a different kind of animal or food.

Analyzing the myth fragment on the abstract plane of the events encoded, we discover a nearly perfect structure of agent- rather than patient-centricity. From the point of view of agency, the structure is the mirror image of the previous one. What stands out is a single central character whose powers to effect transformation in the world are brought out through the parallelism. If the topic were alternatingly or randomly agent or patient, we would not have such a luminous sense of agency, a feel of power, mastery, and control. The effect is produced by the repetitive placement of the linking noun phrase in the role of grammatical subject or agent. Here again the discourse logic of parallelism acts simultaneously at the level of sensibility and intelligibility, being part of the tangible similarities within segments of the actually occurring discourse and also operating at the level of thought. This is not axiomatic propositional argumentation, but neither is it fully the logic of the concrete, something that arises from the organization of experience as the discourse history adapts to a physical environment.

It may be thought that these examples are atypical of myths more generally in Shokleng culture and elsewhere. In fact, they are unusual in the degree of perfection of the patient- and agent-centricity they display. Careful inspection of the materials in question, however, shows that parallelism of various sorts is the rule rather than the exception in these myths—an observation that confirms the claims of Hymes, Tedlock, Sherzer, Woodbury, and others—and that the parallelism dealing with agency and patiency in particular is an important aspect of the broader phenomenon.

To determine just how important, it would be of interest to compare different discourse instances that are regarded as tellings of a "single myth." Preferably, those tellings would be separated in time and be produced by different speakers, albeit within the same community, so that one could get an empirical sense of the continuity in culture through the replication of discourse. What continues to characterize discourse over long periods would presumably be more central with respect to the patterns of similarity and difference that are constitutive of what we mean by "culture." Fortunately, in the case of the first fragment transcribed and translated above, we have evidence in the form of a transcription made of a telling that occurred sometime between 1932 and 1934, during the field work of Jules Henry (1935). Over forty years separate the two instances in question; the instances are known to have been produced by different speakers; and they were recorded by different means—Henry transcribed from dictation; I tape-recorded a spontaneous narration. Nevertheless, striking similarities have emerged. I have phonemicized the transcription and segmented the 1933 version into clauses and have retranslated it giving the side-by-side Shokleng and English format.

The Origin of Honey (Shokleng, circa 1933)

1. mõg cï hã wũ kòzèy tẽ gèg mũ	1. As the bee gathered leaves
2. tẽkũ wũ glũ tẽ wũ ti nu tẽ mũ	2. the toucan followed it.
3. hãñãglò tã mõg tẽ wèg tũ tẽ	3. However, he did not see the hive
4. kũ wũ tã tawig mũ	4. and he arrived
5. kũ wũ tã mõg tẽ wèg tũ nũ tẽ ke wũ tã mũ	5. and he said: "I did not see the hive,"
6. kũ wũ kuyag wũ ti li kèn	6. and the *baitaka* [another bird] did as he did.
7. ti nu mõg cï tẽ tõ kòzèy gèñ	7. As the bee was gathering leaves
8. tẽkũ wũ tã wèl ti nu tẽ mũ	8. he really followed him.
9. hãñãglò wũ tã ti wèg tũ tẽ	9. However, he did not see the hive
10. kũ wũ tã katẽ mũ	10. and he came back
11. kũ wũ tã tawig mũ	11. and he arrived
12. kũ wũ tã mõg tẽ wèg tũ nũ tẽ ke wũ tã mũ	12. and he said: "I did not see the hive."
13. kũ wũ kãnkãl wũ mõg tẽ tõ kòzèy gèñ	13. And the *maracana* [Portuguese, another bird] when the bee was gathering leaves
14. tẽkũ ti tẽg	14. then he went,
15. tẽkũ mõg tẽ nu tẽg man mũ	15. then he went after him again,

16. kũ wũ tã mõg tẽ wèg mũ
17. kãnkãl hã wũ mõg tẽ wèg mũ

18. kũ wũ tã ẽ tãwi
19. tẽkũ mõg tẽ wèg nũ mũ
20. hãñãglò tã kòzï ki nẽ ke wũ tã mũ
21. tẽkũ òg nãli to mũ mũ
22. kũ wũ òg pètï mũ
23. hãñãglò òg òg ya tẽ to mlày gèke mũ
24. kũ wũ òg glũ glũ tẽ mõ to katèg
25. ã hã mã ã mèg mò tèg ke

26. kũ tã to katẽ mũ
27. kũ wũ tã pètï mũ
28. hãñãglò ti mèg tẽ mlày mũ
29. kũ wũ òg ẽ tõ pèzïn yè to kamàg nõne
30. hãñãglò klagmluñcè tẽ wũ
31. ẽ mà zi zi klò tẽ wũ tã

32. kul tõ wãñẽnun kũ
33. kũ wũ tã klò tẽ pètï mũ
34. pèzïn kũ tã zẽ tõ yunke mũ

35. kũ wũ tã wèl zòkòñãn
36. kũ tã pèzïn man mũ
37. kũ tã wãkè nũ yè ẽñ cõ mõg tẽ to tẽ lò
38. pètï yè ke tẽ
39. tã to tẽ mũ
40. kũ wũ tã òg mõ ne to agèlmẽg nũ mũ ke tã òg mõ mũ
41. kũ wũ òg ti mõ ẽñ cõ mõg pèzïn ke
42. kũ to gèlmẽn wã ke wũ òg ti mõ mũ
43. kũ wũ òg ti mõ ẽñ ñõ pèzïn yè yè katã ke wũ òg ti mõ mũ
44. kũ tã to katẽ
45. kũ pètï mũ
46. òg mõ pèzïn
47. kũ òg òg mlè tã ñã mũ

16. and he saw the hive,
17. it was the *maracana* who saw the hive,

18. and he arrived
19. then he said: "I saw the hive.
20. However, it is inside rock."
21. Then they all went
22. and they all pierced (it).
23. However, their beaks would break against (it),
24. and they said to the toucan: "Come here;
25. it is you who will bring your axe (beak)."

26. And he came
27. and he pierced (it).
28. However, his beak broke.
29. And there were many of them piercing (it).
30. However, the woodpecker
31. had his ceremonial mother's stone pestle

32. wrapped in a blanket
33. and he pierced the pestle,
34. (he) pierced (it) and came out the other side,

35. and he really turned it around
36. and he pierced (it) again
37. and he said: "Now I will go to the hive
38. in order to pierce it."
39. He went
40. and he said to them: "What is this noise all about?"
41. And they said to him: "I'm piercing the hive
42. and that's what all the noise is about."
43. And they said to him: "Come to pierce it for me."
44. And he came
45. and (he) pierced (it),
46. for them (he) pierced (it)
47. and he ate (it) with them.

48. mũñãglò òg wũ lègñïl tẽ mõ ti
    mõ nẽm tũ òg tẽ
49. kũ ti tõ hã we
50. kũ òg yo gòy tẽ òg yo pèyu wã
51. tẽkũ wũ tã ẽ hã ẽ tõ gòy pèyu
52. tẽkũ wũ tã ẽ hã gòy tẽ kaklan
    yè tẽ gèke mũ
53. gèke kũ wũ òg ti tõ òg tõ ẽ mõ
    mõg tẽ ki ẽ mõ nẽm tũ hã we
54. kũ òg yo gòy nẽwi wã

55. tẽkũ wũ òg ñãn kagag mũ
56. kũ wũ òg ti mõ gòy tẽ ãg to hã
    nẽ ke wũ òg lègñïl tẽ mõ mũ
57. kũ wũ tã i gòy tẽ kuwòl kò

58. ẽñ cẽg hà hã wũ gòy tẽ kaklag
    gèke mũ
59. tẽkũ wũ òg ñãn kaga
60. tẽkũ wũ òg kòzï tẽ kòzï pagpè
    mẽ wũ òg mẽ kahun mũ
61. mũñãglò ciklè hã wũ òg li kèn

62. mẽ kòzï pagpè tẽ tẽ kahun
    kànãtẽ
63. ñãglo wũ lègñïl tẽ katẽg tẽ ñã

64. kũ wũ tã ciklè tẽ mã
65. kũ wãñmèyu mũ
66. ñãglo tã lègñïl tẽ wũ ciklè tẽ
    wèg tũ tẽ
67. tẽkũ wũ tã pènẽ màg tẽ tõ
    wïmke mũ
68. ñãglo ciklè tẽ wãñmèyu

69. kũ wèg ñã
70. ñãglo lègñïl tẽ pènẽ màg tẽ
    ñãnyïn
71. kũ tã gòy tẽ kaklag mũ
72. kaklan kòlkũ tã klẽ tõ tòmke
    mũ
73. ke tẽ tã tẽ mũ
74. kũ ciklè tẽ to katẽg mũ
75. kũ wũ tã pènẽ màg tẽ tõ
    wïmke mũ

48. However, they did not give it
    to the hummingbird.
49. And he saw this
50. and he hid the water from them.
51. When he had hidden the water
52. then he would regularly go to
    drink the water.
53. Thus it was and because they
    gave him nothing at the hive
54. therefore he did that to the
    water.

55. Then their mouths were dry
56. and they said to the humming-
    bird: "Is the water near us?"
57. And he (said): "No, the water
    is far away.

58. I who fly well regularly drink
    the water."
59. Then their mouths were dry.
60. Then they would lick rocks that
    were damp all over.
61. Meanwhile, the *ciklè* [another
    bird] did the same as them.

62. He went about licking the
    damp rocks.
63. However, the hummingbird
    was coming

64. and the *ciklè* heard him
65. and he hid himself.
66. But the hummingbird did not
    see the *ciklè,*
67. so he tilted back the lid [lit.,
    "big turtle"].
68. Meanwhile, the *ciklè* was
    hidden

69. and (he) was seeing.
70. Meanwhile, the hummingbird
    tilted back the lid
71. and he drank the water.
72. (He) drank (it) and then put the
    lid back.
73. Thus it was and he went
74. and the *ciklè* came to (it)
75. and he tilted back the lid

76. kũ tã hi hi hi hi hi gòy wem gòy wem gòy wem ke wũ tã mũ

76. and he said: "Hi hi hi hi hi, I see water, I see water, I see water."

77. kũ wũ òg mã kũ to kamũ mũ

77. And they heard (this) and came to (it),

78. nãli kamũ kanè mũ

78. every one of them came.

79. mũñãglò lègñïl tẽ to katẽ mũ

79. Then the hummingbird came

80. kũ tã ẽ pènẽ màg tẽ man

80. and he got his lid

81. kũ gòy tẽ klẽ nẽ mũ

81. and sat (it) on top of the water.

82. hãñãglò wũ òg kakòmõ

82. However, they paid no attention.

83. òg wũ ti li kèn mũ

83. They did the same.

84. tõ wïmke man mũ

84. (They) tilted back the lid again.

85. kũ wèg tẽ lègñïl tẽ towañ mũ

85. Seeing this, the hummingbird desisted.

86. ñaglo wũ òg gòy tẽ ki kamàg kò

86. Meanwhile, many were at the water

87. kũ wũ òg mẽ kaklag mũ

87. and they drank all about

88. òg ñãn kaga tẽ yògï kò

88. because their mouths were very dry.

89. hãkũ òg tõ gòy tẽ kònãg mũ gèke wã

89. That is why they regularly go to look for water.

To compare the two myth tellings, it is necessary to examine the remainder of the fragment presented earlier, which I will do below. However, it may be remarked that the 1975 fragment is taken from the beginning of the myth and in that telling the entire opening sequence found in 1933 (lines 1–20) is missing. It is as if the initial portion broke off in the replication processes that have occurred over a forty-year period. Lines 1–18 of the 1975 instance instead show a similarity to lines 21–29 of the 1933 instance.

In 1933, the pattern of parallelism in relation to the piercing of the hive is greatly reduced with respect to the 1975 telling. The basic clause pair—in which description of an attempt to pierce the hive is followed by a description of the resulting broken beak—occurs only twice, in lines 22–23 and 27–28. This contrasts with the five to seven occurrences in the 1975 telling. Does this reflect an attenuation of the patient-centricity in the 1933 myth? No—in fact, the opening lines 1–20 of the 1933 myth display a strong patient-centricity manifested in the logic of discourse parallelism. Here there are three parallel units (lines 1–5, 6–12, 13–20), but they concern the event not of piercing the hive but rather of finding or "seeing" it. In each unit there are clauses, first, describing the following of the bee (lines 1–2, 7–8, 13–15); second, reporting the seeing or not seeing of the hive (lines 3, 9, 16–17); third, indicating the return to the other birds (lines 4, 10–11, 18); and, fourth, quoting the speech of the bird in question that reports his success or failure (5, 12, 19–20). The parallels involve morphological, lexical, and syntactic similarities, and in some cases are nearly verbatim repetitions (for example, lines 4 and 11 or 5 and 12).

As in the case of the 1975 fragment, what ties together the various clauses here, converting them into a continuous thought, is the hive. In both cases, moreover, the topic or center occurs in the position of transitive object: at the plane of events, the fragment is again entirely patient-centric. What stands out luminously against the background of narration is the object, the thing to which something is done, the entity that is affected by transformations occurring in the world.

Interestingly, the other major object in this series of clauses is the bee, which in Shokleng is lexically identified with honey and hive through the form *mõg*. In its first two occurrences (lines 1 and 7), it is found together with the modifier *cï*, "insect," hence, "honey insect," but in its next full occurrence (line 13) it assumes its normal short form as *mõg*. The parallelism at the sensible level of discourse form expands the patient-centricity of the discourse by bringing into the same line of thought two ideas that in English are lexically distinct: bee and hive.

If we were studying exclusively the content of the myth, we would note the differences between the 1933 and 1975 tellings that involve events. The 1975 telling contains no mention of discovering the hive. From a discourse-centered point of view, one observes not only this difference but also a key similarity. Both instances treat the center as patient; they both foreground the object to which something is done, the recipient of actions originating from agents that are less central to the continuity of the narrative. Moreover, the amplified parallelism of the 1975 telling seems to correct for the absence of the opening patient-centric sequence of the 1933 telling. What remains similar between the two is the salience of the hive as an object, brought out through the force of discourse logic. What differs concerns the myth conceived as content, obeying the logic of the concrete.

The obvious differences between these tellings concern the opening segments. The remainder of the 1975 telling shows remarkable similarity to its 1933 counterpart. One can observe here the continuity of culture at the level of actually occurring discourse. Despite their separation by over forty years of history, there are numerous tangible similarities at the discourse level, involving morphology, lexicon, and syntax, with the similarities in some clauses tending toward identity. The line numbering of the transcription picks up from the fragment given earlier.

Fragment of the Origin of Honey (Shokleng, 1975)

19. wãñmlïce wũ kacin tã tòge nẽ

19. The *wãñmlïce* [a kind of woodpecker] was this small [gesture with finger]

20. kũ lã ẽ nõ zi klò pèyu mũ

20. and he hid his mother's stone pestle.

21. pẽyu kũ tã cobertor tòg tõ tã wãñẽnug

21. (He) hid (it) and he covered (it) over with a blanket.

22. kũ tã pètï gèke mũ

22. And he would pierce it,

23. pètïn pigzïn

23. (he) pierced (it), (he) pierced (it) repeatedly,

24. kũ tã zẽ tõ yunke wãñkòto tã mẽ làglum gèke mũ

24. he pierced (it) through repeatedly to the other side.

25. tòge kũ nũ òg mõ pètï tẽg ke

25. (He) said: "And now I will pierce (it) for them."

26. kũ tã to tẽ mũ

26. And he went to (it).

27. to tẽ lò òg to cï nõne to ẽ ya mlànmlòñ

27. (He) went to (it) and they were lying around with their beaks broken

28. kũ tã pètï mũ

28. and he pierced (it).

29. caklẽgu tẽ òg mõ tã kòzï tẽ pètï ñã

29. He pierced the rock for the woodpeckers.

30. tã ki tõ lumke

30. He pierced all the way through

31. kũ tã to mẽ peg̣zïn kũ tòge

31. and he pierced (it) all about and stopped.

32. kũ mẽ ko ke mũ

32. And (they) ate all about

33. kũ òg mẽ ko nõ

33. and they were eating all about.

34. òg wũ to ti kàgze

34. They were pleased with him because of it

35. kũ òg e e e e

35. and they said: "E e e e

36. wãñmlïce wũ ãg mõ mõg pètï mũ

36. *wãñmlïce* pierced the hive for us."

37. kũ òg mẽ ko mũ

37. And they ate all about

38. to òg ñãn kagag mũ

38. because of this their mouths were dry.

39. lègñïl tẽ mõ òg neñ mũ

39. They did not give (it) to the hummingbird

40. kũ tã gòy kònã tẽ mũ

40. and he went looking for water.

41. gòy mèl tòge lò katèle

41. There along the riverbed he came

42. kũ tã wèg mũ

42. and he saw (it),

43. gòy tẽ we

43. (he) saw the water,

44. kũ tã kaklag mũ

44. and he drank (it).

45. kaklag tẽ tã nẽzeñ mũ

45. After drinking (it), he closed (it).

46. gòy tẽ klẽ tã tõge ẽ pènhèl màg
47. kũ tã klẽ tõ tomke
48. kũ nẽm mũ
49. kũ òg ti tawi
50. kũ òg ti mõ lègñïl gòy u we mã gèke mũ

51. tã i
52. ñãglò òg tõ ko
53. tẽkũ òg ñãn kagag mũ

54. lègñïl gòy we mã

55. kũ tã i
56. ẽñ cẽg hà hã wũ gòy tẽ wèg gèke mũ
57. gòy tẽ kuwòl kò gèke mũ

58. ñãglo òg wũ ẽ ñãn kagag tõ ẽ kàglò
59. kũ caklẽgu tẽ ti klẽ pènu tà ti nõnã tẽ nõ

60. kũ òg tògtẽ mẽ gòy tẽ kònãg mũ
61. ẽ ñãn kagag

62. kũ gòy mèl nu tẽ pagpè mẽ ka- hun òg nõ

63. ñãglo lègñïl tẽ ñïl ke katẽ

64. ciklè wũ ti klãkè hã klẽ nã
65. kũ tã ti yàgklẽ tã katã
66. ẽ pènhèl màg tẽ tã klẽ tõ wïmke
67. kũ tã kaklag mũ
68. kaklag kũ tã mẽ wãñkàpèg tã tẽ mũ
69. kũ tã wèg tẽ
70. tã to katẽ
71. tã zanñïg mũ
72. zanñïg kũ tã kaklag mũ

46. Atop the water he put his big lid
47. and he covered (it) over
48. and (he) left (it).
49. And he came to them
50. and they said to him: "Hummingbird, have you been seeing any good water?"

51. He (said): "No."
52. However, because they ate (it),
53. therefore, their mouths were dry.

54. "Hummingbird, did you see water?"

55. And he (said): "No.
56. I who fly well regularly see the water
57. the water is far away," (he would say).

58. Meanwhile, their dry mouths were tormenting them
59. and the woodpeckers' tongues hung out the sides of their mouths

60. and they looked all about for water
61. because their mouths were dry.

62. They went down the riverbed licking (wherever it was) damp all over.

63. Meanwhile, the hummingbird came buzzing along.

64. *Ciklè* was above his cave
65. and he came above him.
66. He tilted back his big lid
67. and he drank (it).
68. After drinking he washed himself all over
69. and he was seeing.
70. He came to (it).
71. He lifted (it) up.
72. (He) lifted (it) up and he drank (it).

73. kaklag ñã	73. (He) was drinking (it).
74. tã hunke	74. He stopped.
75. kũ tã ñã ñã	75. He was standing there.
76. tã wel kaklañ man mũ	76. He really drank (it) again.
77. kaklag ñã	77. (He) was drinking (it).
78. tã wel kaklañ man mũ	78. He was really drinking (it) again.
79. wãhã ẽ ñãn kagag mẽ tũ	79. Now his mouth was not dry,
80. kũ tã e e e gòy wem gòy wem ke	80. and he said: "E e e I see water, I see water."
81. mũlò ki mòl	81. Then (they all) came running,
82. passarinho ki mòl	82. (all the) birds came running.
83. ti paklẽ tẽ tõ klẽ tõ wïmke	83. (They) tilted back his lid
84. kũ zu mũ	84. and (they) threw (it) aside.
85. ñãglo tã zumke gòy tẽ	85. Meanwhile, the water flowed out
86. kũ òg mẽ kaklag mũ	86. and they drank (it) all about.
87. kaklañ kane mũ	87. They finished drinking (it)
88. kũ òg to ciklè tẽ kàgzèg mũ	88. and they were pleased with the *ciklè* because of it.
89. kàgze	89. (They) were pleased
90. kũ ti mõ e e e e e ciklè wũ ãg mõ gòy wèg mũ gèke mũ	90. and (they) were saying to him: "E e e e the *ciklè* saw water for us."

Anthropologists sometimes despair of the empirical solidarity or reality of their object of study—culture, as that which is transmitted across the generations by means of social interaction—but an example such as the one above attests to the validity of the concept. Simultaneously, however, it illustrates the difference between the classical conception of culture, as an abstract system of meaning, and the discourse-centered view, wherein culture resides in and is transmitted by means of actually occurring discourse. The 1933 and 1975 tellings are both similar and different, and the similarities and differences can be traced to the actual discourse, together with the patterns of semiotic interpretation of them. The notion of culture as an abstract system, in this case construed in terms of a "myth," as an entity existing at the ideal plane, introduces unnecessary theoretical problems and distracts attention from the empirical investigation of publicly accessible forms.

In some cases, the similarities between the 1933 and 1975 instances involve nearly verbatim repetition. This is true especially of the quoted speech, as has been observed elsewhere (Urban 1984:321). Compare:

1933 (line 58):   ēñ cēg hà hā wũ gòy tē kaklag gèke mũ
1975 (line 56):   ēñ cēg hà hā wũ gòy tē wèg gèke mũ

Or:

1933 (line 57):   . . . gòy tē kuwòl kò
1975 (line 57):   gòy tē kuwòl kò . . .

A difference here is the fact that these two clauses, while part of the same instance of reported speech, are reversed in the two tellings. Another close similarity in reported speech is:

1933 (line 76):   kũ tā hi hi hi hi hi gòy wem gòy wem gòy wem ke . . .
1975 (line 80):   kũ tā e e e gòy wem gòy wem ke

Here the difference concerns the number of repetitions of the phrase "(I) see water."

The major similarities between these instances, however, do not reside exclusively or even primarily in the verbatim repetition of clauses. They are also to be found in the sequencing and parallel array of lexical items and their grammatical roles. This is what gives us the impression of an underlying conceptual structure. There is, for example, the repeated use of the verbs "to pierce" (*pèti* or *pèzïn*); "to see" (*wèg* or *we*); "to drink" (*kaklag* or *kaklañ*). There is also the repeated occurrence of various nouns and noun phrases, such as "honey/hive" (*mõg*); "water" (*gòy*); and "hummingbird" (*lègñïl*). Through their repetitive sequencing, their parallel array, the given discourse instance appears to embody a conceptual structure, but that structure is grounded in patterns of discourse-internal similarity and contiguity. And the similarities between tellings over time—in this case over forty years—are themselves grounded in these patterns.

This is not to deny a significance to concrete logic. If honey and water are regimented in accord with the discourse logic of parallelism, they are also naturally linked. As ethnographers of central Brazil know, consuming large quantities of honey produces thirst; indeed, the Indians very often dilute honey before consuming it (Lévi-Strauss 1973:52). There is a sensory foundation, an experiential anchoring to the sequential contiguity between the halves of this longer stretch of discourse. At the same time, such structures underspecify the empirical richness of patterning of the myths that the discourse-centered approach brings out, patterning that also manifests itself in the replication of discourse over time. This latter patterning pertains not only to brain structures, but to the structures of culture as a malleable, adaptable organization of semiosis.

In the midst of such discourse patterns, one can single out, at the quasi-philosophical plane, the intense overall patient-centricity of the two discourse instances in question. Both are dual-centered, the first portion focusing on bee/hive/honey and the second on water. In 1975, "water" (*gòy*) as an overt or anaphorically deleted form dominates the discourse with approximately 25 occurrences in transitive object position and none in transitive subject position. It provides the continuity of the narrative, although there is competition for the center from "hummingbird," occurring in transitive subject position some 14 times and in object position once, with other occurrences in intransitive subject position, and also from *ciklè*, with occurrences in some 12 transitive subject slots. On balance, however, the discourse is about what happens to the honey/hive and to water, not about what the birds did. The honey/hive is "seen" and "pierced," water is "drunk" and "seen." Although there are significant elements of agent-centricity, the world emerges most crisply through the discourse as a world of entities to which things are done or happen, rather than as a world of prominent and powerful agents, who go along affecting and transforming numerous facets of the world. Even though the hummingbird and *ciklè* are overwhelmingly agentive, all of their actions center around the water—and they are not the only agents who act upon it.

From the point of view of social and cultural anthropology more generally, however, the isolation of an instance of cultural continuity and change in actual discourse, together with the establishment of formal patterns that give shape to a conceptual structure, is too narrow to allow us to examine the broader totality of culture, what from a discourse-centered point of view is the discourse history characterizing a community. It is necessary to move from local analyses to more global characterizations. While it is not yet possible adequately to demonstrate such a move, the analysis of the instances in question nevertheless suggests its direction. If the relationship of similarity between two instances that are viewed as distinct tellings of the "same myth" involves the similarity in patient-centric patterning (i.e., in the parallelism of role relations of the centers or topics), does this patterning extend across discourse instances viewed as "different myths"? In other words, are there similarities that characterize a range of discourse across the broader sweep of culture, in this case, a patient-centric bias that characterizes the complex of discourse, giving rise to a world view or philosophical orientation in the culture more generally that is distinct from that of other cultures?

In the fragment from "The Giant Falcon" (Shokleng, 1975) given earlier, parallelism of an intensely agent-centric variety occurs. As can be seen from an inspection of the longer discourse in which this fragment is embedded (chapter 3), however, the agent-centric episode is atypical. To a Western sensibility—sensibility here indicating the felt character of the sensuous, concrete experience of discourse parallelism—the protagonist seems strangely passive, the obedient executor rather than originator of commands. The same sensibility is characteristic of much of the discourse in Shokleng culture.

In fact, no mythic discourse collected thus far among Shokleng shows a consistent agent-centricity, such as that found, for example, among the Bella Coola Indians of the Northwest Coast of North America, as reported by Boas (1898). Numerous examples could be chosen, the one selected here, "The Tradition of SE'lia" (Boas 1898:50–53), being a reasonable representative of the agent-centric bias. While the myth is given entirely in English, we get a sense of the parallelism of grammatical roles in which the center appears. Owing to its length, only the first half is reproduced.

Fragment of the Tradition of SE'lia (Bella Coola, 1898)
 1. In the beginning our world was dark.
 2. At that time Tōtosōn´x descended from heaven,
 3. and reached our world on a mountain near the river Wa´k·itemai (Fraser River).
 4. Here he built a house,
 5. in which he lived in the company of the Raven.
 6. The latter had a black canoe which was called "Raven."
 7. The two resolved to travel
 8. in order to find people.
 9. They descended the river
10. until they came to the sea.
11. After some time they reached a house
12. which was covered inside and outside with shells.
13. The totem-post of the house was also covered with shells.
14. It shone like the sun.
15. They saw a canoe on the beach,
16. and this too was completely covered with abelone [*sic*] shells.
17. A chief, whose name was PElxanē´mx ("abelone man"), invited them to enter his house.
18. As soon as Tōtosōn´x reached this place,
19. the sun rose.
20. If he had not found the place of the abelone chief,
21. there would be no sun.
22. Tōtosōn´x did not wish to stay.
23. He looked at the house,
24. and saw something turning about on top of it.
25. When they came nearer,
26. he saw that it was a Mink,

27. which was running about on the roof.
28. Many people were inside the house.
29. When Tōtosōn´x approached and saw the beautiful canoe,
30. he wished to have it.
31. He offered the chief their canoe in exchange.
32. This offer was accepted,
33. and Tōtosōn´x travelled on with the abelone canoe.
34. The Raven staid [*sic*] with the abelone chief.
35. Tōtosōn´x continued his travels,
36. following the course of the sun.
37. First he travelled southward,
38. and came to the post which stands in the west of our world.
39. From here he travelled on,
40. and reached the copper country, which is situated a little farther to the north.
41. When he saw the country from a distance,
42. it looked like fire.
43. When he came near,
44. he saw a house which was built of copper.
45. On the beach there was a canoe,
46. which was also made of copper.
47. The chief was sitting in front of the house,
48. and invited him to come in.
49. A carved post in the shape of a man was standing in front of the chief's house.
50. It also was made of copper.
51. Then Tōtosōn´x offered to exchange canoes with the chief.
52. The chief took the abelone canoe,
53. while Tōtosōn´x took the copper canoe.
54. The chief also gave him a large box made of copper,
55. and he gave him his daughter La´liayōts in marriage.
56. Besides this, he gave him olachen [a type of fish],
57. which was to serve as food for his daughter.
58. In the copper box were all the whistles and other paraphernalia of the sisau´k· ceremonial.
59. He travelled on,
60. and reached our country in the north.
61. When he arrived,
62. the sun began to shine for the first time.
63. He met a chief,
64. to whom he gave the sisau´k· whistles.
65. Wherever he met people,
66. he presented to them the whistles of this ceremonial.
67. Thus he met the Haida, the Tsimshian, the Git'amā´t, the Gitlōp, the Xa´exaes, the Hē´iltsuq.
68. He travelled on,

69. and reached Wa´nuk (Rivers Inlet).
70. There he threw the olachen into the water.
71. They multiplied,
72. and since that time there have been many olachen in that river.
73. He travelled on,
74. and came to Nux·îts, to SōmxōL, and to Ts´i'o, on the lake above Rivers Inlet.
75. He gave the chiefs of these places the sisau´k· whistles.
76. He arrived at Asē´ix, in Talio´mx·.
77. Here he left whistles and olachen.
78. He did the same at Q'oa´px and Nū´ikᵘ! in South Bentinck Arm.
79. Then he travelled down the fiord to the little island QEˉnk´ilst, at the mouth of South Bentinck Arm.
80. Here he left the sisau´k· whistles.
81. Finally he came to SEˉlia, near the entrance to South Bentinck Arm.
82. He liked this place very much,
83. and was surprised not to see any people.
84. He travelled on,
85. and reached the mouth of Bella Coola River.
86. Here he staid [*sic*] four winters.
87. He used his whistles,
88. and performed the sisau´k· ceremonial.
89. At the end of this time a quarrel arose between him and the chief at Bella Coola,
90. therefore he turned back.
91. When he came to SEˉlia,
92. he stopped and built a house.
93. The house resembled in shape that of the chief La´lia.
94. He called the house "La´lia."
95. His wife, the daughter of the chief of the copper country, had many children.
96. They increased rapidly,
97. and became the tribe SEˉliamx·.
98. He invited the neighboring tribes to a feast.
99. He performed the sisau´k· ceremonial.
100. He never gave feasts in honor of his youngest son, Señxag·ila.

The internal parallel organization of this myth is built around traveling, the main figure linking together the 9 parallel units being Tōtosōn´x. Despite this difference, the discourse shows an intriguing similarity to the opening portions (lines 1–20) of the 1933 "Origin of Honey." Both are concerned with discovery, or "seeing" the world, and there is in each case little action or jostling about. In the Bella Coola discourse, we are situated in a serene world, whose wonders—an abalone-shell canoe, a mink atop a house, a country that from a distance looks "like fire," a large copper box, and so forth—are apprehended for the first time. Intuitively, the myth is about making contact with a new and uncharted world. Similarly, lines 1–20 of the 1933 "Origin of Honey" are concerned with probing and apprehending the world—in this case, specifically, the previously unknown hive. The narrative depicts a first encounter with this mysterious entity. The similarities can be traced to the lexical parallels within the discourse instances themselves. The first 20 lines of the 1933 "Origin of Honey" are dominated by the verb "see," which occurs 7 times. Similarly, "see" is a principal verb in the Se′lia tradition. As in the first 20 lines of the Shokleng myth, it occurs 7 times in this fragment.

Despite this similarity, these instances are distinct in another regard. Whereas "The Origin of Honey" is essentially patient-centric, the various events being woven together by the continuous presence of the honey/hive and water, "Tradition of Se′lia" is essentially agent-centric. The single entity that ties together the narrative is the ancestor Totosōn′x, who appears in some 41 transitive clauses, if Boas's translations are reasonably accurate. Moreover, Tōtosōn′x is decidedly an agent. Of the 41 transitive appearances, he is the subject in 36 (88%). In only 2 is he the direct object, in the remaining instances being the indirect object of the verb "to give." There is no patient that comes close to competing with this agent for the center— or even another major agent, although Raven makes an appearance initially. The myth is thus decidedly agent-centric and even, at points, approximates the ideal type of agent-centric structure discussed earlier.

While no single prominent patient emerges from this narrative, an intriguing similarity can be found among some of the patients. They are containers (houses, canoes, and boxes) of a peculiar perceptual saliency, shining "like the sun," or looking "like fire," because they are covered with abalone shells or fashioned from copper. The agents in "The Origin of Honey" similarly form a class—they are all birds. There may be a more general tendency, or constraint on the discourse logic of parallelism, that in such strongly agent- or patient-centric myths the corresponding patients or agents, while multiple and thus not qualifying as a center, nevertheless tend to be elaborated according to a principle of similarity.

The contrast between these myths is parallel to the metaphysical subject-object contrast. In the Shokleng myth, attention is concentrated on the object (honey/hive and water), and one is interested in the subjects (the various birds) only insofar as they bring us into contact with the object. The discourse illuminates the object by probing it through various subjective experiences, for example, the various birds endeavoring to "see" the honey/hive. In contrast, in the Bella Coola myth we are located, so to speak, inside the subject. We peer out at the world through his eyes, seeing what he sees: abalone-shell canoes, copper boxes, and so forth. The discourse illuminates the subject by following him and bringing us into contact with his manifold perceptions of the world outside. There is nothing fully comparable to this agent-centricity among the Shokleng.

It is not possible to investigate in detail each of the recorded Bella Coola and Shokleng myths to determine their relative agent- and patient-centricity. We can imagine, however, that there may be similarities in the patterning of mythic (or even nonmythic) discourse within the broader cultural wholes. This is a byproduct of a possibly general principle of culture, conceptualized as a discourse history, namely, that discourse instances within a culture can come to resemble one another in certain respects through iconicity. This gives rise to the possibility of systematic variation between one culture and another.

Given the difficulty involved in analyzing every myth telling, an alternative test—and one that furnishes evidence of linkages between the microscopic level of discourse and the macroscopic level of culture that is of interest to social anthropologists—could be found in the possible implications of a systematic bias as regards agent- or patient-centricity within the culture as a whole. In other words, what general consequences ought to follow, if the discourse within a culture does tend to be biased toward agent- or patient-centricity? Three such consequences or implications can be brought out here.

(1) *Animacy Levels.* Silverstein (1976a; cf. Dixon 1979) has elaborated the idea of a referential or noun phrase hierarchy, which is useful in cross-linguistic investigation. Some of the properties of this hierarchy may be relevant for deducing consequences of agent- and patient-centricity. Within the hierarchy, certain noun phrases are seen as universally good agents, others as better patients. A simplified version of the hierarchy is given in figure 5.

As we move up the hierarchy, animacy increases, and with it the probability that a noun phrase will play the role of agent, that is, will occupy transitive subject position in an active construction. Correspondingly, as we move down, animacy decreases, and with it the probability of finding the noun phrase in an agentive role. The inverse relationship obtains with patiency. These linguistic results should correspond to patterns of discourse-internal parallelism. A beehive, for example, ought to make a good patient. Consequently, a myth with the noun phrase "beehive" as its center ought to tend toward patient-centricity. Analogously, a human ancestor is a good agent. A myth with such a named ancestor, for example, Tōtosōn´x, ought to tend toward agent-centricity.

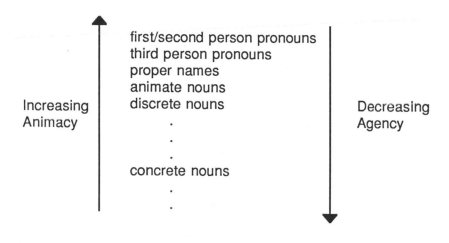

Fig. 5. Animacy or noun phrase hierarchy

The principal implication proposed here is that the centers or topics of mythic discourse are proportionally more animate as the bias within the discourse tends toward agent-centricity. Correspondingly, the more patient-centric the bias, the more discourse is likely to have as its center inanimate objects or entities of lesser animacy. This is in some measure confirmed by an examination of the Bella Coola and Shokleng myths recorded to date.

When the centers are of roughly equal animacy on the noun phrase hierarchy, the difference between an agent- and patient-centric bias should still be detectable. The results of an attempt to distinguish between central Brazilian and Bella Coola myths in this regard have been published elsewhere (Urban 1981a). Both cultures have myths centering upon a young boy becoming a man. In the Bella Coola Salmon-Boy myth, the agency levels tend to be high, the noun phrase appearing as transitive subject in between 60% and 80% of the total number of occurrences in which it is either transitive subject or object. In contrast, in the central Brazilian stories dealing with "The Origin of Cooking" (Lévi-Strauss 1969b)—the center here again being a young boy making the transition to manhood— the corresponding figures range from 30% to 40%.

A possibly related consequence is the use of the highly animate first person singular pronoun, "I." While the results are by no means conclusive, it is of interest that among the Shokleng it proved to be impossible to collect narrative life histories, where the discourse center is first person.

Speakers would invariably shift the center to the community or to other individuals, or they would stop with the extended narration of a single event, usually one in which they played little or no role. This is what one would expect in a culture whose mythic discourse is biased toward patient-centricity.

(2) *Animacy Shifting and Hyperanimacy.*[6] There is a tendency in every mythology for animacy levels to be modified, for animals to speak the way humans speak, for transformations between humans and animals to occur, for objects to become agents. Similarly, there is a tendency to modify the traits or characteristics of everyday entities, as in the creation of giant animals or humans or the fusion of animal with human traits. One may suspect that these modifications, affecting the animacy level and agentivity of entities, correlate in some way with agent-/patient-centric bias. However, one characteristic of mythologies that bears an obvious correlation with agentive bias is the formation of what may be called hyperanimate entities, of which the Old Testament God is an example.

By hyperanimate entity is meant a being, as encoded in a noun phrase, endowed with extraordinary powers of control over events and actions. Such a being is an agent par excellence, possessing the ability to create, to destroy, to modify, without simultaneously being affected. The hyperanimate entity is usually an agent in event types, rarely a patient. One may include in this category what are known as culture heroes, as well as true gods. The empirical claim is this: one should find hyperanimate entities in the same proportion as one finds an agent-centric bias in mythological discourse in a culture. Correspondingly, such entities ought to be less prominent in, or indeed altogether absent from, a culture governed by a patient-centric bias.

The Bella Coola myths recorded by Boas contain at least one entity that qualifies as hyperanimate, although others, such as the Salmon-Boy, qualify in varying degrees. That entity is the Sun, who is known as Senx, and also called Tā́ata (our father), Smai'yakila (the sacred one), or SmayalṓLla" (Boas 1898:29). He is for Bella Coola a creator figure, who possesses extraordinary powers of agentive control, "making," "telling," "giving," "teaching," and "forbidding," in short, constituting the world as it is presently known. He is also the agent who, in the village origin traditions, "sends down" the first ancestors to earth. Sun is by no means a perfect agent. In "The Salmon" myth, discussed above, for instance, he is put in the role of patient by Salmon-Boy, who thereby demonstrates his own agentive powers. Sun is also, in certain traditions, originally "liberated from a box" by Raven. On balance, however, the Bella Coola Sun is seen as an especially powerful agent, capable of exercising control over virtually everything in this world.

Shokleng myths, in contrast, contain no entities of comparable animacy, though analogous creation scenes do occur. The differences in the way creation occurs are especially salient. Shokleng mythology includes a lengthy origin account (known as the *wãñēklèn*), considered in more detail in chapter 4. The myth recounts the creation of the tapir, jaguar, and snake. In each case, however, the creation is effected not by a single hyperanimate actor, but always by a succession of actors.

In the jaguar creation, for example, one actor fashions an image of the jaguar from a certain type of wood; a second actor arrives and paints a portion of the animal; a third actor arrives, painting an additional portion, and he is followed by a fourth, who completes the painting; finally, the jaguar is instructed as to how it ought to behave, in a passage reminiscent of some Bella Coola episodes, and it proceeds to cry out, imitating a certain bird. But it is evident from a study of the discourse that the center of this protracted creation episode is the jaguar itself, the patient. The episode is patient-centric, as is "The Origin of Honey" (discussed above). The succession of birds searching for and endeavoring to pierce the hive is analogous to the succession of agents, each effecting some transformation of the wood into the jaguar.

The complementarity of these conceptions of "creation" is worth remarking. In Bella Coola, creation or transformation occurs effortlessly, with the creator-transformer himself performing multiple acts. The creation, however, as in the Judeo-Christian Genesis tradition, is only effortless thanks to the vast agentive power of the creator-transformer. In Shokleng, in contrast, creation appears as an arduous task, being accomplished only with the help of multiple agents. The arduousness of creation may be viewed as a product of the lack of agentive power of the creators. Whereas Bella Coola focus upon the agent, and upon his capacity for control, Shokleng focus upon the patient, and upon the multifaceted problem of effecting a transformation of it.

(3) *Individuation and Cross-Narrative Continuity.* A third consequence stems from the inherent asymmetry in the relationship between agents and patients. Good agents appear to be universally more natural centers for narrative than good patients. This is so because, whereas the range of actions of which a powerful agent is capable is virtually without limit, the range of effects that a patient can undergo is more circumscribed. Doing something to an entity very often changes its nature. When an entity is affected in too great a degree, we no longer recognize it as the same. Hence,

there is a natural tendency, under a patient-centric bias, for the center of a narrative to fragment. In contrast, a good agent can continue, in theory indefinitely, to perform acts without experiencing any corresponding change in identity. Indeed, an entity typically becomes all the more salient, achieves an even more well-defined identity, the more it acts.

Under an agent-centric bias, therefore, one should find entities or characters who transcend the specific myth (cross-narrative continuity), and whose identities or "personalities" are comparatively sharply defined (individuation). It is as if these mythological characters achieve an independence from the collection of tellings constituting a single myth. They have a life of their own, apart from the specific narrative. In contrast, under a patient-centric bias, the tendency is for specifically mythological characters to be myth-bound, that is, to appear only in a specific myth, having no independent life, and to be less individuated or unique. From inspection of a corpus in terms of cross-narrative regularity and individuation, we should thus, in some measure, be able to predict the degree of agent- or patient-centric bias governing it and to check this prediction against an analysis of the agency of centers at certain levels of animacy.

The Bella Coola mythology contains various examples of mythological entities whose existence transcends the single narrative. Sun has already been mentioned in this regard; he makes appearances not only in village origin traditions, but also in "The Salmon" and in several other distinct myths, although, curiously, nowhere is he fully the center of a myth.[7] Similar to Sun is Raven, who likewise makes appearances in several distinct narratives, though he is not so unequivocally a strong agent. One could also mention the Sneneiq, oversized necrophagous humanoid creatures, who appear in several myths. However, in this case we are dealing not with a single individual, but with a species of mythological entities.

Seemingly as a result of cross-narrative continuity, many of these Bella Coola entities take on a life of their own, independent of the specific text. As Boas observes, Bella Coola have in some measure evolved a system, "in which a number of supernatural beings have been coordinated" (Boas 1898: 27). Simultaneously, these beings show signs of individuation, though here the matter is far from clear-cut. While Sun typically occupies a lofty, fully controlling position, in "The Salmon" myth his schemes are thwarted by Salmon-Boy. Raven, in at least one myth, is a tragicomic trickster figure, but in the village origin traditions he appears as one of those placid purposive ancestors, such as originally were responsible for populating this world. Nevertheless, the degree of individuation, at least of the Sun, is much greater than anything found in the Shokleng corpus.

Insofar as could be determined, Shokleng mythological entities are entirely myth-bound. None of them achieves an independence comparable to that achieved by the Bella Coola Sun. Jaguar appears in one myth as a humanlike character, but there is no connection between this entity, who, incidentally, appears in no other myth, and the jaguar created in the above-mentioned myth. The latter is the actual, prowling jaguar found today. The same myth-boundedness obtains in the case of every other Shokleng mythological entity. In the lengthy origin saga, certain individuals carry over from one episode to the next, so that we may detect some cross-narrative continuity here. Still, it is remarkable how little one comes to know these characters as individuals, and, indeed, what a minor role they play in the overall saga.

*W*hereas concrete logic and the brain structures detected by Lévi-Strauss are associated with the generic characteristics of human thought, the discourse logic of parallelism gives rise to structures of public thought, and these structures vary from one community to the next, albeit in accord with such constraints as the noun phrase hierarchy. Despite its externalized character—its participation in tradition and in the replication of culture over time—the parallel patterning of discourse does pertain to the realm of thought, to the intelligible as well as to the sensuous. And it is no less imaginable that public thought operates through discourse-internal parallelism, through a logic of similarity, contiguity, and difference, than it is to imagine that it operates through axiomatic propositionality and relations of consequence or entailment, or through the sensuous logic of the concrete.

CHAPTER 3

Consciousness, Norm, and Metadiscourse Parallelism

Parallel arrays within mythic discourse occupy a peculiar position with respect to thought. Unlike the salient parallelism of chants, singing, and other marked speech styles, where consciousness or awareness is attracted to the repetition and internal patterning of similarity and difference, much of the parallelism in myth is unobtrusive. The myth is experienced as linear narrative, a story, not as a poetic structure built up from units that are repeated with variation—such as the units punctuated by traveling in the Bella Coola "Tradition of SE´lia" or those involving the effort of birds to locate the hive in the Shokleng "Origin of Honey." Nevertheless, parallelism exercises its sway, produces an aesthetic experience of felt power to the discourse, lends its persuasive or compelling force to the thought shaped by it. Because it operates just beneath the surface of consciousness, by suggesting connections rather than by explicitly stating them, parallelism enables the discourse to participate simultaneously in the intellectual and practical realms, to embody thought and to guide conduct.

In his essay "Myth in Primitive Psychology," Malinowski (1954:96) proposes a connection between myth and practical action, between "the sacred tales of a tribe, on the one hand, and their ritual acts, their moral deeds, their social organization, and even their practical activities, on the other." This proposition has been echoed by numerous social anthropologists, unsatisfied with the purely intellectual approach to mythic discourse. However, because Malinowski focuses entirely upon the content of myth, he is unable to see how the formal arrangements of parts in mythic discourse might contribute to its practical functions.

While myths may be replicated for their own sake, for their intrinsic aesthetic appeal—and in this sense they are culture, simultaneously as they transmit culture—it is also possible that they contain within them instructions or messages as to how to behave, messages that are transmitted, almost parasitically, along with the aesthetic form itself. The present chapter focuses upon one of the mechanisms by which a myth may guide conduct, a mechanism that is dependent upon the internal aesthetic properties of discourse, as in the case of agent- and patient-centricity, and that does not rely exclusively on content, as in the approach that views myth as a metaphor of social organization. The mechanism is especially effective in small-scale, acephalous communities because its normative character is covert rather than overt, requiring inferences rather than being bluntly stated.

The specific focus here is quoted speech and its possible role in guiding a specific form of conduct, namely, the use of language itself.[1] As a semiotic system, language has the unusual property of allowing its users to speak about speech as well as about other types of action. As a consequence, discourse containing instances of reported speech simultaneously embodies an understanding of the relationship between speech and action. The speech that is reported is connected to other reported action: for example, the speech may be a description of action that has taken place or that will take place, it may be a command to carry out action, it may be a lie contradicting other action that has taken place or will take place. By studying these relationships, one gains access to native representations of the functions of language use, that is, to how the relationship between speech and action is conceptualized by the users of the language.

The representation of a language-use function, such as lying or deceiving, brings that function into partial awareness. The awareness can be made explicit with the addition of a referential statement, such as "language can be used to tell lies." In the same sense, a fully conscious norm requires explicit referential coding: "you should never tell a lie." Without the latter, a normative conclusion might still be inferred from the discourse, for example, if it appeared that telling a lie resulted in untoward consequences for the teller, but, in the course of a larger myth, such a partial, inferentially based awareness might sink into the broader sea of narration, leaving behind only a trace.

There is a mechanism, however, by means of which awareness can persistently be rekindled, forced to hover between referential consciousness and ephemerality, between explicitness and the hopelessly opaque. The mechanism, as an empirical phenomenon, simultaneously gives us confidence that the native representation of functionality is not a fortuitous adjunct of the myth, but rather part of its design. This mechanism is the parallel array of relationships between reported speech and reported action. By repeating that relationship, the connection is impressed upon the mind, the inference to normativity brought closer to the surface. Simultaneously, however, the norm remains implicit, suggested rather than stated. For this reason it escapes the contrariety to which rule-making is subject.

This is not to deny that myths also deal with conceptual issues, such as the agent- and patient-centricity discussed earlier, or the structural oppositions of life and death, up and down, nature and culture, discussed by Lévi-Strauss. From a discourse-centered point of view, myths can have multiple functions and a given function can be more pronounced in some instances than in others.[2] While the demonstration of parallelism in this chapter focuses primarily on discourse instances related to what is thought of as a single myth, work has been done as well on a number of additional myths. The results generally confirm the parallelism of relations between reported speech and reported action, but they suggest that the parallelism is more apparent in some cases than in others. Not all myths normatively encode instructions about language use in equal measure.

The word "parallelism" is used here to describe discourse-internal similarities in the relationships between reported speech and reported action, but this usage stretches the usual conception in some cases beyond recognition. Parallelism has generally meant similarities between discourse segments that are sequentially juxtaposed. In the case of relationships between reported speech and reported action, such juxtaposition in fact sometimes occurs—as in the quoted speech of lines 66–72 below: the related action occurs in the immediately following lines 73–79. But more elaborate architectures of similarity are also found. The action to which the opening quoted speech in lines 1–6 is related, for instance, occurs immediately adjacent to it but also through the discourse, including the end. Other speech-action relationships are embedded within this one. This relationship is nevertheless "parallel to" that between the quoted speech and related action in 66–79. We cannot point to a compact linear adjacency. Nevertheless, the concept is retained here not only because it does apply in the strict sense in some cases, but also because it captures the continuity between such complex discourse architecture based on similarity and its elementary manifestations in compact adjacency.

A myth providing an especially salient example of parallelism in speech-action relations is the 1975 "Giant Falcon" narrative, a fragment of which was given earlier.

The Giant Falcon (Shokleng, 1975)

1. kuyankàg tẽ wũ ẽ nũgñẽn tẽ mõ tã
2. yugug tõ

1. Kuyankàg said to his brother:
2. "When the falcon,

3. kòǹgàg tē òg wun kũ òg ko gèke ñã
3. who has been carrying off men and eating them,

4. li ēñ cō ken
4. does this to me,

5. kũ mã ēñ kukò tē tu yè tapã
5. you go up there to get my bones."

6. ke tã ē nũgñēn tō klañmàg tē mö
6. So he said to his brother Klañmàg.

7. gèke mũ tēkũ
7. So it went,

8. ti tazïl tēkũ
8. (and) he would ascend,

9. ti tazïl tēkũ
9. (and) he would ascend,

10. wũ tã ci ka ti mō tã
10. and, after a long time, he said to him:

11. ēñ cazïl
11. "When I go up there,

12. kũ mã ēñ kukò tē tu yè tapã
12. you must go to get my bones,

13. kũ a tō tu
13. and when you carry (them back),

14. kũ katèle
14. and descend (to here),

15. kũ mã klē tà zag
15. then you must put them on a mountainside way over there."

16. ke tã ti mō mũ
16. So he said to him.

17. ē tō mãg mũ tēkũ
17. He (the brother) listened to him,

18. kũ ti kukò tē kòñãg taplï mũ
18. and he went up to look for his bones.

19. yuguy zãl
19. With the falcon feathers

20. ē tō win tō
20. he had stored away,

21. tã wãñmē kòzãg mũ
21. he covered himself

22. tē kaglòn
22. (and then) he tried to fly.

23. taplï ñã
23. (He) ascended.

24. ē tēg u
24. He flew well

25. tēkũ tã katèle mũ
25. and then (he) came back down.

26. katèle kũ
26. When he came back down,

27. tã òg mō tã
27. he told the others:

28. kòñka low hã wũ tũ nē
28. "The sky's hole is over there;

29. kũ mã kulag ki ēñ yè lēl
29. wait for me tomorrow."

30. kũ tã kulag tēkũ taplï
30. So the next day he ascended.

31. ē nēga tòg tē mē tã kòzãg
31. He covered his arms with falcon feathers

32. kũ tã tē kaglòn
32. and he tried flying.

33. tã kòñka low nē
33. He (said): "The sky's hole is over there;

34. tõg ki mã ēñ yè lēl
34. wait for me there,"

35. ke tã mũ
35. he said

36. kũ tã taplï mũ
36. and he ascended.

37. taplï ñã
37. (He) was ascending.

38. zàg tug klē ñã mũ	38. Above the dry araucaria pines,
39. klē ñãñã tã taplï	39. above them he ascended.
40. kòñka low tē lòlam mũ	40. He entered the hole in the sky.
41. kòñka low tē lòla	41. (He) went through the sky's hole,
42. kũ tã lò escada tõge tã tē	42. and there (the ground) was like ladders.
43. kũ tã lò tazï	43. And he went through,
44. kũ ẽ zãl tē nũñ kũ win tē	44. when (he) took off his feathers, and put them away,
45. tã ãmẽn tē lò tē	45. he went along the path
46. lò wũ òg wãle tē	46. and their camp,
47. yugug tõ kòñgàg tē òg wãle tē nẽ	47. the camp of the manlike falcons, was there.
48. òg wãle tē ki yugug tē ki ka- màg nõ	48. In the camp, there were many falcons,
49. kũ tã mẽ òg wèg ñã	49. and he looked at them.
50. hã tõ ti nũgñẽn kukò hã wũ zè wãzï	50. (He thought): "Surely it was for his brother's bones that the baskets had been woven."
51. kũ tã zè wãzï tag	51. And he (thought): "They were newly woven for (that purpose),"
52. kũ tã zayàn kũ cò	52. and he (thought): "They hung inside (them)."
53. kũ mẽ wèg ñã tã tē	53. And he went looking around (him).
54. ti tē	54. As he went along,
55. lò wũ òg gèlmẽn mã	55. he heard their noise.
56. ti tõ to katē	56. As he was coming along,
57. ñãglò tà zi wũ katē	57. a woman came.
58. kũ zi ti mõ	58. And she said to him:
59. ne to a katē nũ wã ke mũ	59. "Why have you come?"
60. ẽñ cõ kòñgàg kataplï mũ	60. "I have come for the man who came up here,
61. ãtã kukò kònãg katē wã.	61. for his bones I have come.
62. hã ka tã ña	62. Where are they?"
63. ke mũ	63. (he) said.
64. hã wã yayà to zayàn kũ cò	64. "They are hanging from the yayà tree.
65. wãzï tag wã tã zayàn kũ cò	65. In the newly woven baskets, they are hanging."
66. ge tē tē zi ti mõ	66. Afterward, she said to him:

67. kũ mã ẽn cañ	67. "And you kill me.
68. ẽn cañ	68. When (you) kill me,
69. kũ mã ẽñ cõ gòy man mò tã	69. take this water I have brought
70. kũ mã a mèn mõ mã kulam	70. and make soup for your husband,
71. kũ mã ti mõ nẽm	71. and give it to him,
72. kũ mã ti mlè kaklag gẽ	72. and eat it together with him."
73. kũ tã mã	73. And he listened,
74. kũ zi tañ mũ	74. and (he) killed her.
75. zi wẽ tẽ li ke	75. He did as she said.
76. kũ gòy mò tẽ tã kulam	76. With the water he brought he made soup,
77. kũ tã ẽ mèn mõ zi nẽm ge nẽ	77. and he gave it to his husband.
78. zi hãlike tã katã	78. He came looking like her,
79. kũ tã li ke mũ	79. and he did this (as she said).
80. kũ tã katẽ mũ	80. And he came.
81. ti katẽ	81. As he came along,
82. tẽkũ zi lẽl	82. she came (back) to life
83. kũ zi mèn tẽ to tẽ mũ	83. and went next to her husband.
84. ñãglò tã nõ tẽ pègñẽn tã katẽ	84. Meanwhile, he came, circling about.
85. ti katẽg	85. As he was coming along,
86. tà ũ zi wèl katẽ	86. another woman came along.
87. kũ zi ti mõ	87. And she said to him:
88. hã ne to a katẽ nũ wã ke mũ	88. "Why have you come?"
89. ẽñ cõ kòñgàg kataplï mũ	89. "I have come for the man who came up here,
90. ãtã kukò kònãg katẽ wã.	90. for his bones I have come.
91. hã ti kukò ti hã ka ña.	91. Where are his bones?"
92. hã wã amẽn ka tã ka	92. "By the path,
93. yayà mlày to zayàn kũ cò	93. hanging from the broken *yayà* tree.
94. wãzï tag ki wã tã ñã	94. They are in the newly woven basket."
95. ke kũ zi ti mõ	95. (She) said this, and then she said to him:
96. ẽn cañ lò	96. "(You) kill me.
97. ẽn cañ tẽ	97. When (you) kill me,
98. mã ẽñ cõ gòy man mò tã	98. you take this water I have brought
99. kũ mã a mèn mõ mã	99. and you (say) to your husband:
100. ẽñ cõ ẽñ pãn cicil yakan yò zi	100. 'Give me the instrument for

	removing thorns from the feet [archaic usage];
101. yè nũ tõ ẽñ pãn cicil yaka	101. I want to remove thorns from my feet [archaic usage].'
102. ke lò ti mõ	102. Say this to him."
103. kũ tã zi tañ mũ	103. And he killed her.
104. zi tañ tẽ tã	104. When he killed her he,
105. tã tẽ mũ	105. he went.
106. gòy man mò tã	106. He took the water
107. kũ tã zi mèn ti mõ tã	107. and he said to her husband:
108. ẽñ cõ ẽñ pãn cicil yakan yò zi	108. "Give me the instrument for removing thorns from the feet [archaic usage];
109. yè nũ tõ ẽñ pãn cicil yaka	109. I want to remove thorns from my feet [archaic usage]."
110. kũ tã zi mõ zig mũ	110. And he gave it to her.
111. ñãglò zi tõ ẽ pãn ki nènlãl kunũñ yò tõ zi wẽ wã	111. She must have been talking about removing the thorns from her feet.
112. kũ zi yògcal	112. And she was pretending
113. ẽ pãn tẽ mẽ òn ge nẽñã	113. to squeeze her foot.
114. tã katẽ mũ	114. He came along.
115. ti katẽ	115. And when he came,
116. tẽkũ tà tañ mũ tẽ	116. the woman he had killed
117. zi lẽl	117. came back to life.
118. zi lẽl	118. When she came back to life,
119. mũñãglò tã katẽ mũ	119. he came along.
120. katẽ mũ	120. (He) came along.
121. amẽn tẽ lò yi tã katẽ ge ñã	121. He was coming along the path, it is said,
122. tã ki tawig mũ	122. and he arrived,
123. ñãglò yi yugug tẽ òg kamàg kò	123. and the falcons were numer- ous, it is said,
124. yugug tẽ màg kò	124. the falcons were big.
125. kũ yi tã yugug tẽ mẽ òg nẽkukèg	125. And it is said that he de- stroyed the falcons.
126. kò tõ yi tã òg pènũ ge kũ	126. He threw a stick at them and said:
127. wãcõ mã yè kòkàg	127. "You will become a *kòkàg*
128. kũ mã peñ ko we kè	128. and you will eat the *jacutinga* bird."
129. ũ pènũ kũ yi tã	129. He hit another, it is said, and he said:
130. wãcõ mã yè yugug màg	130. "You will become a *yugug* *màg*
131. kũ mã põn ko we kèke	131. and you will eat snakes."

132. ũ pènũ kũ tã
133. wãcõ mã yè tàtà
134. kũ mã cãgõñ ko we kèke
135. ũ tã kò tõ pènũ kũ tã

136. wãcõ mã yè yatàñ
137. kũ mã nèn kukrè ko we kèke
138. ũ pènũ man kũ yi tã

139. wãcõ mã yè kòkàg
140. kũ mã kòñãl ko we kèke
141. tã mẽ òg pin kan mũ
142. kũ tã ẽ nũgñẽn kukò tẽ tẽ katèle
143. tu
144. kũ yi tã nañ katèle gèke ñã

145. apla tawig
146. kũ yi tã ti tõ ẽ mõ wẽ ti li ke tũ

147. ti tõ ẽ mõ wẽ tẽ li ke mã katã

148. zàg òg tõ geñ yò ka tã zãg mũ

149. ti kukò tẽ
150. ẽ nũgñẽn kukò tẽ ka zãg mũ

151. kũ òg tõ mẽ zàg tẽ gèg mũ gèke
152. tẽkũ òg wèg mũ
153. tẽkũ òg tan

154. tẽkũ gẽl tẽ òg wèg mũ
155. kũ gẽl tõ kòñgàg tòge tã kacin nẽ
156. kũ tã tï mũ
157. ẽ tèl
158. tẽkũ tã hu tã nã wèg nãmò

159. tã mã

160. kũ ẽ mõ to tẽ mũ
161. ti nẽm hòn

132. He hit another, and said:
133. "You will become a *tàtà*
134. and you will eat little birds."
135. He hit another with a stick and he said:

136. "You will become a buzzard
137. and you will eat rotten flesh."
138. He hit another again, and, it is said, he said:

139. "You will become a *kòkàg*
140. and you will eat monkeys."
141. He finished hitting them.
142. And he descended with the bones of his brother.
143. Carrying (them) on his back,
144. it is said, he was spiraling downward,

145. until he reached the ground.
146. And, it is said, he did not do as he was told (by his brother).

147. He returned without doing as he was told.

148. Where they go to gather araucaria pine nuts he put them,

149. his bones,
150. his brother's bones (he) put there.

151. And they would gather pine nuts,
152. and then they saw (him),
153. and then they told (the others about it),

154. and then all the children saw.
155. And he (the brother) looked like a small child-man.
156. And he died.
157. When he died,
158. he said: "(You) will not see me again."

159. When he (the other brother) heard (about this),

160. he went to him.
161. He placed him (the bones) well,

162. tā kakò mō
163. tï mũ
164. ãg tèl gèke tògtē yè

165. ãg tèl kũ wèg tũ tē gèke
     tògtē yè

166. ti tèl hã wā
167. ñãglò ti tõ un
168. ti tõ zãg
169. lò wũ ãg tèl tògtē wũ
170. tà katē gèke tē gèke wā

171. ñãglò ti hã wũ u tũ tē

172. hākũ ãg tï gèke tògtē
173. tà katē wañ kũ tē
174. kũ ti tõ hã tan hã wũ
175. ēñ wèg mã nĩ gèke mũ hã wũ
176. hu tã nã wèg nãmò

162. but it did no good.
163. He died.
164. It is for this reason that
     we die.
165. It is for this reason that, when
     we die, we are not seen
     again.
166. It was this death.
167. However, had he done it well,
168. had he put (the bones) away,
169. then, although we would die
170. (we) would always come back
     from there.
171. However, because he did not
     do it well,
172. therefore when we die,
173. we never come back again.
174. And it was he who said this:
175. "You who are looking at me
176. will not see me again [archaic
     usage]."

The last lines of this myth articulate with clarity and precision the intellectual problem with which it grapples:[3] "It is for this reason that we die. It is for this reason that, when we die, we are not seen again. It was this death." From a structuralist point of view, the issue is life and death, here correlated with spatial displacement—the up and down movement—and the problem is the reversibility or irreversibility of a transformation. Why is death an irreversible transformation? Why do we die but not come back? The concrete logic of spatial relations is brought to bear in producing an answer. The answer is that the transformation was once reversible, like spatial displacement, but that it became irreversible. Just as the movement from down to up can be canceled by the reverse movement from up to down, so could death be canceled by the reverse process of birth and growing up, in this case of the "child-man" from the bones. However, death became like displacements in time rather than in space. Just as the past slips away never to be made present again, so does death irrevocably remove an individual from this world.

There is another logic that is articulated here. This is the logic underlying the explanation as to why death became irreversible: "And, it is said, he did not do as he was told (by his brother). He returned without doing as he was told . . . because he did not do it well, therefore when we die, we never come back again." The logic of this explanation pertains not to the concrete sensuous realm of space and time, but to the world of social relations and, specifically, to a norm of language use—obeying and disobeying commands. Irreversibility is the result of a failure to execute commands properly. The present-day constitution of the world, of reality, is understood as a consequence of a past relationship between language use and deed.

While the propositions encoded in the discourse suggest a philosophical or quasi-scientific account of reality, a solution to an intellectual puzzle, there is more. The irreversibility of death is not just a curiosity; it is a terrible tragedy. If the failure to follow an instruction is the cause of that tragedy, then that failure is to be condemned. There is a moral embedded in the consciously articulated proposition, but that moral is a conclusion that listeners must infer. They must reason from the tragic consequence back to the cause, in this case, back to a relationship between speech and action, between commands and their execution.

Because this moral conclusion must be inferred, it is susceptible to failure. One may or may not become aware of the normative implication; if one does, the sense of doubt that the message was intended still lingers. Consequently, the inference may be allowed to recede from consciousness in the face of an intrinsically interesting story. But if the inference is reinforced, if the relationship between speech and action, between command and compliance, is not just a one-time occurrence—if it is, in short, part of the structural design of the discourse—then it may be forced to linger in awareness, to hover between absolute certainty and plausible inference. In fact, the myth in question deals not just with one instance of command and compliance, but with an array of them. It makes this array the basis of its own internal aesthetic organization. Each instance of quoted speech contains a command that is related to a description of the action that ensues. From the relationship between the reported speech and action, the listener is able to draw a normative conclusion. That conclusion, while not wholly inescapable, presses itself upon the listener, and it is a conclusion that can be applied to actions in the listener's own life.

Discourse logic is relevant to one of the classic problems of social anthropology: how society, in Durkheimian terms, is able to regulate the conduct of individuals.[4] It does so, in the case of this and related instances, by slipping normative messages about how individuals ought to behave into speech in such a way that the message can be inferred. The message is suspended in the realm between consciousness and unawareness, and thus appears not as a rule imposed from the outside, but rather as part of the social being of the individual, as self-regulation.

The lesson takes hold not for its own sake, but because it is carried in

Table 1. *Quoted Speech in "The Giant Falcon" (1975)*

Block	Lines	Speaker	Hearer	Functional type
1	1–6 10–16	brother$_1$	brother$_2$	command
2	27–29 33–35	brother$_2$	unspecified others	command
3	58–73	brother$_2$ woman$_1$	woman$_1$ brother$_2$	question/answer command
4	87–103	brother$_2$ woman$_2$	woman$_2$ brother$_2$	question/answer command
5	126–140	brother$_2$	falcons	command
6	158 174–176	brother$_1$	onlookers	prophecy

discourse that takes hold, that fascinates intellectually and aesthetically, that grips the mind while it grips the emotions. The lesson must therefore be intrinsically related to the intellectual structure, to the operation of Lévi-Straussian mythic thought, on the one hand, and to the aesthetic organization, on the other. In social anthropological terms, discourse becomes part of the social glue that binds individuals to collective norms.

To demonstrate this empirically, it is necessary to show that the normative lesson is part of the aesthetic architecture of the discourse. This involves consideration, first, of the quoted speech, and then, second, of the described action to which it is related. The telling contains six principal blocks of quoted speech, where a block consists of quoted speech represented as part of a relatively continuous linguistic interaction with the participants remaining constant. In addition to the quoted speech, the telling contains one instance of inner thought (lines 50–52). The principal blocks are listed in table 1, where the reported speaker and hearer are indicated, along with the functional type of the reported utterance. The apparent center of this myth is Klañmàg, the addressee of the opening quote. He is referred to here as brother$_2$. The opening speaker, Kuyankàg, is referred to as brother$_1$.

The striking feature of the quoted speech contained in the myth is the preponderance of imperative forms. In each of the first five blocks, the quotations involve commands. Blocks 3 and 4, which are themselves parallel units, actually involve multiple commands. Block 3 contains five commands: "And you kill me. When (you) kill me, take this water I have brought and make soup for your husband, and give it to him, and eat it together with him." Block 4 contains three commands, one of which is a command to issue a command: "and you (say) to your husband: 'Give me the instrument for removing thorns from the feet [archaic usage]; I want to remove thorns from my feet [archaic usage].' Say this to him." Block 5 actually contains ten separate commands. In all, there are some twenty-two discrete quoted commands in this myth, each encoded in at least one clausal segment.

Commands do occur in discourse that forms part of other myths. In an investigation of five distinct Shokleng myths (Urban n.d.), at least one imperative within reported speech occurred in each case. However, in no other Shokleng narrative investigated to date does the imperative so thoroughly penetrate the internal parallel organization. One finds instead other represented functions of language, such as truthfully reporting what one has seen, a function that dominates the parallelism in the 1933 "Origin of Honey" discussed in chapter 2. The "Giant Falcon" myth is unique in using the imperative form as its central architectural principle.

In contrast to the propositional explanation contained in lines 164–173, the parallelism of command forms is not abstract. It is concretely encoded in relationships between the overt linguistic forms of constituent segments of the discourse. The various commands share recognizable surface characteristics of the imperative, including second person (*mã*) subjects, which may or may not be deleted, and imperative verbal inflections, with or without the imperative sentential particle *lò*. The following examples, one chosen from each of the first five blocks, illustrate this.

5. kũ mã ẽñ kukò tẽ tu yè tapã   5. you go up there to get my bones

34. tòg ki mã ẽñ yè lẽl   34. wait for me there

67. kũ mã ẽn cañ   67. and you kill me

98. mã ẽñ cõ gòy man mò tã   98. you take this water I have brought

128. kũ mã peñ ko we kè   128. and you will eat the *jacutinga* bird

The role of quoted imperatives with respect to the structural design of the myth is confirmed by an empirical investigation of other instances regarded as tellings of the "Giant Falcon" myth. Because the other instances were all collected over the period from 1975 to 1982, we lack the dramatic evidence of cultural continuity spanning forty years that we had in the previous chapter. Nevertheless, comparing the telling above (here labeled 1975a) with another produced by a different speaker (here labeled 1975b), we can detect numerous instances of nearly verbatim repetition in the quoted material, indicating again that cultural replication involves the production of similarity in the surface forms of the discourse.

1975a	tòg ki mã ẽñ yè lẽl	wait for me there
1975b	tòg ki mã ẽñ yè lẽl ke	wait for me there, (he) said
1975a	kũ mã ẽñ cõ gòy man mò tã	take this water I have brought
1975b	kũ mã ẽñ cõ gòy man mò tã	take this water I have brought
1975a	ẽñ cõ ẽñ pãn cicil yakan yò zi	give me the instrument for removing thorns from the feet
1975b	ẽñ pãn cicil yakan yò zi	give me the instrument for removing thorns from the feet
1975a	hu tã nã wèg nãmò	(you) will not see me again
1975b	hu nã tà tã ña wèg nãmo	(you) will not see me again

This is not to deny that the instances are also similar in terms of content. However, there are numerous ways in which the constituent propositions could have been phrased; the content could have been retained without the form. In fact, however, the form itself tends to be replicated with some precision. What confirms this in the last two examples cited above is that these instances of quoted speech involve obscure lexical and grammatical forms that are not interpretable, except through inference, by the speakers themselves. From a discourse-centered point of view, the replication of culture, studied empirically through publicly accessible discourse, is the replication simultaneously of form and content.

Having established a pattern of parallelism in the reported speech, namely, that each instance involves a command, it is now possible to turn to the relationship between the reported speech and action. The proposal put forth until now has been that the discourse is organized aesthetically around the command-compliance relationship. From a discourse-centered point of view, that proposal can be sharpened. The reported action not only describes the compliance or failure to comply with the action commanded; the liguistic form of the description itself resembles the linguistic form in which the act was commanded. There is an internal parallelism between the reported speech and the described action.

This can be seen most transparently in the case of blocks 3 and 4, where the descriptions of action immediately follow the reports of the commands. In block 4, for example, line 96 is related to line 103, 98 to 106, 99 to 107, 100 to 108, and 101 to 109.

96. ēn cañ lò	96. "(You) kill me"
103. kū lā zi tañ mū	103. And he killed her
98. mā ēñ cò gòy man mõ tā	98. "you take this water I have brought"
106. gòy man mõ tā	106. He took the water
99. kū mā a mèn mõ tā	99. "and you (say) to your husband"
107. kū tā zi mèn ti mõ tā	107. and he said to her husband
100. ēñ cõ ēñ pãn cicil yakan yò zi	100. "'Give me the instrument for removing thorns from the feet' [archaic usage]"
108. ēñ cõ ēñ pãn cicil yakan yò zi	108. "Give me the instrument for removing thorns from the feet [archaic usage]"
101. yè nū ēñ pãn cicil yaka	101. "'I want to remove thorns from my feet'"
109. yè nū tõ ēñ pãn cicil yaka	109. "I want to remove thorns from my feet"

In the first three instances, the differences between reported command and described action involve imperative-to-declarative shifts and second-to-third person pronominal substitutions within the same syntactic construction, with the nouns and verbs held constant. In the latter two instances, the similarity reaches identity, the difference concerning the quoted status: the earlier line is a quote within a quote, the later line a simple quote.

The parallelism is not always perfect. In the case of block 3, line 72—wherein the woman orders the man to drink the soup together with her husband—is not complemented by a corresponding action description, although the other commands are. However, there is a general statement covering the whole sequence in line 75: "He did as she said." Compliance with the command is here explicitly described, not inferred from the parallelism between the reported speech and reported action.

There are two other exceptions. Block 2 in which brother$_2$ orders the onlookers to wait for him is not complemented by a description of their actually doing so. However, this appears to be a failure in the replication process. Examination of another telling (1975b) produced by a different speaker shows that the parallel relationship does exist in that case, although the original command there was issued to his wife, not to the group of onlookers.

ti plũ zi ti yè lēl   his wife waited for him
ñãglò tã wãñwi katèle   while he came back down

We find in the different tellings various gaps and inconsistencies of this sort, from which we are tempted to construct an ideal myth, in relation to which the actually occurring instances are only imperfect reflections, shadows on the cave wall. Such a view, however, creates more problems than it solves. While a given instance may be an imperfect replica of another, to posit an abstract type is to introduce the problem of how change in myths can occur over time and of how the abstract type can be transmitted. If, alternatively, culture is seen as residing in the publicly accessible instances themselves, then one can appreciate that the copying process is imperfect, that some aspects can be deleted, others added through embellishment. Change in the composition of the collection of public instances, housed in the externalized mind of the community, results in change in the "myth" as entity.

The other important exception to the rule that the reported command is accompanied by a parallel description of action occurs in the case of block 5, where brother₂ shatters the giant falcons,[5] ordering the pieces that result to become birds of prey. In no telling that I have examined is there a description of the subsequent action, that is, of the birds actually eating the prey in question. However, listeners are able to infer the results from their empirical knowledge of the world. Each bird of prey described here is well known, and Shokleng also know that the birds in question in real life do eat what they were commanded to eat in the narrative. The buzzard, for instance, really eats "rotten flesh," and the *kòkàg* really pursues and eats the *jacutinga* bird. Moreover, the behaviors described are salient and differentiating features of these birds. The hearer is able to draw an inference regarding command and compliance that is based on knowledge external to the discourse itself. The inference confirms the pattern of parallelism found in the other instances, namely, that the command is obeyed.

The command is obeyed in all cases, that is to say, except the first, and even here one finds elements of the command-compliance pattern, with overt surface parallelism between the reported speech and described action. The opening statements instruct brother₂ to ascend, the linguistic forms used (*tapã*, *tazïl*, *taplï*, and *cazïl*) being grammatical variants, and the subsequent action describes the ascent. The brother is instructed to carry on his back (*tu*) the bones (*kukò*) and to descend (*katèle*) with them, and he in fact does so (lines 143–145). The parallels here are as direct as in the case of block 3.

However, brother$_2$ was commanded to put the bones on a mountain "way over there" (the demonstrative *tà* = "there" coupled with an elongated vowel with falling intonation). He put (*zãg*) the bones, but not on the mountain "way over there." Instead, he put them "where they go to gather araucaria pine nuts." Brother$_2$ apparently did not know the significance of this command beforehand. Moreover, he did try to follow the command as faithfully as possible. Nevertheless, he failed, as the speaker indicates: "he did not do as he was told." The consequence is a terrible one: instead of returning to life, brother$_1$ dies, never to come back again. Worse yet, death more generally becomes irreversible.

The issue of consequence is critical in transforming the descriptive parallelism of speech-action relations into a normative one. In the case of blocks 1, 3, and 4, it is not just a question of following or failing to follow the instructions. From a normative point of view, compliance or noncompliance has consequences: faithful compliance with the instruction results in good or desirable consequences, noncompliance, even in the case of a slight deviation, in unfortunate, even tragic consequences.

The relationship between normativity and consequence accounts for what is otherwise hopelessly opaque in the narrative: the middle two episodes surrounding the woman. Shokleng narrators were puzzled by these as well. Why should the woman tell the man to kill her and then to perform the duties she would ordinarily perform in relationship to her husband? Especially enigmatic is the fact that the duties in question involve a confusion of roles. The man takes on the behavior and even the appearance of a woman. One narrator remarked that he did not understand what this could be about. It is precisely the strangeness of the episode that fascinates, that leaves listeners wondering in astonishment, even though they may have heard this numerous times before.

Despite the strangeness, or perhaps because of it, the listener is able to draw an important conclusion. While the addressee of the command within the story does not know beforehand the consequences of his compliance or noncompliance, just as the listener does not, he nevertheless endeavors to do as precisely as possible what he has been instructed to do. What the listener infers is that precise execution of an instruction leads to a desirable consequence, in this case, the reversibility of death. The dead person can be brought back to life again. This inferred consequence can be compared with the result of failure to comply, namely, that death becomes irreversible. Here the consequence is tragically negative, even though the noncompliance was unwitting, not the result of a conscious rebellion against authority. As formulated in the story, emphasis is on the precise execution of instructions, on carrying them out faithfully and in all details.

While the norm in question seems to call for blind compliance with instructions in all cases, evidence suggests that the norm is a qualified one. The evidence concerns the question and answer routine at the beginning of blocks 3 and 4, where the man asks the woman where his brother's bones are. The pragmatic issue involved here is whether brother$_2$ can trust the woman, since only commands coming from someone who can be trusted should be obeyed. It is apparent that brother$_2$ already knows where the bones are, or at least thinks that he knows, as is indicated in the reported thought (lines 50–52). In 1975b, the device of reported thought is not used. Instead, brother$_2$ is described as seeing his brother's bones hanging in a newly woven basket, from which blood is dripping. In any event, the question and answer routine may be an indication to the listener that brother$_2$ has taken the necessary steps to ensure that he can trust the woman. His compliance with her commands is not blind, but rather grounded in confidence, just as his compliance with brother$_1$ is based on the certainty of solidary social relations.

Chapter 1 poses the problem of the interpretability of discourse, suggesting that interpretation consists in the recognition of similarities and differences between the specific instances and others, and the placement of the instance within a network of perceived interconnections in the broader culture or discourse history. The present chapter argues that the 1975a "Giant Falcon" encodes a normative lesson about orientations to language use and that its 1975b counterpart confirms this lesson, showing it to be part of the internal design of the discourse, which is replicated over time. An intellectual or philosophical fascination with death as a transformation and, specifically, with its irreversibility is also part of its replicable characteristics. We may wonder whether the conjunction of these two in the collection of instances constituting the "Giant Falcon" myth is fortuitous, or whether, in fact, it reveals something about the macroconfiguration of Shokleng culture.

The myth is, after all, culture-specific. Generations of Shokleng Indians, interacting within their communities in southern Brazil, evolved the collection of telling to which the 1975a "Giant Falcon" is related. That evolution required innumerable replications, which gradually transformed and reshaped the discourse-internal patterning, deleting here and embellishing there, producing an aesthetic organization that could hold the attention. Does the specific internal patterning reflect that local evolution? Or does it reflect more broadly human tendencies and concerns?

Lévi-Strauss focuses on the panhuman aspects of myths, proposing that in them one can detect the operation of human thought more generally. In fact, the intellectual or philosophical issues underlying the 1975a

"Giant Falcon" form part of the widespread "Orpheus" tradition, whose North American distribution has been charted by Åke Hulkrantz (1957). Hulkrantz mentions that the differentiating features of this tradition are (1) "that the living person tries to bring the deceased back with him to the land of the living," and (2) "that the living person is a close relative or friend of the deceased." In many cases—in the ancient Greek tradition, for example—the question of return and failure to return is connected with the issue of obeying and failing to obey commands. However, this is not always so.

A striking example is furnished by a myth from the Coos Indians of Oregon, "The Revenge against the Sky People," which has been investigated by J. Ramsey (1977, 1983:76–95). The tale is a transformation of "Seal and Her Younger Brother Lived There," which is the focus of an earlier analysis by Hymes (1968, 1981:274–308). In the Coos variant, a man goes up to the sky to bring back his brother, who has been killed and carried off by the people from above. As in the Shokleng story, the protagonist takes on the role of an old woman after killing her and, in his disguise, attempts to fool the old woman's husband. Dramatic tension builds around the question of his ability to carry out this imitation successfully. In the end he succeeds and manages to bring his brother back to life upon his return to this world.

A key point of interest is that the Oregon variant, while so similar in terms of the overall action sequence, does not intertwine with the command-compliance pattern. The lesson regarding language use seems to be different. It concerns the concrete acting out of behavior patterns that are verbally described. The hero knows how the old woman behaves, and consequently how he himself should behave, only through her verbal responses to his questions. He has no opportunity actually to observe her conduct. The lesson of this myth thus seems to be the following: if you can learn how to behave properly through questioning, and if you can actually instantiate this verbal learning in concrete behavior, then desirable consequences will follow.

Despite the differences in normative lessons, the Coos myth is so similar to the Shokleng tellings in its intellectual structure that the similarities cannot be due to chance. Such similarities led Lévi-Strauss to conclude that mythic discourse transcends the local circumstances in which it is found; far from being local, the myth reflects underlying brain structures or principles of thought. How could two such similar narratives have grown up in distinct local contexts, far removed from one another geographically? The hypothesis of invention and diffusion is plausible, given the widespread character of the Orpheus tradition, but one would still wish to know why the diffusion occurs. Why do different communities wish to copy, tell, and retell narratives with closely similar intellectual structures?

From a discourse-centered point of view, the Lévi-Straussian and diffusionist positions are not incompatible. The diffusion may occur because the intellectual issues encoded in the discourse tap into a basically human fascination with the world, with its perceived organization and transformations. There are, in other words, cross-cultural constraints on the production of discourse, such that certain types are more intrinsically interesting, more prone to be replicated, than others. They possess features that transcend the local context and appeal to individuals whose local experiences, whose discourse histories, may be different. This is what makes them especially suitable as embodiments of culture, conceived as that which is transmitted across the generations by means of social interactions. For discourse to be the object of replication, it must be built in accord with structures that are able to transcend, in some measure, the local contexts of its production.

Of course, it is not possible finally to decide whether characteristics of the discourse make a myth diffusable, or, alternatively, whether we only read back into the discourse its special characteristics after the fact of diffusion. Perhaps the latter is a fortuitous or random process, not steered by discourse-internal features. Or, again, perhaps it has to do with social relationships, power, and the like. We cannot finally know, at least not at this stage of anthropological knowledge. At the same time, however, we are not hopelessly in the dark either, since, as discourse replication within cultures becomes a focus of empirical investigation, we realize how susceptible myths are to change, how portions may break off—as in the Shokleng "Origin of Honey"—and become separate narratives, and how continuity and replication are the products not so much of a lack of creativity as of a hard-won victory over the forces of entropy and flux. The replicable aspects of mythic discourse appear as a singular achievement.

That is what makes them, from a social anthropological point of view, such effective carriers of norms: the norm rides along with the more broadly human appeal, insinuates itself into the intellectually and aesthetically satisfying qualities of the myth, and gets replicated along with those qualities. Though the myth is not consciously understood as a normative lesson, it can become one. At the same time, since the "editing" effects to which replication is prone could easily cancel out the normativity, there must also be a motivation for transmitting the lesson. Even if the replicators are not fully conscious of transmitting a norm, part of their motivation must be to induce others, and perhaps even themselves, to behave in accord with so-cially approved rules of conduct.

In emphasizing the broadly human appeal of the intellectual structures, one must remember, simultaneously, that the Coos and Shokleng myths are distinct: they encode different normative lessons and they are also intellectually distinct. The Coos man is able to bring his brother back: death in this case is not irreversible. The Coos hero succeeds while his Shokleng counterpart fails, an outcome possibly in keeping with the agent-centric bias prevalent in the Northwest of North America. Moreover, the method of coming back to life is specific in the Shokleng case: the brother's bones were to regrow into the figure of the dead brother; death was to be canceled by rebirth.

This latter theme is consonant with the specific evolution of discourse that occurred in the communities on the southernmost extension of the central Brazilian plateau. There the principal life-cyclic ceremonies focus upon death and upon the replenishment of society through birth. Shokleng even express a belief that young children who die are reborn. While the broad intellectual structures of the "Giant Falcon" tap into panhuman concerns, the specific shape of the structure as coded in the Shokleng myths reflects the local evolution of culture—conceived as a discourse history—in this small corner of the world.

We can move outward from local Shokleng concerns with death and replacement to broader characteristics of the discourse that are nevertheless not fully universal. In particular, we can point to the tendency to attach covert normative lessons to discourse that has overt aesthetic and intellectual value, something that is not specific to Shokleng, but that is nevertheless not universal. Why leave the listener to ponder, infer, and reflect? Why not simply formulate the norm of language use explicitly? After all, it is difficult enough for analysis to reveal the regularities that are inferable from the relationships between reported speech and action. To leave listeners to their own devices in this regard is to risk failing to communicate the norm at all.

If there is a risk of failing to communicate the norm because it is too implicit, because it is too delicately formulated, there is also an opposed risk—namely, that an explicitly formulated norm can be explicitly rejected. In the absence of hierarchy or a system for enforcement of rules, any endeavor to formulate rules is itself a contestable political act. The formulation is an instance of discourse usage, and participants can attribute pragmatic significance to it, seeing the rule as something that benefits its formulator. So how can what is in the collective interest be expressed in such a way that it is understood to be in the collective interest? The answer is that the normative moment must be only an implicit, pragmatically inferable part of something else.

This is where the aesthetic and the normative merge: myths are something that listeners find fascinating because of their artistic, not their regulative, qualities. They want to learn about the events in the magical world to which they have been given privileged access. To package an implicit normative statement within such an attention-getting device is to ensure that the overall discourse will be listened to and thus that an inference regarding norms may be made. Because the norm is only implicit, it can simultaneously escape the beacon of public consciousness that sweeps the arena of discourse for evidence of self-interest. Myths are perfect vehicles for getting norms past that censor. They are well-suited for societies, such as Shokleng and Coos, which lack the bureaucratically regimented structures of authority in which rules can be laid down, the penalties for violation made explicit, and the violators punished.

CHAPTER 4

Time, Continuity, and Macroparallelism

*I*n the case of myth, cultural continuity implies the replication of discourse over time: some current stretch of discourse is similar to one that has come before it. Continuity such as this is an objective phenomenon, a matter of fact; it is not necessarily part of the subjective sense within a community of maintaining a link to the past, a tradition that it carries on. An individual can be aware of the replication process—aware that the two instances are tellings of a single myth, for example—but this awareness is not necessarily socially generalizable. If a community is to maintain a felt sense of continuity, then the awareness must be encoded in publicly accessible signs that go along with the replication process and that form part of the replicated discourse. Such signs are metasigns, whose meaning is a message regarding how other signs are to be interpreted. The signs of continuity call attention to replication, suggesting to their users that the process is one involving the production of discourse instances similar to or identical with ones with that have come before them.

At least from the point of view of such metasigns, not all cultures have an equal interest in continuity. While it may be true definitionally and empirically that every culture depends on replication—in the accepted understanding of culture as socially transmitted beliefs, values, and ways of acting—it is not necessarily the case that public discourse defines itself in terms of continuity. An alternative possibility that is realized in lowland South America, in the region north of the Amazon and into its far western headwaters, is that the metadiscursive self-definition of discourse stresses not continuity but rather complementarity within a dialogical process, value being placed on how two or more instances of discourse, produced by different individuals, form parts of a larger whole. While self-definition in terms of continuity is not absent altogether, it is backgrounded. In central Brazil, however, the issue of continuity is brought to the fore, made part of an expressed understanding of community life.

In connection with the question of foregrounding and backgrounding, the similarity between cultural continuity, on the one hand, and the phenomenon of parallelism, on the other, is instructive. Like cultural continuity, parallelism involves the replication of units over time.[1] This is true at least in spoken discourse and in performance more generally; even visual parallelism may involve a temporal unfolding, as the eye moves from one component to the next. The time scale of replication is shorter—seconds and minutes rather than months and years—and the units are regarded as parts of the same continuous discourse or phenomenon. Nevertheless, like cultural continuity, parallelism involves the replication of units perceived, at least in some measure and respect, as similar.

Parallelism, however, can assume differing degrees of saliency. That involving agency and patiency is tacit, part of the relatively unconscious structures that shape thought, that lead to differences in philosophical attitude. Cultural continuity may be similarly tacit, a fact of life but one to which no special importance is attributed. The parallelism of quoted speech is more prominent; it persistently reinforces patterns and leads to actual inferences, but remains just outside the beacon of consciousness. So, too, may the process of continuity press itself upon the participants, instilling in them an awareness of tradition and replication, without formulating it in propositional metasigns. Finally, in the case of the marked speech styles to be examined subsequently, parallelism is overt: it is saliency-producing and attention-getting. One cannot miss its presence; it is there to be noticed. In a similar way, cultural continuity may be made overt, in the limiting case, the explicit object of propositional discourse.

The most transparent case, however, may not be the most effective in producing a *feeling* of continuity. It is possible to encode, in actually occurring discourse, a referential statement to the effect that "the present instance of discourse usage is an act of cultural replication." The particle *yi*, "it is said," in the 1975 "Giant Falcon" discussed in chapter 3 does this in some measure, and there are other overt statements (such as, "my father told me this story") that accomplish the goal in varying degrees. Such referential statements may contribute to a feeling of continuity, but they may also produce a sense of distance from the discourse, as if it were removed from the present, part of a past that is not fully alive. Consciousness achieved through propositionality can be distinguished from the feeling of continuity, which is produced by metasigns that are nonpropositional. While consciousness and feeling may be present simultaneously, it is also possible for one to inhibit the other: propositional metasigns can disjoin the individual from the discourse, giving it a folkloric rather than lived-in feel.

Why should a culture, or a given instance of discourse as the embodiment of culture, encode a representation of its own functionality? Why should it wish to tell its users that they are engaged in producing cultural continuity? The answer I will give subsequently is that the self-representation of functionality has to do with culture-specific models of social solidarity operating in a society. The metasigns not only create a sense of continuity; they create as well a sense of community, of how the society is put together, of how the individual is subordinated to the group. In the case of solidarity based on a model of cultural continuity—the model characteristic of central Brazil—the idea is that people are held together by the tradition they share. Metadiscursively to mark discourse instances as traditional, as handed down across the generations, is simultaneously to overcome the clash between the instances produced within a generation. Individuals may dispute whose discourse is more traditional, but the dispute already accepts traditionality as its norm; it eliminates conflicts as regards other claims. In the continuity model, the basis of social cohesion is likeness, which extends across time and space. While metadiscursive representation may be one thing and the facts of discourse another—so that change may occur even as continuity is asserted—the idea of likeness suggests how discourse, and by extension society, ought to be put together.

The characterization of continuity given above can be viewed in relation to the contrast between "cold" and "hot" societies that has been proposed by Lévi-Strauss (1966) and criticized by J. Hill (1988:3–5) and T. Turner (1988:235–239). In the literature, cold societies are understood as those that "resist historical change" (Hill 1988:4). The criticism is correctly made that cold societies in fact undergo change all the time and, indeed, that change is even recorded in myth as a form of social consciousness analogous to history (T. Turner 1988:236). I have no intention of contradicting these recent criticisms, which have greatly increased our understanding of small-scale processes. At the same time, the view of coldness put forth here is distinct from that criticized in recent research. In the present context, such societies may be understood not as those that "resist historical change," but rather as those that represent their basis of cohesion in terms of continuity. And there is an important difference. The present discussion focuses on metadiscursive representations: does the discourse represent itself metadiscursively as continuous with the past, as shared across time and space? This metadiscursive question can be distinguished from one focusing on the discourse per se: is the discourse produced today the same as that produced forty years ago? Is A's discourse the same as B's? Both need to be distinguished in turn from the content of the discourse—is there talk about change?—which is what seems to be meant by the "social consciousness" of change. Finally, all three need to be distinguished from the question of change in the nondiscursive aspects of culture: in tools, ecological practices, body ornamentation, and the like. We can equate cultures, finally, only by collapsing these distinctions.

From a metadiscursive point of view, hotness refers not to societies that undergo change, since, as Lévi-Strauss critics have correctly pointed out, all societies undergo change. It refers instead to the metarepresentation of discourse as "modern," as new and unique, distinct from what has come before. Under a modernist metadiscourse, cohesion is not the precipitate of sameness or likeness across space and time; it is the crystallization of difference, continuously evolving difference. It is Durkheimian organic solidarity, but in which difference is a diachronic as well as a synchronic fact. Hotness is, indeed, organicity viewed diachronically, that is, in terms of the self-representation of relationships among discourse instances in terms of temporally unfolding distinctiveness.

When it comes to the metadiscursive representation of continuity, as found in central Brazil, it is of interest that the analogy between cultural continuity and parallelism, as forms of replication, is useful not just to the outside observer, but also within the culture for self-understanding and for the normative promotion of solidarity. A key feature of discourse makes this possible: it can be used to tell about the past and about the diachronic process of how the past becomes present—in other words, to narrate history, representing in discourse the time line leading from the past to the present and into the future. Consequently, the referential content creates an awareness of the possibility of continuity or change. But that representation of time is also itself an actually occurring, temporally unfolding discourse instance. By constructing discourse in parallel fashion, it is possible to make time seem to be composed of like units succeeding one another and so to suggest its replicating, repetitive quality—to represent, in other words, cultural continuity—without explicitly asserting it. Continuity can become a sensible phenomenon, encoded in the concrete experiential realm of actually occurring discourse.

The kind of parallelism involved here is distinct from that in agent- and patient-centricity, where the basic unit is the clause. It is also distinct from that in reported speech, which has to do with units constructed from the metadiscourse-discourse relationship. Finally, it is distinct from the elementary parallelism of meter, intonation, and rhyme, which has elsewhere been termed microparallelism. The parallelism of history takes as units larger chunks of time—and hence of discourse—many clauses that taken together represent a historical episode. This segmentation of discourse into larger units that are similar to one another can be termed macroparallelism.

The present chapter argues that one key Shokleng myth, the origin myth known as the *wãñēklèn*, is constructed in this way and that it functions to produce the sensation of cultural continuity, while simultaneously embodying that continuity. This discourse is of special interest because it stands on the border between myth and ritual. The term *wãñēklèn* designates the mythic story of origin of the modern-day Shokleng, which may be told in ordinary narrative style, as in the case of the myths investigated earlier, but the term also designates the ritual act of performing the telling, which occurs during ceremonies in the central ritual space of the village and involves two performers, who recite the myth syllable by syllable in dialogic fashion.

While the focus of this chapter is macroparallel structure, it is important to note that the macrostructure is built on the microparallelism of intonation, stress, and rhyme, at least in some measure. One unit of macroparallelism, excerpted below as section B.2.1 from a 1975 telling (not a dialogic performance), shows this.

Origin Myth (Shokleng, 1975, Section B.2.1)

1. wãgyò to zàgpope tõ patè ẽñ yo katèle
2. glè yò ki kala
3. kũ ne to agèlmẽg wũ mũ ke mũ
4. iwo ẽñ cõ kõñgàg kale yògï mã

5. kũ ẽñ cõ ẽñ mãg yè
6. kàplug kèg
7. mũ lõ ti kï tũ
8. ẽñ cõ wèg mũ
9. kũ ẽñ cõ ẽñ mãg yè
10. zàg tèy kèn

11. kũ ẽñ cõ ti làn ke
12. kũ kàgnãg
13. kũ tõ gèlmẽg nẽ wã

14. kũ ã yïyï tẽ hãlike tẽ ke mũ

1. Relative Zàgpope Patè arrived in front of me,
2. (he) arrived in the dance plaza
3. and he said: "What is all of this noise about?"
4. "I hear the sound of many men coming

5. and so for my creation
6. (I) fashioned *kàplug* wood.
7. However, he did not call out,
8. I have seen,
9. and so for my creation
10. (I) fashioned araucaria pine wood

11. and I painted it
12. and (I) erred
13. and that is what all the noise is about

14. and what would your name be?" he said.

15. iwo ēñ yïyï hā wū zàgpope ke   15. "My name would be Zàgpope,
    tē
16. ēñ yïyï hā wū patè ke tē   16. my name would be Patè."
17. ū ke mò yè ēñ ñō ēñ māg làn   17. "Well then come help me to
    yè kala ke mū   paint my creation," he said.

The position of this episode with respect to the broader history will become apparent subsequently. Described here is part of the endeavor to
make the first jaguar. In this episode, one man, named Zàgpope Patè, arrives and hears a ruckus and asks what is going on. He is told and is then
asked to help paint the jaguar, to which he contributes certain designs.
These designs are those used by one of the groups during the ceremonies
for the dead, in which this myth is performed.

Elements of microparallelism can be found, for example, in lines 5 and
6, which form a rhymed couplet:

kū ēñ cō ēñ māg yè

kàplug kèg

The *yè*, "for," in Shokleng rhymes with *kèg*, "to fashion," and there is
also a parallel in the meter. The major stress in each line occurs on the
penultimate syllable, and the stress corresponds with a tonal peak. The
intonational contours in each case are roughly the same.

A similar couplet occurs in the following two lines, 7 and 8:

mū lō ti kï tū

ēñ cō wèg mū

Once again the rhyming is in the final syllables. However, primary stress
in these lines is on the ultimate syllable, and this corresponds with the tonal peak. In other words, lines 7 and 8 represent, insofar as stress and intonation are concerned, an inversion of the pattern found in lines 5 and 6.

The pattern of lines 5 through 8 is reflected in the pattern of lines 9
through 12. Lines 9 and 10 are identical to lines 5 and 6 except for the
substitution of a two-word phrase:

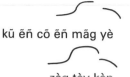

kū ēñ cō ēñ māg yè

zàg tèy kèn

Here there is similarly a primary penultimate stress corresponding with the tonal peak and a secondary final stress corresponding with a falling intonation. Lines 11 and 12 are wholly distinct in semantic terms from lines 7 and 8; indeed, the final syllables do not even rhyme. However, in terms of intonation and stress they are modeled on lines 7 and 8:

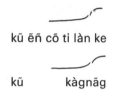

kū ēñ cō ti làn ke

kū   kàgnāg

The general formula for microparallelism in these lines may be represented as follows:

$$5 = 6 : 7 = 8 :: 9 = 10 : 11 = 12$$

Is there a meaningful correlate to this purely formal structure, based on the sensible characteristics of the discourse, that is, on intonation, stress, and vocalic parallelism? Like lines 9 and 10, lines 5 and 6 make a positive affirmation, in response to the earlier question: "What is all of this noise about?" In 5 and 6, the speaker asserts that he attempted to fashion a certain type of wood, known as *kàplug*, into an animal, in particular, as is revealed later in the narrative, into a jaguar. Lines 7 and 8 point to the failure of this attempt: "However, he did not call out, I have seen." In lines 9 and 10, the speaker refers to his second attempt to make a jaguar, this time using wood from the majestic araucaria pine (*Araucaria brasiliana*). The lines are nearly identical to 5 and 6 in terms of linguistic segmentation as well as meaning.

5. kū ēñ cō ēñ māg yè	5. and so for my creation
9. kū ēñ cō ēñ māg yè	9. and so for my creation
6. kàplug kèg	6. (I) fashioned *kàplug* wood
10. zàg tèy kèn	10. (I) fashioned araucaria pine wood

This attempt again fails, because, as lines 11 and 12 indicate, the speaker was about to paint it, but he made a mistake. The sensuous characteristics of the actually occurring discourse, therefore, form a pattern in a manner analogous to that between the semantic meanings of the corresponding lines. The intonational and stress inversions mirror the semantic inversion associated with "attempt" and "failure."

Episode B.2.1 (1975) shows an overall rhetorical structure that grows out of this microparallelism. It does not involve lines of fixed lengths. Nor is the microparallelism uniform throughout the episode. Rather, it occurs at the center of the episode and involves short lines with no pauses in between—the lines here are isolated by means of intonation, meter, stress, and grammatical segmentation. In the opening and closing portions of the episode, the lines are longer and are marked by pronounced pauses (>1.0 sec. in duration).

The rhetorical structure proposed for this fragment is displayed graphically in figure 6. The numbers correspond to lines in the above transcription. The letters correspond to major groupings of lines based upon grammar and semantic content. From a formal point of view, lines 1 and 2 are unmarked descriptive statements made by the narrator. Line 3 is set off from them through its characterization as a quotation by means of the final *ke mū,* "said." Hence, 1 and 2 are grouped as A, and 3 is grouped as B. The particle *iwo* sets off lines 4–13. It indicates a change of speaker within a quotation, so one knows that these lines, and, indeed, line 14 as well, were spoken by someone distinct from the person quoted in line 3. Consequently, 4–13 are grouped together under C. Line 14, like line 3 and line 17, is set off by the quotative *ke mū,* "said." Moreover, the quoted material in line 14, like the quoted material in line 3, is set off formally as a question, in opposition to lines 4–13 and 15–16. Consequently, it is assigned the letter D. Lines 15 and 16 are distinguished by the change of speaker particle and also by their linguistic parallelism. They are grouped as E. Finally, line 17 is set off by the quotative and is formally marked as a command. The internal hierarchical organization of lines 5–12 has already been discussed.

The segmentation of this episode into five parts has a semantic correlate. In A the narrator describes an event, the arrival in the dance plaza of Zàgpope Patè. The latter is quoted as having asked a question in B: "What is all of this noise about?" In C this question is answered at length by the main character, who himself asks a question of the newly arrived Zàgpope in D. This question is answered in E, and in F the main character issues a polite command to Zàgpope.

The discussion here is technical, but technical concern is a necessary

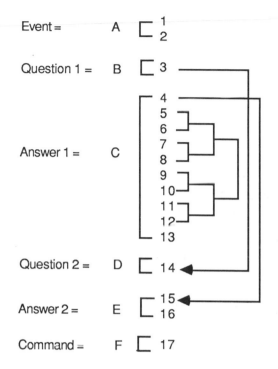

Fig. 6. Rhetorical structure of B.2.1 (1975)

prerequisite to getting at the broader problems of the representation of historical time and its relationship to discourse time, and of cultural continuity and its relationship to discourse parallelism. The fragment transcribed represents 50 seconds out of a total of approximately 70 minutes. It thus takes up about 1.2% of the total time. In ethnohistorical time, it is a representation of one of the events that occurred between the first emergence of humans from beneath the ground until the period somewhere in the early nineteenth century, after which the fully historical narratives begin.

Listening to this fragment, one senses its poetic quality through the intonation and rhythm, even without knowledge of the actual content. The time line of the concrete discourse has a feel to it, a sensuous texture based upon its repetition of units, its arrangement of similarities and differences into a hierarchical structure. That texture is more pronounced than in the case of ordinary myth tellings, such as described in chapters 2 and 3. The texture stands out more, calls attention to itself, makes the listener aware of the musical qualities—so much so, indeed, that the actual semantic content fades in and out, achieving greater luminosity here, less there. The structure of the concrete discourse is overlaid on the structure of historical time in such a way that the two blend together, becoming commensurate in status with respect to consciousness.

This is aided by the fact that the semantic content is itself difficult to understand. The sentences are often complex syntactically, and they contain archaic words and expressions that render them at points opaque from the point of view of everyday speech. There are also references to customs that have not been practiced for more than a hundred years. Access to all of this information requires a familiarity with the native exegetical tradition, which was still maintained within Shokleng culture during the period from 1974 to 1982. The important point here is that the relative opacity of the semantic text combines with the relative salience of the musical qualities to enable both to emerge into awareness.

There is a hypnotic quality to the discourse, which is interwoven with the historical time that is described. I have observed elsewhere (Urban 1989) that the narrator during the 1975 telling actually entered into an almost trancelike state, as if he were back in the world described in this myth, or, alternatively, as if that world were made present. This time-travel quality is associated with peculiarities in the pronominal usage, which can be discerned in the fragment transcribed above. Although line 1 is not an instance of quoted speech but rather a description of a historical event, the narrator uses the first person singular pronoun: "Relative Zàg-pope Patè arrived in front of *me*." This substitution of first for third person does not occur consistently throughout the myth, and it is not consistent across different tellings. It is part of the same fading in and out quality that one finds in relationship to the relative foregrounding and backgrounding of semantic content and sound. Nevertheless, it is a regular feature of narration that has been transmitted across the generations, as can be verified by a study of the adumbrated translation of a different fragment of the origin myth, recorded around 1933, that was published by J. Henry (1964 : 148–150).

Even at this microplane, one appreciates that the discourse is associated with a subjective sensibility, a feeling of parallel unfolding that is linked to the creation of a sense of cultural continuity. The sensuous qualities of the sound foreground the subjective sense of discourse time. But at the same time the semantic content floods consciousness with historical time, immerses narrator and listener alike in the earliest events that transpired in the community. While semantically describing the past in propositional form, the discourse creates a feel for the parallel qualities of the passage of microtime. Within this general interweaving of two time lines, the pronominal shift from third person to first person enhances a sense of continuity in which past and present are brought together.

However, it is the macrostructure of the discourse that suggests the connection between discourse parallelism and the repetitive quality of history and hence instills a sense of cultural continuity, situating the community and its members within the flow of time. The Shokleng origin myth is an enormous and complex work of art, in which blocks such as B.2.1 (1975) constitute units, exhibiting similarity with units parallel to them on both the formal plane and the plane of content. This macroparallelism can be seen by examining the relationships between B.2.1 and the other fragments with which it exhibits internal similarity, namely, B.1.1, B.2.2, and B.2.3.

B.1.1 occurs prior to B.2.1. In this episode, as in B.2.1, a man named Zàgpope Patè arrives while efforts are underway to make the first jaguar. He asks what the ruckus is all about and is told. He is then asked his name and afterward told to help paint the animal. As described in the portion of the discourse following this fragment, however, the animal turns out to be not the jaguar but rather the first tapir. It is for this reason that the events described in B.2.1, B.2.2, and B.2.3 become necessary. All three involve the making of the first jaguar. In any case, examination of B.1.1 shows that it is parallel to B.2.1 in both linguistic form and semantic content.

Origin Myth (Shokleng, 1975, Section B.1.1)

1. wãgyò tõ zàgpope tõ patè ẽñ yo katèle	1. Relative Zàgpope Patè arrived in front of me.
2. ne to agèlmẽg wu mu ke mũ	2. "What is all of this noise about?" (he) said.
3. iwo ẽñ cõ kõñgàg kale yògï mã	3. "I hear the sound of many men coming
4. kũ ẽñ cõ ẽñ mãg yè	4. and so for my creation
5. ẽñ cõ kàplug kèg	5. I fashioned *kàplug* wood
6. kũ ẽñ cõ ti làn ke	6. and I painted it
7. kũ kàgnãg	7. and (I) erred
8. kũ tõ gèlmẽg nẽ wã	8. and that is what all the noise is about
9. kũ ã yïyï tẽ hãlike tẽ ke mũ	9. and what would your name be?" (he) said.
10. ẽñ yïyï hã wũ zàgpope ke tẽ	10. "My name would be Zàgpope,
11. ẽñ yïyï hã wũ patè ke tẽ	11. my name would be Patè."
12. ke mũ mò yè ẽñ ñõ ẽñ mãg làn yè kala ke mũ	12. "Well then, come help me to paint my creation," (he) said.

The parallel between B.1.1 and B.2.1 is unmistakable. Many of the lines are actually identical or nearly so: compare B.1.1 line 1 with B.2.1 line 1:

> B.1.1 Line 1: wãglò tõ zàgpope tõ patè ẽñ yo katèle
> B.2.1 Line 1: wãglò tõ zàgpope tõ patè ẽñ yo katèle

B.2.1 line 2 has no counterpart in B.1.1. But B.1.1 lines 2–5 are nearly identical to lines B.2.1 lines 3–6. This is true not only of the morpheme by morpheme segmentation of the lines, but also of the intonation and meter, as described earlier. The new material in B.2.1 that is not simply a replication of what has come earlier in B.1.1 occurs in lines 7–10. Then the parallel resumes, with B.1.1 lines 6–12 matching B.2.1 lines 11–17.

Episode B.2.1 actually builds both semantically and formally on B.1.1. There is in B.1.1 an analogous rhymed couplet in lines 4 and 5, with penultimate stress, followed by a couplet with final primary stress in lines 6 and 7. However, this is the entire extent of the internal microparallelism. There is no subsequent repetition of this pattern, such as occurs in B.2.1. The overall comparison can be summed up in the following proportions.

> B.1.1   4=5:6=7
> B.2.1   5=6:7=8::9=10:11=12

B.2.1 builds upon B.1.1 not only in terms of a semantic incorporation, but also in terms of a poetic incorporation, which involves a structure of similarity and difference grounded in the concrete, sensuous qualities of the actually occurring discourse. B.2.1 is an amplification of B.1.1.

When we move to the relations between B.2.1 and the following episodes, B.2.2 and B.2.3, the parallels are even closer. The described events are actually identical, with only the character who arrives having changed. There is an occasional difference in which a line is added here, another deleted there, but what one senses is the repetitive quality of discourse time—a quality created through replication of the discourse materials in great detail—overlaid on the repetitive quality of historical time.

Origin Myth (Shokleng, 1975, Section B.2.2)

1. wãgyò tõ zàgpope tõ patè wãmõhà tõ zẽzẽ ti no katèle	1. Relative Zàgpope Patè's companion Zẽzẽ arrived in front of him.
2. ne to agèlmẽg wũ mũ ke mũ	2. "What is all of this noise about?" he said.

3. iwo ēñ cō kōñgàg kale yògï mā   3. "I hear the sound of many men coming

4. kū ēñ cō ēñ māg yè   4. and so for my creation
5. ēñ cō kōñgàg kòmāg nē hà we   5. I truly fear the men
6. kū ēñ cō ēñ māg yè   6. and so for my creation
7. kàplug kèg   7. (I) fashioned *kàplug* wood.
8. mūlō ti kï tū   8. However, he did not call out.
9. ēñ cō wèg mū   9. I have seen
10. ēñ māg yè   10. for my creation
11. ēñ cō zàg tèy kèn   11. I fashioned araucaria pine wood

12. kū ēñ cō ti làn ke   12. and I painted it
13. kū cō to gèlmēg nē wā   13. and that is what all the noise is about

14. kū ã yïyï tē hālike tē ke mū   14. and what would your name be?" he said.

15. (ēñ yïyï hã wū zàgpope ke të [throat clear])   15. ("My name would be Zàgpope" [throat clear])
16. iwo ēñ yïyï hã wū zēzē ke të   16. "My name would be Zēzē."
17. hà we kū nū ti mō   17. Truly it is and I (said) to him:
18. ū ke mò mā ēñ ñō ēñ māg làn yè kala ke mū   18. "Well then, you come help me to paint my creation," I said.

Origin Myth (Shokleng, 1975, Section B.2.3)

1. wãgyò tō zàgpope tō patè wāmōhà tō nūklèg tō kïy ti no katèle   1. Relative Zàgpope Patè's companion Nŭklèg Kïy arrived in front of him.
2. ne to agèlmēg wū mū ke mū   2. "What is all of this noise about?" he said.

3. iwo ēñ cō ēñ māg yè   3. "I for my creation,
4. ēñ cō kōñgàg kale yògï mā   4. I hear the sound of many men coming,

5. ēñ māg yè   5. for my creation
6. kàplug kèg   6. (I) fashioned *kàplug* wood.
7. mūlō ti kï tū   7. However, he did not call out,
8. ēñ cō wèg mū   8. I have seen,
9. kū ēñ māg yè   9. and so for my creation
10. ēñ cō zàg tèy kèn   10. I fashioned araucaria pine wood

11. kū ēñ cō ti làn ke   11. and I painted it
12. kàgnãg   12. (and) erred
13. kū tō gèlmēg nē wā   13. and that is what all the noise is about

14. kũ ã yïyï tẽ hãlike tẽ ke mũ   14. and what would your name
                                            be?" he said.
15. ẽñ yïyï hã wũ nũklèg ke tẽ   15. "My name would be Nũklèg,
16. ẽñ yïyï hã wũ kïy ke tẽ   16. my name would be Kïy."
17. ũ ke ẽñ mãg làn yè kala ke mũ   17. "Well, come help me to paint
                                            my creation," (he) said.

From the view of culture as a system of abstract meanings, which can be read through language, the phenomenon of macroparallelism makes no sense. Such a view in fact compelled the ethnographer J. Henry (1964: 148) to remark that "for generations [the origin myths] have not been the bulwark of much that is vital in [Shokleng] culture, but they contain echoes of things that may have been important at one time." He goes on to observe that "the incidents are confused and repetitive . . ." But while the content of this myth may describe customs that are no longer current, it is nevertheless consistently held up as the high point, the flower of Shokleng culture—its single greatest intellectual achievement. Why?

The answer is not to be found in the view of culture as an abstract system of meanings. What that view regards as "repetitious," the discourse-centered approach shows to be structured. The structure is one that resides in the concrete form of the discourse as well as in its content. It is a structure of parallels. This can be seen from a careful study of the relations between the episodes B.1.1, B.2.1, B.2.2, and B.2.3, as mapped out in figure 7. In this figure, the lines in each of the episodes are arrayed from left to right, the numbers corresponding to those in the transcriptions. The time line of the discourse flows from left to right, and from top to bottom, and this flow simultaneously models the time line of history. The vertical columns show parallels up to identity between the individual lines in one episode and those in other related episodes. An asterisk indicates that a given line in one episode differs by design from the corresponding line in the preceding episode. Such design differences are established by comparing different instances, regarded as distinct tellings of the myth, as is done below. In the case of the third vertical column from the right, for example, one finds the following.

B.1.1 11. ẽñ yïyï hã wũ patè ke tẽ   11. "my name would be Patè"
B.2.1 16. ẽñ yïyï hã wũ patè ke tẽ   16. "my name would be Patè"
B.2.2 16. iwo ẽñ yïyï hã wũ zẽzẽ   16. "my name would be *Zẽzẽ*"
          ke tẽ
B.2.3 16. ẽñ yïyï hã wũ *kïy* ke tẽ   16. "my name would be *Kïy*"

While the speaker of the utterance is the same in B.1.1 and B.2.1, there is a different speaker in B.2.2 and still another speaker in B.2.3. Other dif-

```
B.1.1  1     2    3  4      5              6   7   8   9   10 11      12

B.2.1  1  2  3    4  5      6   7*  8*  9* 10* 11 12 13 14 15 16      17

B.2.2  1*    2    3  4  5  6  7  8  9  10 11 12    13 14 15 16*  17 18

B.2.3  1*    2  3  4  5      6   7   8   9  10 11 12 13 14 15* 16*    17
```

Fig. 7. Parallelism between episodes in origin myth

ferences, such as the form *iwo* (indicating a change of speakers) that occurs in B.2.2, reflect "errors" in the replication process.

It is important not to dismiss these "errors" in replication, because they play a role not only in discourse-internal parallelism, but also in the relations between different instances over time. Most of the differences have to do with an added or deleted morpheme, and occasionally an added or deleted clause. An effort is made within the discourse instance to replicate the parallel units as precisely as possible, but absolutely precise replication is not possible. Nevertheless, it is apparent from these examples that discourse-internal replication is a matter of *form* as well as *content*. The narrator does not simply try to retell the event using different words. He tries to use exactly the same words and to array them in precisely the same syntactic form. Moreover, he makes an effort as well to replicate even the sound characteristics—the rhythm and pitch contour. Replication as observed within the utterance is a matter of the concrete form of the discourse, not just its underlying "meaning." Concrete replication may not occur perfectly, but it is in the concrete replication that the poetic structure of the narrative is to be found.

The emphasis on perfect concrete replication characterizes not just discourse-internal relationships, but also relationships between instances over time and across space. There is a tacit belief in Shokleng culture, which is occasionally stated explicitly, that the *wañēklèn* must be memorized and recited verbatim, syllable by syllable. Each instance should perfectly match every other analogous instance that has come before it. Insofar as these instances actually approach identity, the *wañēklèn* constitutes evidence of the continuity of culture, of the ability of individuals over time to replicate socially learned behaviors, and to replicate them faithfully. The belief can be compared with the facts of replication. B.2.1 (1981) is the analogue to B.2.1 (1975), told by the same person nearly seven years later. I requested this narration, and in fact line 18 is a didactic aside to me. It points out a connection between this character and one that occurs in another section of the myth. B.2.1 (Wãñēkï, 1982) is the analogue to B.2.1 (1975) but told by a different individual, maximally removed from the first narrator in social terms.

Original Myth (Shokleng, 1981, Section B.2.1)

1. wãgyò tõ zàgpope tõ patè no katèle
2. kũ yi tã wũ
3. ne to agèlmẽg wũ mũ ke mũ

4. iwo ẽñ cõ ẽñ mãg yè
5. kõñgàg kale yògï mã

6. kũ ẽñ cõ ẽñ mãg yè
7. kàplug kèg
8. mũlõ ti kï tũ
9. ẽñ cõ wèg mũ
10. kũ ẽñ cõ ẽñ mãg yè
11. ẽñ cõ zàg tèy kèn

12. kũ ẽñ cõ ti làn ke
13. kũ kàgnãg
14. kũ tõ gèlmẽg nẽ wã

15. ã yïyï tẽ hãlike tẽ ke mũ

16. ẽñ yïyï hã wũ zàgpope ke tẽ
17. ẽñ yïyï hã wũ patè ke tẽ ke mũ

18. (tõ pata tõ patè tõ yugug pènũ hã wã)
19. kũ tã ke mò mã ẽñ ñõ ẽñ mãg làn yè kala ke mũ

1. Relative Zàgpope Patè arrived in front
2. and it is said he (said):
3. "What is all of this noise about?" (he) said.

4. "I for my creation,
5. (I) hear the sound of many men coming,

6. and so for my creation
7. (I) fashioned *kàplug* wood.
8. However, he did not call out,
9. I have seen,
10. and so for my creation
11. I fashioned araucaria pine wood

12. and I painted it
13. and erred
14. and that is what all the noise is about.

15. What would your name be?" (he) said.

16. "My name would be Zàgpope,
17. my name would be Patè," he said

18. (Pata Patè who shot the falcon).
19. And he said: "Well then, come help me to paint my creation," (he) said.

Origin Myth (Shokleng, Wãñēkï 1982, Section B.2.1)

1. ti kòñka hà tõ zàgpope ti no katèle
2. ti glè yò ki kala
3. ne to agèlmẽg wũ mũ ke mũ yi tã

1. Kinsman Zàgpope arrived in front of him,
2. (he) arrived in his dance plaza.
3. "What is all of this noise about?" he said, it is said.

4. iwo ēñ cō kōñgàg kale yògï mā

4. "I hear the sound of many men coming

5. kū ēñ māg yè
6. kàplug kèg
7. mūlō ti kï tū hà

5. and so for my creation
6. (I) fashioned *kàplug* wood.
7. However, he really did not call out,

8. ēñ cō wèg mū
9. kū ēñ cō zàg tèy kèn

8. I have seen,
9. and so I fashioned araucaria pine wood

10. kū ēñ cō ti làn ke
11. kū kàgnāg
12. kū tō gèlmēg nē wā

10. and I painted it
11. and erred
12. and that is what all the noise is about."

13. ke tā ti mō mū
14. ā yïyï tē hālike tē
15. ēñ yïyï hā wū zàgpope ke tē
16. ēñ yïyï hā wū patè ke tē
17. ke ñāg hà we kū yi tā
18. ū ke mò ēñ ñō ēñ māg làn yè kala ke mū

13. He said to him:
14. "What would your name be?"
15. "My name would be Zàgpope,
16. my name would be Patè."
17. Thus it truly was, it is said.
18. "Well then, come help me to paint my creation," he said.

The degree of similarity across time and space is remarkable. Through a study of these transcriptions, one can appreciate that cultural sharing is the product of replicating across time and disseminating throughout the community instances that are nearly identical to one another. Figure 8 shows a line-by-line comparison of the instances, set up by analogy with the myth-internal comparisons shown in figure 7. As in the case of discourse-internal parallelism, the match is not perfect. A line is deleted here, another is added there. Similarly, analogous lines may be identical or nearly identical, differing in only a morpheme or two, as shown, for instance, in the relationships between the third lines of each episode.

1975 3. kū ne to agèlmēg wū mū ke mū

3. and he said: "What is all of this noise about?"

1981 3. ne to agèlmēg wū mū ke mū

3. "What is all of this noise about?" (he) said

1982 3. ne to agèlmēg wū mū ke mū yi tā

3. "What is all of this noise about?" he said, it is said

On balance, the differences across time and space seem to be of the same order as those across parallel units within the instance.

One difference, however, should be noted. In line 1 of B.2.1 (1975) and B.2.1 (1981) the archaic term *wāgyò*, "relative," is used, but in B.2.1 (1982), which was produced by a different speaker, the relatively contem-

1975	1	2		3		4	5	6	7	8	9	10	11	12	13		14	15	16			17
1981	1		2	3	4	5	6	7	8	9	10	11	12	13	14		15	16	17		18	19
1982	1	2		3		4	5	6	7	8		9	10	11	12	13	14	15	16	17		18

Fig. 8. Replication of the origin myth over time

porary term *kòñka hà*, "kinsman," is used instead. The term *wãgyò* is incomprehensible to all but those who have been indoctrinated into the exegetical tradition that goes along with origin myth telling. It is possible that the producer of the 1982 instance knew this, but was simplifying for his audience, in which I was included. At the same time, however, one can appreciate how change in discourse might occur over time, especially where there is less emphasis on reproducing the form in all its concrete richness. The discourse would gradually adjust to changes in habits of speech that have originated elsewhere. Ordinary speech would be continuously reshaped in accord with the changing configuration of similarities and differences that make up the culture or discourse history.

The emphasis on precise replication in origin myth telling simultaneously leads to the semantics of the discourse diverging, over time, from present-day realities—the discourse can be related to those realities only through new exegesis that must be constructed to render it intelligible. This accounts partially for Henry's (1964:148) sense that the origin myths "for generations . . . have not been the bulwark of much that is vital," but that "they contain echoes of things that may have been important at one time." What Henry missed, however, because of his focus on semantic content, is that the origin myth not only encodes culture; it *is* culture. The tradition that is shared is the concrete form of the discourse. Cultural sharing consists in the replication of discourse instances over time and their dissemination throughout the community. When someone tells the origin myth, he is not only telling about culture; he is actually replicating it.

Ideally, we should have evidence of continuity over a longer time span, not just seven years but a half century or more. While Henry did not publish transcriptions of the myths collected in 1932–1934, he did publish an "abridged" translation of one fragment (Henry 1964:148–150). The translation appears to be reasonably literal, although he has obviously omitted materials and elaborated here and there for purposes of clarity. Nevertheless, a careful study of his translation in comparison with the 1975 instance I recorded shows what is in all probability nearly verbatim repetition. In Henry's translations one can detect the form of the discourse collected in 1975. The examples are from a subsequent portion of the myth.

1975 wãgyò tõ zàgpope tõ patè òg du katèle
1975 wãgyò whose name is Zàgpope came down behind them
1933 In the meanwhile, wangdjô² whose name is Thekpopé came down after me

1975 òg glè yò ki kala mũ
1975 (and he) entered their dance plaza
1933 and entered my dance ground.

1975 ũ tõ kõñgàg nũ ke ña ke mũ
1975 "What man is this one?" (they) said
1933 When I saw this I said, "What man is it?"

This close parallelism continues throughout the action. As part of his abridgment, Henry (1964: 149) observes in relation to the section that "the same procedure is gone through with two more men." Similarly, the 1975 instance contains three parallel units in this place. The salient difference in the passage cited above concerns the pronominal usage. The 1933 narrator has taken on the first person, as in the 1975 fragments transcribed earlier, but in this portion of the 1975 instance the narrator has faded out into the third person again.

Continuity in the *wãñēklèn* is not just a matter of precise replication of discourse over time. It is also a matter of content, which links the discourse via private but publicly correctable images to the nondiscursive world. The discourse tells the story of humankind from the beginning of time—the emergence of the first ancestors from beneath the earth—to the historical period. The myths are chronicles, and they generally unfold in accord with historical time. The process of discourse replication is also the locus of collective memory; it is the mechanism by which events long since transpired are reinserted into the present life of the community.

The discourse is not simply a chronicle, however. There are four distinct myths that make up the 1975 and 1981 *wãñēklèn* cycles. These can be replicated independently. A comparison of the 1975 and 1981 narrations shows that, when they are told together, they follow a fixed order, as if they were parts of a single continuous story. However, each of the first three goes back to the creation, to the earliest period of humankind, and traces events up the historical period. The three instances are thus parallel to one another, as if the act of emergence itself were not unique but rather repeatable, replicable like culture itself. These three form the core of the *wãñēklèn* cycle. The last, which deals with comparatively recent events, is also the shortest and is not known by everyone. It is possible that it has not yet won a fixed place among the components of the *wãñẽklèn* cycle. The first three are disseminated widely and tell parallel stories of community history.

Each of the three also shows an internal macroparallel structure. Labeling each distinct episode with a capital letter, and indicating each parallel repetition by means of an attached number, the linear unfolding of the first *wãñẽklèn*—both 1975 and 1981—may be represented as follows, where B.1.1 through B.2.3 correspond to the fragments analyzed above.

A.1 A.2 A.3 B.1.1 B.2.1 B.2.2 B.2.3 C.1 C.2 C.3 C.4

This is the global macroparallel structure of the first of the Shokleng origin myths.

Each episode in this sequence has a semantically describable coherence, correlated with the macrorepetition. The A episodes deal with the discovery of the world after the emergence. In each case, someone ascends, sallies forth into the world to discover some aspect of it (e.g., grass or a kind of bird), and brings evidence of this discovery back with him to show the others. The B episodes, similarly, involve the making of an animal, B.1 the tapir and B.2 the jaguar, as shown above. In C preparations are made for a great war among Shokleng themselves. Each parallel episode describes the arrival of a new figure, who explains that he is mad because there are no women left to marry and talks about how he is preparing for war.

Despite the semantic coherence of these episodes, it is important that the global structure emerges from local relations, that is, from formal macroparallelisms such as described above. In other words, the structure is based upon the sensible characteristics of the discourse—the distributions of actual morphemes and lexemes and their syntactic arrangements. Global structure, in this sense, is an aspect of the actually occurring discourse as a meaning-bearing sign vehicle.

The first myth is the basic one and is also the longest of the four, taking some 28.3 minutes in the 1975 telling, or 40.5% of the total narrative time. It is rivaled by the second, which takes 26.1 minutes, or 37.3% of the narration. In contrast, the third has a total length of only 10.2 minutes, or 14.6% of the overall time, and the last accounts for just 5.3 minutes, or 7.6% of the total.

The second myth has its own global structure, which is, however, related to that of the first. Continuing the representation of episodes by means of an alphabetic sequence, that structure may be formalized as follows.

D.1 D.2 D.3 D.4 E F.1 F.2 F.3 G C.1 C.2 C.3 C.4

The D episodes describe the arrival of different personages, shortly after the initial emergence, each of whom bestows some gift (e.g., a particular kind of fiber blanket or dance ornament). Episode E shows no internal macroparallelism. It deals with a boy whose father died falling from a tree while trying to fetch fledgling birds for his son. The G episode similarly shows no internal macroparallelism, dealing with an encounter with the Guaraní Indians. In F, there is a contest in which different persons test their skill at eluding arrows. The person in F.3 gets hit, terminating the sequence. But the parallels are simultaneously a matter of content and of form.

The last part of this second myth is identical to the concluding set of episodes in the first two. By means of this sequence, the first two themselves are brought into parallel alignment. They begin differently, but they conclude with the same events—those leading to the great war among Shokleng and to the dispersal of the bands, which is coupled with the entry of the historic Shokleng bands into the forest and their abandonment of the savannas. The global structure, built up from formal relations at the local level, thus extends across the individual myths that make up the cycle, giving shape to the entire *wãñēklèn* sequence.

This intermyth structuring is continued with the third component of the *wãñēklèn* cycle, whose opening portions are parallel, albeit not identical, to the opening portions of the first. Interestingly, both the second and third hark back to the first myth and show no parallelism with one another. This confirms the prominence of the first myth at the levels of both subjective evaluation and the formal properties by means of which they are interrelated. The global structure of the third may be represented as follows.

A.4 H.1 H.2 B.3 B.4 I

The opening episode A is a discovery of the world episode, parallel to the beginning of the first myth. The H episode concerns fire: two times in succession the fire goes out at night, and the main character suffers the bites of mosquitoes. In each case, fire is later restored, in the first instance by the arrival of someone who possesses fire, in the second by the main character having mastered the art of making fire himself. B.3 and B.4 concern the making of animals—a wild cat and a snake, respectively; these episodes run parallel to those in the first myth. Finally, the concluding episode is again one with no internal macroparallelism. It deals with the transformation of a man into a capybara.

The fourth myth of the *wãñēklèn* cycle shows no evidence of internal macroparallelism. There are obvious ways in which it could be transformed and brought into alignment with the other three, but this has not yet occurred. The discourse has the earmarks of a relatively recent addition to the set. Moreover, the events it recounts pick up where stories in the first two leave off. The nonparallel character of this myth, and of some episodes in the first two, may be significant in connection with the problem of cultural continuity. It seems intuitively obvious that not all historical events can be seen as replicas of certain general types, at least not initially. There is a unilinearity or idiosyncrasy to history, especially with respect to relatively recent events, which have not had time to undergo interpretation and assimilation into a larger scheme. The nonparallel episodes capture this idiosyncrasy.

The set of myths constituting the *wãñēklèn* cycle may itself have grown by a process of historical accretion, as the forces of poetic ordering operated to shape the old materials into more refined poetic form. New materials would have been added, as may be occurring in the case of the fourth myth. These new materials would gradually be assimilated into the older structures. If so, then, in addition to reflecting the processes of cultural continuity and change, the Shokleng origin myth would also in this case embody them; and the process could operate despite the conservative force exercised by the emphasis on precise replication. A comparison of the 1975 and 1981 tellings shows that replication over time is most precise for the portions of the discourse that participate in internal parallelism: nonparallel episodes are least replicable over time.

In any case, the general macroparallel structure of the entire 1975 telling is laid out in figure 9. This is a remarkable structure. Although it has never been represented to Shokleng in this graphic form, it is something that they appreciate aesthetically, a mark of intellectual accomplishment making the *wãñēklèn* the pinnacle of Shokleng artistic development. The structure is something that the mind comes to apprehend only gradually, through numerous encounters; and for this very reason it captivates and holds interest. One knows that something is there, but how can one comprehend the enormity of it?

This is not the kind of intellectual task that is within the competence of every native speaker. Indeed, there is evidence for a hierarchy of mastery. Some Shokleng men, even prior to the first peaceful contact with whites in 1914, had failed adequately to memorize the myth and were never able to perform it in the ceremonial sphere. Among those who did memorize it, there were differing degrees of certainty with which they had internalized the structures and differing levels of appreciation for the art form itself. The two individuals whose narrations I have employed here were

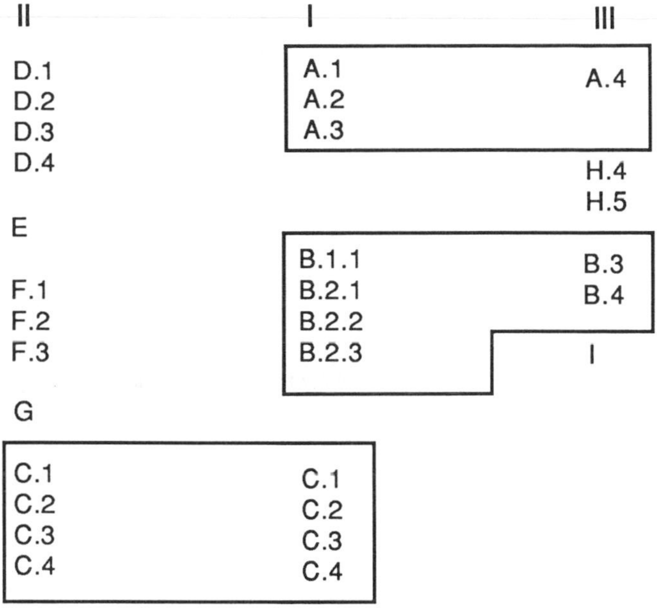

II	I	III
D.1	A.1	A.4
D.2	A.2	
D.3	A.3	
D.4		H.4
		H.5
E		
	B.1.1	B.3
F.1	B.2.1	B.4
F.2	B.2.2	
F.3	B.2.3	I
G		
C.1	C.1	
C.2	C.2	
C.3	C.3	
C.4	C.4	

Fig. 9. Global structure of the Wãñẽklèn

masters of the art form. Moreover, of these, one had the higher level of appreciation.

Nevertheless, even for those who are not capable of fully understanding it, the *wãñẽklèn* exercises a sway, a fascination. Hearers always know that they are in the presence of something important, something monumental, something that inspires, in Durkheim's terms, "reverence for the collectivity," for its transcendence of the powers of mere individuals. Here is a collective product whose artistic characteristics cannot be attributed to any single person, contrary to the ideology of "hotness" that dominates Western thought. The *wãñẽklèn* seems to require a feeling for continuity. It is therefore something whose significance can be linked to the overall significance of Shokleng culture.

Jakobson (1960:356) refers to the "poetic function" of parallelism, whereby a "focus on the message for its own sake" is created. The discourse becomes a source of fascination apart from the semantic meaning it communicates. The *wãñẽklèn* can be understood in terms of this aesthetic function, which is built up from discourse-internal iconicities. Each fragment becomes a sign vehicle that draws attention to another fragment that has come before it. Individuals in the presence of the discourse sense these iconicities, and the iconicities in turn draw them into it, acting as a source of attraction, a glue that binds individuals to it. That glue is its source of power, its ability not only to bind given individuals to itself, but simultaneously, because they are bound to a common object, to bind individuals to one another. The poetic function is the source of a true social solidarity in addition to a represented one.

If anthropologists are to understand culture, they need to understand the properties of discourse that make it attractive. Not all discourse instances are equal in this regard; some do not take hold at all, disappearing instead into the flow of events. Others have a wider appeal, inducing replication over time and through space. The most powerful properties manage to free themselves from a specific language and emerge irrespective of the phonological, morphological, and syntactic segmentations that a full interpretation may require. Aspects of the *wãñēklèn*—for instance, the dyadic performance characteristics discussed below—participate in this extralinguistic forcefulness. An appreciation of the full power of this artistic construct, however, requires a feel for the language, and, indeed, for the layers upon layers of parallelism. This is what makes the *wãñēklèn* such a good repository of Shokleng culture.

The poetic or aesthetic function, however, does not adequately capture the role of the *wãñēklèn* within the living community. Macroparallelism is also a metasign that communicates a specific meaning about the discourse instance in which it is contained. The signs call attention to or foreground the relationships among the events that are described, and those relationships lead overwhelmingly to a single conclusion: that the events themselves are similar. Despite the fact that they occur later in a linear unfolding, they are modeled on what has come earlier. History is not a line made up of unique points; it is a series of events that are similar, in greater or lesser degree, to one another. The making of animals occurs repeatedly— and it *occurs repeatedly in the same way.*

This is the meaning of continuity. It is not that past leads to present; it is that the present is like the past; it replicates it just as the discourse instances themselves are replicated. In "hot" models, the present is unique, distinct, just as the discourse instances are; each is ideally different from those that have come before it. In the Shokleng model, emphasis is not on uniqueness or distinctiveness but on similarity, and the message of similarity is encoded in discourse-internal macroparallelism. Macroparallelism creates a feel for time that is grounded in likeness rather than uniqueness, in continuity rather than disjunction. One who is fascinated by the *wãñēklèn* is simultaneously fascinated by the sense of continuous time, by the spirals of history proposed by the early eighteenth-century Italian thinker Giam-battista Vico, rather than (or as well as) by the linearity of Darwinism. These functions depend on the properties of discourse itself.

Subsequent chapters turn progressively toward the embeddedness of discourse within the richer context of social life as studied by social an-thropologists; in this context, it is of interest that the *wãñẽklèn* stands on the border between the everyday and ritual or ceremonial discourse. Like the myths considered in earlier chapters, the *wãñẽklèn* can be told around the fire in the household, and, in fact, the myths analyzed here were collected in such contexts. But the myth is also part of a dyadic ritual performance, involving two men, who sit facing each other in the dance plaza: one shouts out one syllable of the myth, and he is echoed by the second, who repeats that syllable, and so forth. The discourse unfolds in an internally replicated fashion. Line 14 of B.2.1 (1975), for example, would appear as:

kũ kũ ã ã yï yï yï yï tẽ tẽ hã hã li li ke ke tẽ tẽ ke ke mũ mũ
and and what what would would your your name name be be he he
    said said

There is a leader in this dyadic performance, and the replicator copies him. While two elder men may perform the *wãñẽklèn*, the performance also involves older men paired with younger ones, and in those cases it is the elders who are the leaders, the younger who are the replicators. The discourse performances are both models and also instantiations of the rep-lication process. The younger performer is locked to the older, more skilled performer, forced to copy syllable by syllable the discourse produced by his elder. The copying process ensures that replication is as faithful as possible.

While the dyadic performance may occur at other times, it is obliga-torily associated with the *ãgyïn* ceremonies, which are performed after the death of an individual and which serve to reintegrate the widow or wid-ower, who has been in seclusion, into the community. Within the broader matrix of Shokleng culture, death is a key disruption, threatening the con-tinuity and persistence of the community. Correspondingly, the *ãgyïn* and the *wãñẽklèn* performance within it are conceptualized as methods for re-establishing that community, for reasserting continuity with the past. At the level of content, the *wãñẽklèn* is a mythic history, but one that encodes the doings of the ancestors, the forefathers of the present-day community. To tell the myth is to bring the ancestors into the present, to assert the existence of a community with traditions, to bring about continuity with the past.

We can appreciate that the perceived purposes of origin myth telling—to reintegrate the spouse and to heal the rupture produced by death—are consonant with the properties that analysis shows to be present in the discourse itself. Macroparallelism makes salient, brings into sharp focus, the very idea of continuity—semantic continuity between episodes, continuity in the replication of the discourse through distinct tellings, and continuity within the encompassing culture for which the myth is a metaphor.

CHAPTER 5

Style and Social Order

*T*he investigation of macroparallelism underscores differences between the discourse-centered and shared meaning conceptions of culture. Understood as meaning, culture is read *through* the content of spoken words, but an exclusive focus on content precludes understanding form, which may be as important or more important than content to an assessment of the social functions of the discourse. In the case of macroparallelism, form stands alongside content and is replicated together with it. Without a feel for form, the Shokleng origin myth seems, in Henry's (1964 : 148) apt formulation, "not very interesting."

There is a second difference: because content or semantic meaning is what is most transparent to consciousness, shared meaning approaches end up identifying the study of culture with the study of consciousness. Consequently, we find ourselves unable to home in on culture-specific social phenomena that escape awareness—for example, the parallelism of reported speech, which presses itself upon the interpreter, suggesting inferences, but then recedes at the last moment, leaving doubts as to whether the inferred meaning was actually intended. Such phenomena occupy a shadowy existence, lurking in the uncharted regions below the high ground of consciousness. Within the approach from discourse, however, characteristics of actually occurring instances can be shown to exhibit regularity and replicability over time, and hypotheses can be made about their significance based upon their use and similarities to other cultural forms.

There is yet another difference, addressed in this and the following chapters. That difference concerns the connection between discourse and the here-and-now context, that is, the actual social life of the community, which was the principal focus of interest for social anthropology. A preoccupation with content projects the discourse into the realm of abstract, decontextualized meanings or types. A myth, for example, becomes an entity, a story in which one is interested because it is about the world. But being *about* the world, it is not *in* the world; it is removed from it, floating above it. One can appreciate why some social anthropologists were not especially interested in discourse: they were concerned with the richness of an actual present that unfolded before their eyes, so to speak, a present consisting of concrete behaviors, bodily ornamentations, and spatial arrangements. The *aboutness* of myth and discourse more generally must have made them seem otherworldly, removed from the pragmatic anchoring of daily life.

The content of consciousness and the aboutness of words are indisputably important. But if that is all that words are, then it is difficult to make the link between them and actual social life. We must speculate about connections between consciousness and the world, between the content of stories and what the eye sees, between meanings and objects. From a discourse-centered perspective, however, words face both ways: they face toward consciousness and meaning by virtue of their unique distributional properties, but they also face toward the material here-and-now by virtue of their sensible encoding in concrete discourse. By focusing on the tangible aspects of discourse, as well as the content, and placing them within the matrix of an ongoing social life that appears to the senses, discourse can be linked to the traditional concern of social anthropology—namely, the problem of social order.

One concept that is useful in providing a bridge is *style*. As employed here, style means a form of language use characterizable independently of the content or semantic meaning that is communicated,[1] which constitutes a sign vehicle that contrasts with others within a culture. The concept shades imperceptibly into that of *register*, where form and semantic meaning blend into one another. Registers are typically associated with the speech diversity in complex societies that is based on social class and occupation—for example, the speech of doctors, which involves special terms for familiar objects and altered pronunciations of familiar terms. The concept of register in turn shades into that of *genre*, where content comes to the fore, for example, in the distinction between myths and legends, although formal elements are still involved (see Bakhtin 1986; Seeger 1986; Bauman, Irvine, and Philips 1987).

One example of a style, mentioned briefly in the preceding chapter, is the *wañēklèn* dyadic origin myth telling performance. In that style, the lead speaker produces a syllable, which is repeated by the responding speaker. The lead speaker then produces the second syllable, and so on through the entire narration. It is apparent that the communicated semantic content involved here is independent of the style: the origin myth can be told in ordinary narrative style within the household as well as in this special style. Moreover, the style is distinct from others within the same community, notably, from ritual wailing (*zō*), which is equally salient but whose formal characteristics are wholly distinct from those of the *wāñēklèn*.

The proposition put forth here and in subsequent chapters is that an understanding of such styles can help to illuminate the problem of social order. It allows us to comprehend the here-and-nowness of discourse, its immanence or immediacy with respect to the senses, taking discourse out of the abstract, decontextualized plane of content and inserting it into the tangible present of social life. A style is not just an instance of language usage, an instantiation of Saussurean distributions within a discourse instance. It characterizes a potentially infinite set of such instances, and this characterization can be made more or less independently of the semantic meanings attributable to them. Style thus makes possible a classification of discourse that crosscuts classifications based on content.

The concept of style inserts discourse into a plane of analogous social phenomena, such as body painting, hair and clothing styles, ornamentations, postures, and gestures. What is distinctive about this plane is that the cultural phenomena in question are embodied. They are part of what Marcel Mauss (1979) calls "body techniques" (*les techniques du corps*), which may become part of the content of consciousness when they are named by means of language and discourse and so reflected upon, but which exist first and foremost in the realm of the senses. They are culture as inscribed in the physical person rather than, or in addition to, the mind. They represent a realm of physical experience that reflects a direct and immediate control by culture over the body.

In light of the earlier discussion of hot and cold societies, it is intriguing that style has received a somewhat different treatment within the American social scientific literature than is proposed here. Osgood (1960:293), for example, proposes that style be looked at as an individual's "deviation" from a social norm. This characterization is appropriate in a hot society, where emphasis is placed upon uniqueness with respect to diachronic relations (new "styles") and also synchronic patterning. The alternativity of styles—the fact that there is more than one to be chosen from—allows them to be marshaled in the service of uniqueness in hot societies. This is so even though the essence of style is not to be a deviation or error with respect to a norm, but rather one of a set of alternative norms. To produce a new style is to produce a new norm, one that is recognizable and copiable, one that can characterize a potentially infinite class of discourse instances.

In a cold society such as Shokleng, the alternative norms are not marshaled in the service of individuation, uniqueness, and novelty any more
than are the norms governing clothing, ornamentation, posture, and the
like. They may reflect a social categorization scheme, but they do not provide an embodied sense of individuation. Rather, they instill a sense of
participation in traditional ways of being and doing, in collectively prescribed and replicated patterns of conduct. One does not seek to produce a
new style, based upon ones that have come before it, but to perform as
faithfully as possible the style that has been handed down.

The embodied character of discourse styles can be seen in Shokleng origin myth telling and ritual wailing. The dyadic origin myth style involves
not only an interpersonal coordination of syllable production, but also
various controls over the actual sound production. First—and most obvious among the sensible, embodied characteristics—is the production of
syllables through abrupt diaphragmatic explosion, the syllable being articulated with unusual force, as in a shout. Second, accompanying this explosion is a constriction of the pharynx and larynx, such as twentieth-century
Americans would recognize in the shouted signals emitted by quarter-
backs at the beginning of each play in football. This lends a harsh or gruff
quality to the articulation. Third, the pitch level of sounds is held relatively constant, with an occasional modulation, a feature that adds to the
repetitive quality, to the production of units essentially like each other.
Fourth, the syllables are articulated with equal stress, which again eliminates potential differences among the syllabic units, making them all conform to a single model.

This can be seen graphically in figure 10, which shows the composite
waveforms for actual stretches of origin myth telling, one in the dyadic
style and one in the ordinary narrative style. Both recordings were made in
1975 under relatively natural conditions. In the dyadic style depicted
above, each amplitude bundle corresponds to a single syllable. The syllable metering, with each syllable given equal length, can be seen in this
case, but not in the ordinary narration shown below. The amplitudes in
the dyadic performance show more variance than was actually present.
This is due in part to the fact that the lead speaker was closer to the micro-
phone than the respondent. In part it is due to the rocking motion of the
speakers, which brought them closer to and farther away from the micro-
phone at different times.

Although dyadic syllable alternation is probably the critical distinguishing characteristic of origin myth telling, the above features themselves are
capable of producing a recognizable style. One can appreciate this by try-

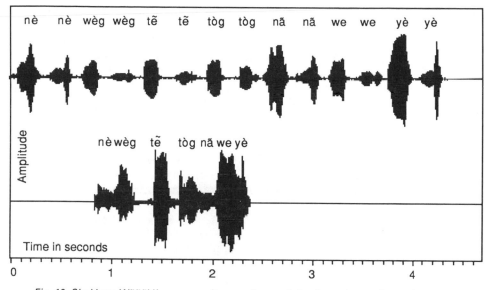

Fig. 10. Shokleng Wãñẽklèn, composite waveforms of dyadic and narrative styles

ing to speak while producing each syllable with a sharp diaphragmatic pulse, giving each a roughly equal length, pitch, and stress, all the while maintaining a constricted larynx and pharynx. These features are salient and unmistakable classifiers of discourse, which any interpreter can pick up on.

However, they are not just recognizable; they are part of the actual bodily techniques of control that the collectivity, in the service of tradition, exercises over the individual. They can be felt in the muscle contractions within the throat, mouth, and abdomen, and in their pure form they are accompanied by aspects of bodily posture—the two individuals are seated facing one another, rocking back and forth in time with the rhythm of syllable alternation. The features embody in a very real and concrete sense the voice of tradition, which speaks through the individual, through the muscular contractions and kinesthetic sensations as well as through the acoustic effects.

In his celebrated article on "The Dualism of Human Nature and Its Social Conditions," Durkheim (1960 [1914]: 328) writes: "Far from being simple, our inner life has something that is like a double center of gravity. On the one hand is our individuality—and, more particularly, our body in which it is based; on the other is everything in us that expresses something other than ourselves." He goes on to explain (1960 [1914]: 337) that:

it is not without reason . . . that man feels himself to be double: he actually is double. There are in him two classes of states of consciousness
that differ from each other in origin and nature, and in the ends toward
which they aim. One class merely expresses our organisms and the
objects to which they are most directly related. Strictly individual, the
states of consciousness of this class connect us only with ourselves, and
we can no more detach them from us than we can detach ourselves
from our bodies. The states of consciousness of the other class, on the
contrary, come to us from society; they transfer society into us and
connect us with something that surpasses us. . . . In brief, this duality
corresponds to the double existence that we lead concurrently: the one
purely individual and rooted in our organisms, the other social and
nothing but an extension of society.

Here the problem is formulated in terms of a dualism of consciousness.
Social sensations originate from outside, from the experience of the other,
and produce a consciousness of the group; bodily sensations originate from
the inside, from the experiences of the self, and produce an individual
consciousness.

However, in the case of origin myth telling, the other has so thoroughly
penetrated the self that the distinction cannot be made. The actual bodily
control comes from sensori-motor mastery, which mastery is achieved by
the individual; but the individual is working for society, for tradition, for
the past. Since the physical patterns are socially learned and transmitted
across the generations, the awareness of bodily sensations resulting from
these sensori-motor coordinations is not individual but social or, rather,
simultaneously individual and social. Nor can the contrast of internal with
external be supported in this view. The sensations come from within the
body, but their true origin lies outside the body in the publicly accessible
discourse and other tangible sign vehicles that have served as the models to
be copied and in which culture resides.

An especially interesting case is that of ritual wailing, which again requires of the individual physical mastery, although that mastery is distinct
from what is required in origin myth telling. First, there is a regular singsong intonation for each line, with the pitch gradually falling off toward
the end. This pitch contour forms a recognizable, if not fully melodic, signal, which is repeated over and over again. Second, there is a glottal
creakiness, in which the vocal cords are controlled to make them vibrate at
a slower pace than in ordinary speech. The creakiness is such as one hears
in the speech of old people. Third, a given instance of ritual wailing usually contains interspersed "cry breaks," which can be of different types, as

described in more detail in chapter 7. These involve a glottal catch initially and/or finally, with a diaphragmatic pulse producing a stream of air that causes friction as it rushes over the glottis. In its pure form, ritual wailing, like origin myth telling, is also associated with other bodily gestures: the performer is typically in a seated position with the hands covering the face.

One may be tempted to associate ritual wailing with the "individual" half of Durkheim's divided self, with forces arising from within the body rather than from culture, but ritual wailing furnishes excellent evidence for the falseness of the internal/external dichotomy. In fact, the wailing is stylized, as subsequent comparative investigation will show, and it is culturally transmitted, as is origin myth telling. It is, in short, again culture taking over the body, manifesting itself not only in consciousness, but also in sensation and feeling, in the fabric of the physical organism.

In light of the earlier discussions of parallelism, it is of interest that a key aspect of bodily control in each case is repetition, the ability to parcel sensori-motor coordination into units or chunks, which can then be repeated. If such repetition functions cognitively—to make the discourse salient, as Jakobson (1960) proposes, or to provide the grounds for inference, as in the metadiscourse parallelism of reported speech, or to serve as a model for the repetitive quality of time, as in the everyday narration of the origin myth—it is also the basis for actual physical ability. The clearest evidence that something has been learned in sensori-motor terms is that it can be repeated. In repetition is mastery, which is evident in the metered production of syllables in the origin myth telling, each syllable being like the others in stress, pitch, and length. It is also evident in ritual wailing in the production of lines with a similar pitch contour, articulated with the characteristic creaky voice. Such units produced over and over and over again reveal the thorough control that individuals have taken over their own physical apparatus. A single replication of a pattern could be chance, a twofold replication happenstance, but repeated replication can only be mastery. It is a sign of mastery.

However, control by the individual is simultaneously control by culture. The style, in a cold society at least, is not an individual invention; and even in a hot society the new style is socially accepted only because of its relationship to styles that have come before it. It does not so much free itself from the past as define itself in terms of the past, even if that definition is oppositional. In the case of ritual wailing and origin myth telling, the styles are cultural inventions that have been handed down across the generations, and, while they may be shaped by the individuals in a given generation, those individuals are also shaped by them. Culture works its way across time and space, seizing control of the physical apparatus of the individual body. One can appreciate why parallelism should be the best example of this seizing of control. If repetition of sensori-motor units is a mark of individual control, it is *ipso facto* a mark of cultural control if the sensori-motor patterns have been copied and socially transmitted.

Because sensori-motor parallelism plays a crucial role in ritual, especially in its dance components, one can appreciate why ritual in turn is regarded as the highest expression of culture. It displays in purest form the mastery that culture achieves over human bodies. Sensori-motor parallelism and coordination become complex sign vehicles that communicate this fact to the individuals, although that communication is achieved at the level of icons and indices rather than semantic contents and consequently occurs outside of full consciousness. The individual feels the control exercised by culture, regardless of the conscious meaning that may be assigned to the activities.

It is true that forms of activity other than ritual involve such socially learned sensori-motor repetition, for example, patterns of activity in work, but ritual is the purest expression of cultural control. It is not subordinated to any other immediate goal than the performance itself. Where the conscious ideology formulates a practical goal for the activity (e.g., the promotion of health or fertility or the bringing of rain) ritual as a means to those ends is nevertheless guided only by the norm of its proper and faithful execution. It is not guided by an immediate practical purpose that might influence the sensori-motor habits themselves. Those habits are regulated only by the past, by tradition, by culture. The success or failure of the ritual is attributed to the perfection with which it has taken place.

For Durkheim (1965 [1915]), the importance of ritual lies first and foremost in the fact of social aggregation. In the case of the Australian Arunta, it is the coming together in one place of the otherwise dispersed community that allows the *intichiuma* to kindle a collective consciousness in the individual. The presence of the group impresses itself on individuals, makes them feel a part of something much greater than any of them in isolation. Many elements contribute to this experience of "sacredness," of the collectivity, including the rhythmical qualities, which lead to an altered state of consciousness; but nowhere does Durkheim point to the manifestation of bodily control through the performance of sensori-motor repetition or to the feelings arising from that control.

Among ritual behaviors, style is especially noteworthy because of its relationship to discourse. Unlike other ritual behaviors, which must get their conscious significance from discourse that is not intrinsic to them (i.e., from exegesis), the marked styles of ritual result in their own publicly accessible discourse, which has its own semantic meanings or content. Not only do they reflect the mastery by culture over the physical apparatus of the human body; they are also the bearers of properly linguistic significance. The discourse suffuses consciousness with meanings; simultaneously, bodily sensations produce their own feeling of mastery, even though that feeling may be kept from consciousness.

Style is characterizable independently of content: the origin myth can be told in ordinary narrative style or in the dyadic *wãñẽklèn* style. Similarly, the meanings encoded in the *zõ* (ritual wailing) style can also be encoded in everyday speech. Style is primarily a matter of the form of discourse, not of its content. Despite their characterizability, however, marked styles are associated with certain contents rather than others. Each is associated with its own consciousness of the world. In principle, the *wãñẽklèn* style could be used to say anything. In fact, it is used only to tell the origin myth. The *zõ* style could be used to communicate any meaning. In fact, it is only used to encode laments for the dead.

Some indication of the conscious content of origin myth telling is given in the preceding chapter. For ritual wailing, the example below is provided. It was produced by a woman approximately eighty years of age whose husband and other close relatives had died years before. I recorded it in 1975 at an *ãgyïn* ceremony for the dead.

Ritual Wailing (Shokleng, 1975)

1. ẽñ kàñka tõ kòñgàg kamàg to ka nẽ gèke yò ka nũ wãñcuke nẽ ñãgyag tẽ
   I used to be in the midst of my male kinsmen, and now I am alone too much;

2. ẽñ cõ ẽñ kàñka òg mlè zògneg mõ nẽ kèke yò ẽñ cõ wèg nẽ gèke kũ nũ òg to plãl kũ kògò nẽ tẽ
   I see that with my kinsmen I was at peace, and I cry for them and I am sick;

3. ñũgñẽn tõ ẽñ ñõgagtòl kòmã yògï lò nũ nõgagtòl ñãgyag gèke kũ
   my brothers wanted me not to suffer, but now I suffer too much;

4. ẽñ cõ ẽ mlè nũgñẽn tũ yògze li ke wãcuke yògagtòl kèke tò nã ka òg kàglẽl nõ hãñãglò òg la ñõgagtòl mã tẽ kèkc tin
   I do not have any more siblings to do thus (as my brothers had done) and alone I suffer. Sometimes it seems that they are still alive, but even near them I suffer;

5. nũgñẽn zi ẽ ñõgagtòl mã kũ ẽñ yògzõ nõñã ẽñ kakutun ẽñ cõ wèg mũ
   ẽñ cõ zi kakutu kũ nẽ ke tũ mã kũ nũ zi to plãl kũ kògò nẽ gèke tin
   when I heard my sister suffering, and I was healthy, I saw that she had
   forgotten me. I cannot forget her and I cry for her and I am sick;

6. ẽñ cõ tã nã ka zi ten yò nã we kũ lò zi nu tẽ mã tẽ kèke nũ zi kakutun kũ
   nẽñ ke tũ mã kũ nũ zi to plãl kũ kògò nẽ kèke tin
   had I seen where she went, I would have gone with her. I cannot forget her and I cry for her and I am sick;

7. ñũgñẽn tẽ tõ ñõ nèn kònã tẽ gèke kũ ẽ tõ nèn we kũ wun kũ ẽ tõ ẽñ we
   yò to ẽn kàgzèg katẽ kèke ẽñ cõ we yò ka ẽñ ñẽ kèke
   my brother would go to look for things for me [i.e., would go out
   hunting for me], and, when he saw something, he would bring it, and
   he would come contentedly to where he had seen me, I would see
   repeatedly;

8. ti tõ ẽñ co katã mã tẽ kèke kũ ti yògzõ nũ kògò nẽ kèke tin
   he seems to come toward me now, and I miss him and I am sick.

The conscious content of this instance consists of memories of the past
juxtaposed against the present, of kinsmen who were once present but who
are now dead, of a time of contentment that has since vanished. A comparison with other instances reveals the similarity of content. Each floods
consciousness with separation and loss, with nostalgia for a bygone era.

Among Shokleng, ritual wailing and origin myth telling, along with
singing, are the most salient speech styles. It is intriguing that they are
related as well in terms of the conscious content they encode. Both tell of
the past and of the dead. Their content deals with times gone by, with
persons who are no longer members of the community, with events that
have transpired.

This is not to say that there are no differences in the conscious content.
In the origin myth, the past goes beyond that accessible through memory.
None of the narrators knew firsthand any of the individuals whose deeds
are recounted. Those individuals are ancestors, whose continuity with the
present members of the community is asserted, but who extend back beyond the reach of direct sensory memory. The individuals remembered in
ritual wailing, however, were known to the living firsthand. The past in
this case is an immediate past that lingers on in memories grounded in direct sensory experience. Those direct memories can be kindled by the
words of living speakers. Moreover, unlike origin myth telling, the specific
content of ritual wailing is not fixed. There are a sufficient number of formulaic elements to suggest a degree of fixity. Still, the specific deeds and

events can be tailored by the speaker, made to express a unique relationship to the dead.

Intriguingly, these objective differences are in some measure overcome by the form of the discourse. This is especially true in the case of firsthand memories versus hearsay. As demonstrated in chapter 4, narration of the origin myth involves pronominal shifting that makes it appear as if the speaker were recounting the memories of direct sensory experience, as in the case of ritual wailing. Where one would expect a third person form ("arrived in front of him"), the first person appears ("arrived in front of *me*"). Whatever the subjective orientation of the narrators in each case, from the point of view of the publicly accessible discourse, at least one key difference is neutralized: the conscious content of origin myth telling, like that of ritual wailing, is represented semiotically as a past personally remembered.

This similarity in the conscious content of these two styles is not, from a Durkheimian perspective, a matter of chance. In fact, consciousness is suffused in each case with the problematic of cultural continuity. In the case of origin myth telling, that problematic assumes a positive form. The conscious content leads its interpreters to ask: how did we get from there to here, from the ancient past to the present living community? And it provides them with a positive answer: we are continuous with that past. In the case of ritual wailing, the problematic is negative: why is the past not like the present? And the answer is a negative one: because those individuals are no longer here today. But the concern in each case is with continuity, and this is the same concern that is reflected subliminally—at the iconic and indexical planes—in the bodily repetition of units of sensorimotor coordination.

What has been said thus far, however, gives no insight into the question of why these particular forms of sensori-motor coordination. One can appreciate that parallelism or repetition of a given sensori-motor unit may be a sign of cultural control over the individual, but why select this particular sensori-motor unit? Why, in the *wañēklèn* style, should the basic unit be a pair of syllables uttered in alternation by two speakers, the syllables being articulated with a constricted larynx and pharynx and produced with a sharp diaphragmatic expulsion of air? Why should the unit of ritual wailing involve a characteristic singsong intonation and creaky voice?

In a well-known dictum, Saussure (1966 [1915]) proposes that in language "there is only difference." Lévi-Strauss translates this dictum to the level of social order, and his translation provides one hypothesis about speech styles. In his explanation of totemism (Lévi-Strauss 1963:77), he proposes that animal species are used as diacritics for differentiating social groups, much as, it can be suggested, styles are differentiating diacritics with respect to categories of person and time: ". . . on the one hand there are animals which differ from each other (in that they belong to distinct species, each of which has its own physical appearance and mode of life), and on the other there are men—among whom the ancestors form a particular case—who also differ from each other (in that they are distributed among different segments of the society, each occupying a particular position in the social structure). The resemblance presupposed by so-called totemic representations is *between these two systems of differences.*" For structuralism, the totemic lesson can be applied to social life more generally: in social order there is only difference. The level of the representational scheme—in the case of totemism, animals, and in the case of speech styles, the distinct sensori-motor coordinations as well as the resultant discourse—forms a system of contrasts or difference. That system maps onto analogous contrasts among persons, places, and times. The social order is differentiated by means of the representational order. There is no positive relationship between a given representation—a given animal or speech style—on the one hand, and the category of person, place, or time to which it is attached, on the other. That connection is purely arbitrary, a function of the correlation between the two planes of difference.

I propose to show that this hypothesis presents an impoverished view of speech styles and probably, by extension, other related "systems of differences," such as body painting and ornamentation, clothing and hair styles, postures, and the like. At the same time, it contains an element of truth, and it represents an advance over the Durkheimian conception. For Durkheim, society or culture is a unified thing; its parts are understood primarily in reference to it. Such a holistic approach, however, provides no motivation for the character of differentiated parts, since they are all essentially alike, each functioning to kindle a consciousness of the whole. In Lévi-Strauss's approach, there is a motivation for specificity, although that motivation is negative and impoverished: the part must be different from others with which it enters into a system of contrasts.

The element of truth in this view is that speech styles do function in some measure as systems of differences, which correlate with other such systems at the level of social categories. Speech styles are indexical sign vehicles that serve to point to or pick out by virtue of actual physical co-presence aspects of the social situation, of space, time, person, and so forth.[2] While picking out one aspect of the social world and pointing to it, the discourse style or other indexical element simultaneously differentiates that aspect from others. Consequently, the style must be distinct from the other styles with which it contrasts. If a diacritic of the social categories of male and female is clothing, then the clothing worn by men must be physically distinct from that worn by women.

Ritual wailing and origin myth telling function as embodied signals of social differentiation of this type. Their sensori-motor coordinations are physically present, imprinted, so to speak, on the body. But they are not imprinted on the bodies of all community members, only those who have reached mature or adult status. This physical co-presence enables the co-ordinations, as well as the actual discourse, to signal maturity as opposed to immaturity, adulthood as opposed to childhood. Even though the social categories are not presented as such to consciousness, they are felt. The repetitive mastery induces a sense of situated status, of location within the collectivity, location that has been achieved over time and through practice. While the social category of adult is broad, it is not co-extensive with the "collectivity," in an undifferentiated sense. For children, indeed, the signals serve an exclusionary function; they mark what the children are not, what they strive to become. They are signals of a possible future rather than of an actual present.

The function of dividing up the present does not contradict the theme of cultural continuity. One can feel oneself to be carrying on a tradition—what members of clan A as opposed to clan B do, what men as opposed to women do, what adults as opposed to children do—without simultaneously feeling oneself to be a member of the collectivity that encompasses these differentiated parts. Even in a cold society, social order need not hinge upon a feeling for the group or for the culture as an entity, as a singular thing. It may rather be grounded in the sense of mastery over the body that is achieved through copying the mastery of others, who have in turn copied it from others, and so on back beyond the reach of memory. Foucault's (1980) microtechniques of power may be generalized, from this perspective, from the control by one individual over another, or by one position over another in a hierarchy of authority, to controls exercised by tradition through an embodied sense of social position, which occurs in acephalous as well as cephalous cases.

Moreover, not everyone within the collectivity has the same class of role models. The two styles considered here are socially distinct: while ritual wailing marks mature members of the community of either sex—that is, a future to which every child can aspire—origin myth telling is performed only by men. Girls cannot model the mastery of their bodies on this image, and that is not something to which they aspire. When men engage in origin myth telling, they feel themselves to be men as opposed to boys. Over time they have achieved a physical and intellectual control that boys lack. But they also feel themselves to be men as opposed to women, and, in this sense, they have achieved a control that women will never have.

We should not imagine, however, that speech styles only signal social categories, that their differentiating function is confined to the field of persons. In addition to differentiating society, they also differentiate time. Adults do not always engage in origin myth telling. While certain embodied signals of socially differentiated status may be present at all times—for example, the lip plugs worn by men—marked discourse styles occur only at some times. As a consequence, they point to those times as special, as distinct from others. Most notable in this regard is the specific association between the styles and the *āgyïn* ceremonies, which are performed in order to reintegrate a widow or widower into the community after a period of seclusion and mourning. Although ritual wailing and origin myth telling occur at other times, they invariably occur at this time. The styles serve to highlight the ceremonial occasion as special, to produce in the performers a sense of this segment of time as unique. The difference is not just between ceremonial and nonceremonial time. It is also between this ceremony, the *āgyïn*, and the other major ceremony to which it is opposed, the *āglan*, in which children two to four years old are "made" (*a han*, literally, "your making") into members of the community. Ritual wailing and origin myth telling never occur at the *āglan*.

In addition to the two already discussed, ritual wailing has three other indexical associations. First, it occurs during the period immediately following an actual death. It occurs not just at the *āgyïn* ceremony, but at any time when individuals feel the pain of the death. Second, it is also a form of greeting, known in the literature as the "welcome of tears," discussed in more detail in chapter 7. While the semantic content of the discourse in this case is still recollections of the dead, the style is co-present not with the event of death, but with comings and goings, with separation and loss of a different sort. Third, as Henry (1964:188) observes, the style is "most commonly heard in the very early morning or evening," and thus has an indexical association with the daily cycle as well. It occurs at the transition points between day and night, the points of separation, so to speak, within this cycle. The style is a marker of what van Gennep (1960) and Victor Turner (1967:93–111, 1969:94–130) call "liminal" phases.

Origin myth telling has, aside from the indexical functions previously mentioned, two additional ones. First, it is performed in order to counteract the possibly harmful effects of a food taboo violation. The idea is that the taboo violation is a breach of continuity. One has broken the rules that have been passed on over time. Since origin myth telling is associated with continuity, its performance can right that wrong, reestablish connections with the past. Further, the penalty for violation may be sickness or death. Hence, performing the origin myth in this context is thought to avert death, just as performing it in the *ägyïn* overcomes a death that has occurred, heals the wounds of the community, and reestablishes continuity. Second, the origin myth is part of the instruction of youth whereby boys are made into adults and, consequently, is practiced in the evenings as part of the process of transmission of culture itself. The context to which it is linked, and which it in turn signals, is related to that of death. If death diminishes the category of adults, this initiation replenishes it.

Structuralism thus gives a partial answer to the question of why styles assume the specific forms they do. In order for them to have a differentiating capability, they must be recognizably distinct. If origin myth telling is to distinguish men from women, then the sensori-motor coordinations involved, as well as the discourse produced, must be distinct from those of ritual wailing. Moreover, the two styles taken together must be distinct from the ordinary, nonceremonial style of language use and they must contrast with the styles used in the *äglan* ceremony, to which the *ägyïn* is opposed. Their positive character is based in part upon their negative, or differentiating, value. Styles are linked to social order in a specific way. If they kindle a sense of control by culture over the body, the body is regimented not to the shape of an undifferentiated collectivity, but to a specific location within society and within time. One is made to feel oneself a certain kind of person—mature as opposed to immature, male as opposed to female—and to be in a certain phase—the *ägyïn* ceremony for the dead, or a state of mourning, or the transitions between day and night. This task of differentiation is accomplished by the styles as sign vehicles. The embodied sensori-motor coordinations within a given style, as well as the resultant discourse, are distinct from those in other styles.

But this form of explanation is highly impoverished, and we feel ourselves not much closer to understanding the reason for the diaphragmatically exploded syllables produced with a tight larynx and pharynx in the case of origin myth telling and for the singsong intonation and creaking voice of ritual wailing. We are beyond the unitary explanation of Durkheim, but not far enough beyond. If the connection of styles to the social order is arbitrary, purely differential, then exchanging the sensori-motor coordinations characteristic of ritual wailing for those of origin myth telling should make no difference. The differentiating function of the wailing style could be accomplished if the discourse were produced dyadically, syllable by syllable, with constricted larynx and pharynx, and a metering of syllables coupled with equistress and a level pitch. Correspondingly, the origin myth might be told with creaky voice, interspersed cry breaks, and a falling singsong pitch contour. In fact, such an eventuality is unlikely, since the motivation is not simply a matter of differences, as suggested, based on comparative research, in the following chapters.

Do styles function analogously to totems, providing a resemblance between "two systems of difference"? Or do they also bring together the socially and temporally distant elements of another locus, thereby enriching it? And, if so, does this drawing together—in the associational sense, which provides a dialectical moment opposed to structural differentiation—allow for creativity and innovation as new linkages are recognized and asserted? In fact, the relationships among styles within the broader configuration of culture are grounded in similarity as well as difference. Ritual wailing and origin myth telling are constructed from features that occur elsewhere, features that have indexical values in those other styles. Ritual wailing and origin myth telling, so to speak, import those features in order simultaneously to sneak in their associated values. In this way, they become, in effect, clusters of icons through which one looks out at the larger history of discourse and draws the indexically relevant meanings into the present.

This is most obvious in the case of ritual wailing, where one feature—creaky voice—functions in the everyday code to index old age, an index that is based on the natural facts of aging. It also occurs in crying, which in Shokleng is called by a distinct term (*plãl* as opposed to *zõ*). In ritual wailing, the feature is stylized and incorporated into learned patterns of sensori-motor repetition; but having been incorporated into the wailing style, creaky voice does not thereby lose its positive association with old age and crying. In fact, it continues to function as an icon, calling up its associations in these other contexts. The same can be said of the cry breaks, which in the everyday code are associated with intense, nearly hysterical, feelings of grief.

Similar arguments can be made regarding the embodied characteristics of origin myth telling. The articulation of syllables with constricted pharynx and larynx, and with abrupt diaphragmatic explosion, also occurs in the everyday code. It indexes an aggressive posture, as when yelling at a dog. The exploded, constricted values occur as well when trekking groups meet after a prolonged separation, when it is unclear whether the groups are still on friendly terms. The style is a form of aggressive greeting, which is imitated in narratives describing these events. The *wãñẽklèn* style draws on these indexical values, suggesting that the mature men who perform the origin myth are bold and aggressive, characteristics that are generally valued within the culture.

The other sound-level characteristics of the *wañēklèn* cycle—dyadic syllable metering, equistress, and flat intonation—seem at first glance enigmatic. As it happens, they occur in a familiar context, namely, in teaching something that must be learned verbatim—for example, teaching their own language to a foreign anthropologist.[3] The teacher utters a syllable, then has the pupil repeat it, then utters another, and so forth. The indexical value is transmitted to the origin myth telling context: the features signal that the telling is in fact an instance of teaching, of the transmission of culture. Indeed, the dyadic syllable-by-syllable method is used in teaching the origin myth itself to young men, night after night, in huts specifically constructed for this purpose. One function of the overall style proposed here—to instill in its users an embodied sense of the continuity of culture—is suggested by the sensori-motor features of the style itself, which are iconic with those of the broader teaching style.

One differentiating function of ritual wailing and origin myth telling is to mark the distinctiveness of the *āgyïn* ceremonies for the dead in relationship to the *āglan* ceremonies that "make" young children members of the community of the living.[4] Neither ritual wailing nor origin myth telling occurs in the latter. However, we do find a style that is related to, if distinct from, the origin myth telling style. Two groups of men stand in lines opposite one another. The men in one line utter in unison a monosyllabic word such as *til*, "tick," or a nonsense vocable. This is repeated by the men in the second line, then again by those in the first line, and so forth for several rounds, after which both lines repeat in unison a short refrain. In this respect, it is like the origin myth telling style, except that it involves only isolated, monosyllabic words lacking syntax.

The two styles are not just distinct; they are obviously related. They look out at one another and in so doing comment on their relevant contexts, that is, death and replacement, even if that comment is made through icons and indices, occurring outside the full consciousness of semantically encoded discourse. The two styles go together, as sides of a coin, but, at the same time, they are also distinct. In the *wañēklèn* one finds a syntax and narrative remarkable for their complexity, indexing the pinnacle of cognitive development, the shining intellectual achievement of Shokleng culture. In the other style, known as *a han*, one finds the simplest monosyllabic lexemic utterances, some of them nonsensical, with no syntax at all, indexing the earliest phase of child development in which there is recognizable evidence of culture. The association of this style with ceremonies for making biological children into social beings is based on the positive characteristics of the style itself, namely, the encoding of how children of this age actually talk, the rudimentary speech being evidence of incipient culture. Similarly, the association of the *wãñẽklèn* style is with the eldest, most cultured members of the community, those who in fact use the most elaborate syntax.

In the case of style, the discourse-centered approach leads us to reject the dictum that in social life "there is only difference." In fact, there is similarity as well, and that similarity functions to draw positive linkages between the various parts of a differentiated social order. In the configuration of discourse instances, here studied specifically through the relationships among styles, we catch sight of the overall order of Shokleng social life. The styles reflect mastery over the physical body by culture, and they also create a differentiated topography of person, time, and situation. For structuralism, however, differentiation thins and narrows the present experience, making it specific in relationship to the general whole, labeling it only as a type of experience. The meaningfulness of the here-and-now is in its specificity, in its distinctiveness with respect to everything else. However, while styles differentiate, they simultaneously create webs of similarity, of positive linkage. Linkages enrich the simple indexical value of the style, make the here-and-now more densely meaningful, and amplify its significance by positive associations with other areas of social space and time.

CHAPTER 6

Stylized Dialogicality
and Interpretability

*N*iels Fock (1963:219–230) many years ago charted a widely distributed form of linguistic interaction, in native South America, known as the ceremonial dialogue. It is concentrated primarily to the north and west of the Amazon basin, where it has been reported for some forty-two societies. In relationship to this widespread pattern, the Shokleng *wãñēklèn*, or dyadic origin myth telling style, is divergent. Not only are Shokleng geographically remote from the heartland of ceremonial dialogue—they occupy part of the southernmost extension of the central Brazilian plateau—but the dialogical pattern involves repetition rather than response. Nevertheless, the broad phenomenon provides a test case for questions of interpretability and motivation of style.

There is empirical evidence, in the characteristics of actual discourse collected from several different cultures, that the phenomenon shows regularities across the boundaries of languages and language families and even across considerable stretches of geographical space, where no analogous cases of ceremonial dialogue are known to intervene. The regularities are of two sorts: first, in the properties of the discourse itself; and, second, in the social contexts in which it occurs. This suggests that ceremonial dialogue may function as a signal of social relations that is nonarbitrary or "motivated" in the Saussurean sense. The interpretability of this signal, moreover, is relatively independent of the interpretability of the semantic content of the discourse in question.

It is possible to think of the discourse as carrying two messages: one semantic or referential, decodable only through mastery of the language in question, the other indexical and iconic, understandable through contiguities and similarities that can be apprehended independently of those forming the basis for language. One is directly accessible to consciousness—indeed, forms the content of consciousness; the other is only indirectly accessible to consciousness, residing first and foremost in the sensuous and phenomenal realms.

While the two messages are decodable through different pathways and are in this sense independent, however, they also co-occur in one and the same discourse instance. Is this co-occurrence fortuitous? The present chapter argues that it is not. The stylistic message is indexical, marking contexts and social relations, but the signal itself is, from the point of view of its concrete characteristics, a "model" of certain characteristics of discourse interactions more generally. It parodies or caricatures those characteristics, as in the political cartoons that represent a prominent public figure by taking one or two physical characteristics—shape of the nose, protrusion of the chin, or bushiness of the eyebrows—and exaggerating them. The overall likeness may be minimal, but the exaggerated characteristics unmistakably suggest the figure.

In the case of ceremonial dialogue, the purpose of the exaggeration, however, is not to ridicule or make fun of; rather, it is to suggest that the other characteristics of the discourse on which it is modeled are also to be found in the present case. In this sense, the exaggeration is not only a "model of" other discourse; it is simultaneously a "model for" the discourse containing the semantic meaning with which it co-occurs.[1] It brings those other characteristics to bear on the present case, creating their presence. The co-occurrence is thus not fortuitous. Ceremonial dialogue is a metasignal, a signal about the discourse in which it is found, telling interpreters how to interpret it.

If there are regularities in the ceremonial dialogical form, however, there are also vast differences. These have to do not only with the formal characteristics of the ceremonial dialogue, but also with the overall function or place of the dialogue within the culture or discourse history of which it is part. In the last chapter, it is pointed out that the Shokleng *wãñẽklẽn* or dyadic origin myth telling style contributes to a model of society understood in terms of cultural continuity and sharing, with the major disruptions focused primarily on death. That dialogue modeled the teaching or learning situation. However, ceremonial dialogue is not especially associated with the modeling of continuity. The present chapter argues that it is also, and perhaps more generally, associated with a model grounded in exchange rather than continuity, in reciprocity rather than transmission.

To examine the problem, I have assembled five reasonably well-documented cases: (1) the classic Carib style of ceremonial dialogue as found among Waiwai of Guiana and Trio of the Brazil-Surinam border, (2) ceremonial dialogues of Yanomamö Indians of the Brazil-Venezuela border region, (3) ritualized dialogic "greetings" of Jivaroan Shuar and Achuar of eastern Ecuador, (4) dialogic gathering house chanting of Kuna Indians of the San Blas islands in Panama, and (5) the dyadic origin myth telling style or *wãñēklèn* of Shokleng.

The classic Carib pattern was known originally through the descriptions of Fock (1963:216–230 and 303–316), who himself observed the phenomenon known as *oho-karï*, "yes-saying," among Waiwai. The materials available include detailed descriptions of the formal linguistic and contextual features, as well as of social purposes, and translations of two actual dialogues. Waiwai ceremonial dialogues typically involve two elder men, who sit on stools opposite one another. One man takes the lead, speaking in short sentences, which among Waiwai are uttered in a "special chant-tone . . . with rising pitch at the end" (Fock 1963:216). After each sentence, or sentence fragment, the respondent utters *oho*, "yes."

A variant of the Carib pattern has been described for Trio by Rivière (1969:235–238, *passim*, and 1971:293–311), who distinguishes three types of dialogue, all of which show certain common characteristics. In the most formal type (*nokato*), two men sit on stools, as among Waiwai. The lead man speaks in short sentences, each containing at the end a rhyming word (*kara* or *tʌme*). The second man responds with a "low murmuring grunt" (Rivière 1971:299). In the least formal type, known as *tesʌmiken*, no rhyming word is used and the respondent utters the word *irʌrʌ*, "that's it." In addition, the speakers need not sit on stools—indeed, women sometimes participate in this kind of dialogue. The intermediate type of dialogue, known as *sipʌsipʌman*, is also formally intermediate, lacking the rhyming word but using either the grunt or *irʌrʌ* in responses.

Regarding Yanomamö ceremonial dialogues, there are reasonably extended accounts by Cocco (1972:326–330) and by Migliazza (1978), a description by Shapiro (1972:149–151), and numerous brief references in other ethnographic accounts. In addition, one such dialogue can be observed in the Asch and Chagnon film *The Feast*. There one sees two men facing in the same direction, one squatting in front of the other, engaging in a rapid back-and-forth dialogue, in which the speaker behind leads with a 1–3 syllable utterance and the speaker in front responds at regular intervals with another 1–3 syllables. Shapiro (1972:150) mentions a more "intense form of ritualized conversation" (*yaimu*) in which partners are "seated together on the ground locked in a tight embrace, sometimes even groin to groin and with legs intertwined." The speech alternation is "so rapid that the two are often exchanging monosyllabic utterances." A photograph in Cocco (1972:327) shows the interlocutors in squatting position facing one another, but a note (1972:326, n. 16) indicates that "the more common custom has been to celebrate the *wayamou* with both parties in a standing position."

The Jivaroan Shuar and Achuar ceremonial dialogues have recently been described in detail by Gnerre (1986), although they were reported earlier by various observers, notably Karsten (1935). Janet Hendricks, who spent two years among Shuar, has also made available a tape of Shuar war dialogues. At least two types of ceremonial dialogue must be distinguished for Shuar and Achuar, a "greeting" used in visits between settlements and a "war dialogue" used when warriors arrive in the house of a leader who takes them into battle. Both types occur inside the house. In greetings, the interlocutors are seated across from one another. The lead speaker utters a short sentence to which the respondent replies with a monosyllabic word (e.g., "yes," "wow," "true"). War dialogues take place from a standing position, with each speaker moving back and forth in time with his speech.

For Kuna, Sherzer (1983) supplies detailed descriptions of "gathering house chanting" performed by chiefs, although there are also older accounts of this *onmakket*, "gathering house," style (e.g., Wassén 1949: 46–54; Holmer 1951: 16–21). Sherzer has also made available tapes and transcriptions of actual instances of this ceremonial dialogue. In Kuna ceremonial dialogues, two interlocutors—the chief and his respondent— lie in hammocks slung next to one another in the communal gathering house. The chief chants a line characterized by a distinctive, generally falling intonation contour (Sherzer 1983: 52–53). As he protracts the final vowel of this line, the respondent enters in with a harmonized *teki*, "indeed," the final vowel here in turn being protracted, at which point the lead speaker begins another line. The entire Kuna performance is distinctly musical sounding.

The Shokleng *wãñēklèn* style has already been reasonably well described. In a manner reminiscent of the Yanomamö case described above, two men sit opposite one another in the middle of the plaza, their legs entwined. One interlocutor leads, uttering the first syllable of the origin myth. The respondent repeats that syllable, after which the first speaker utters the second syllable, and so forth, in rapid-fire succession. Speakers move their heads and upper torsos rhythmically in time with the syllables, which are shouted with extreme laryngeal and pharyngeal constriction.

A distinction can be made between *content-defined* and *form-defined* dialogicality, a distinction made earlier (Urban 1986) in terms of "semantic" versus "pragmatic" dialogues. The latter caused some confusion, and the new terms are introduced more adequately to reflect what is intended. The concept of content-defined dialogicality corresponds with the ordinary notion of dialogue as involving "turns" at speaking (cf. Sacks, Schegloff, and Jefferson 1974), where a turn indicates a contribution on the part of a speaker to the unfolding content of the discourse. A turn typically responds to, amplifies, or otherwise extends the content of a previous turn, as it is accessible to consciousness through semantic meaning. A turn in the content-defined sense specifically excludes what are sometimes called "back channel responses," such as "uh-huh" in English, which do not embellish the semantic meaning of the preceding turn. Not all ceremonial dialogues exhibit content-defined dialogicality of this sort.

However, they do all exhibit form-defined dialogicality. The latter indicates that the production of the concrete discourse—the actual sound substance—involves contributions from two parties, who alternate with some regularity. The contributions in this case need not add content. They can be back channel responses, which punctuate the main speaker's turn, keeping the linguistic interaction going, but not contributing to the overall semantic meaning. They can also be simple repetitions of the words in the previous utterance. By definition, all content-defined dialogicality must involve form-defined dialogicality, but not vice versa.

The South American dialogic complex is characterized by the foregrounding of form-defined dialogicality, with or without content-defined dialogicality. There is a palpable rhythm of alternation. One speaker utters a stretch of speech—a syllable, word, line, or sentence—that constitutes his form-defined turn at speaking. The respondent replies with another stretch of speech—a syllable, word, line, or sentence—that constitutes his turn. The initial turn and response taken as a unit can be called a "cycle." Within a given type of ceremonial dialogue, the cycle is organized in a characteristic way. However, in each case the cycle achieves acoustic prominence through its temporal regularity, making a veritable "beat" discernible.

The extreme cases in this regard are Shokleng and Kuna. Among Kuna, cycles are so long that it becomes difficult to speak of a cycle beat, although, because of the musical character of these dialogues, an actual beat can be tapped out during a given turn. Measurements of two instances show that Kuna cycles are in fact remarkably regular. The cycle may be represented schematically as in figure 11. Sp_1 represents the lead speaker, and Sp_2 the respondent. The cycle begins at time t_1. Typically, the voice of the respondent can be detected at the outset, as he completes a response to the previous utterance. However, his voice trails off with declining pitch and intensity, making it difficult to determine precisely where his response ends. The onset of the lead speaker, however, is unmistakable. He proceeds to chant a line of narrative, consisting on average of 25 syllables. At

t_2, the respondent begins to utter the work *teki*, "indeed," the onset of this word overlapping the drawing out of the final vowel by the lead speaker. At t_3, the lead speaker completes his line, while the respondent protracts the final vowel of *teki* until beyond t_4, when the lead speaker begins the next line. One complete cycle lasts from t_1 until t_4. The waveforms of two consecutive lines of actual Kuna dialogue are shown in figure 12, with the cycle points from the schema in figure 11 appropriately marked.

Measurements of elapsed times involved in Kuna cycles reveal a regularity. A study of one text, containing 11 lines, yielded the following results.

	Average	Stand. Dev.	Maximum Range
$t_1 - t_2$	11.08	1.03	10.2 – 13.5
$t_2 - t_3$	0.59	0.40	0.2 – 1.4
$t_3 - t_4$	4.82	0.40	4.4 – 5.4

An entire cycle lasts about 16.5 seconds. Further study shows that there is variation between different occurrences of this style as regards the average times, but that the differences are not great. Moreover, within a given telling there is consistency despite the divergence between tellings. For example, in the results from a second instance of Kuna chanting, the length of lead speaker/respondent overlap is systematically greater than in the first instance.

	Average	Stand. Dev.	Maximum Range
$t_1 - t_2$	11.54	0.61	10.7 – 12.2
$t_2 - t_3$	2.68	0.43	2.2 – 3.1
$t_3 - t_4$	6.64	0.67	6.1 – 7.4

It is important to recognize that overlaps between turns form an integral part of Kuna ceremonial dialogues. Because the two speakers are actually chanting, their voices may be described in terms of "musical," as opposed to "speech," pitch. At the $t_2 - t_3$ overlap, the two voices harmonize, giving hearers the impression of a totality of discourse created by cooperation. This harmonizing contrasts markedly with the aggressive-sounding overlap between speakers found in Shuar war dialogues.

If Kuna provide a limiting case in the direction of extremely long cycles, Shokleng provide a limit in the direction of short cycles. Here a "turn" consists of uttering only a single syllable. Normally, there is no overlap between turns, as can be seen in the spectrogram of a short stretch of dyadic origin myth telling in figure 10 of chapter 5. Measurements show an average cycle length of 0.58 seconds, as contrasted with the 16–21 sec-

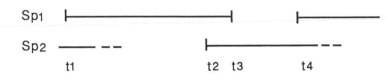

Fig. 11. Schema of the Kuna cycle

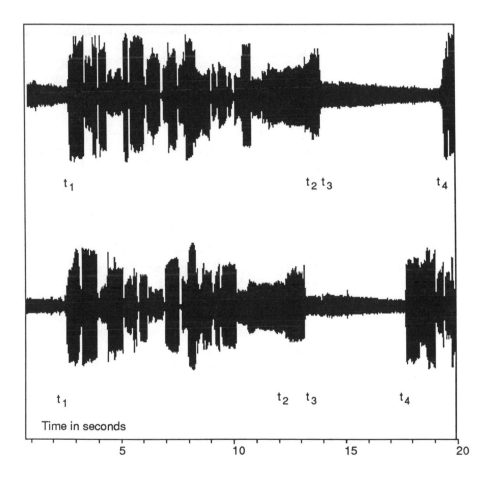

Fig. 12. Waveforms of two actual lines of Kuna ceremonial dialogue

ond cycles among Kuna. The rhythm of cyclicity in Shokleng is simultaneously signaled by head and body movements, as mentioned previously.

The other cases of South American ceremonial dialogue range between these extremes. In the absence of tapes, I have been unable to do measurements on Waiwai and Trio ceremonial dialogues. Nevertheless, the existence of a palpable rhythm of cyclicity is born out by Rivière (1971:298), who refers to even the least formal variety of Trio ceremonial dialogue as "readily distinguishable from everyday speech both by the speed at which it is carried on and by the continual and formalized response of *irʌrʌ*, which gives the conversation a slightly staccato effect." He adds (1971: 309, n. 10): "After I had been among the Trio a few days only and while busy writing in my hammock, my attention was drawn to it by the change in rhythm of the conversation going on around me." Some idea of cyclicity can be had from the brief transcription he supplies (1971:309, n. 14). The lead speaker's turns involve uttering between 5 and 10 syllables, as contrasted with an average of 25 syllables among Kuna and 1 syllable among Shokleng.

Among Shuar-Achuar, in samples measured, the lead speaker's turn typically lasts only 1.37 seconds, during which time he utters on average 7.4 syllables. Average syllable length here is thus 0.19 seconds, and the overall average including response is just 0.21. This contrasts with the Shokleng case, where syllables take nearly 0.29 seconds to produce, and Kuna, where the average syllable length is 0.64 seconds. In Shuar-Achuar cycles there is generally no overlap between lead and response turns. Indeed, there may be a slight (0.20–0.30 second) pause. However, there is often overlap at the other end. The lead speaker frequently begins his utterance as the respondent's trails off. This does not produce a musical effect, as among Kuna. Rather, one senses an aggressive penetration of the respondent's speaking time by the lead speaker. Figure 13 displays the waveform of two cycles of an Achuar ceremonial dialogue, produced from the tape accompanying Gnerre's (1986:315–324) transcription. Two full cycles are shown here, together with fragments of the adjacent cycles. While I have indicated a slight gap between the response in the first cycle and the lead in the second, in fact the latter virtually cuts off the former.

Judging from the descriptions, Yanomamö dialogues seem to vary in cycle length. Analysis of the Asch and Chagnon filmed example suggests that lead speaker and respondent utter between 1 and 3 syllables per form-defined turn, average cycle length being equal to that of the Shokleng *wãñēklèn* (0.58 seconds). Cocco (1972:330, *passim*) refers to repeated occurrence of "trisyllables," while Shapiro (1972:150) mentions an especially rapid form in which the turn is reduced to a monosyllable, as among

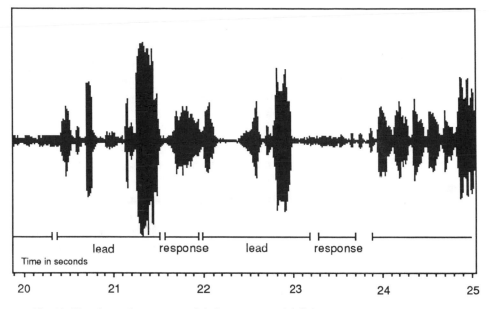

Fig. 13. Waveform of a segment of Achuar ceremonial dialogue

Shokleng. The rhythmical nature of the Yanomamö cycle can be sensed in any case. Acoustically, this dialogue is most reminiscent of Shuar-Achuar ceremonial greetings, though it sounds not unlike the Shokleng *wãñēklèn*.

For each tribe considered here, there is a distinctive form-defined cycle associated with the ceremonial dialogues. Among Kuna, the cycle is long, syllables are uttered slowly and in a chanted voice, and there is an emphasis on harmonic overlap between turns. Among Shokleng, the cycle is short, syllables are uttered rapidly in a shouted voice, and there is no overlap between turns. The other types of ceremonial dialogue range between these extremes. However, Shuar-Achuar dialogues are noteworthy as well for their aggressive character, manifested in the penetration of the respondent's speaking time by the lead speaker.

Despite the diversity, an important similarity underlies all of these dialogues. In each case, alternation between speakers is regularized. Simultaneously, the alternating character itself is foregrounded. This regularization draws attention to the entire linguistic interaction, suggesting that it is noteworthy, something distinct from the ordinary run of events. This is in keeping with the attention-getting function of parallelism discussed in the preceding chapters.

At the same time, the regularized form-defined cycle itself constitutes a separate signal, with its own message, riding along with the semantic message carried in the linguistically segmentable discourse. The regularized cycle caricatures dialogue; it exaggerates the features of everyday conversation in such a way that they can be noticed as a distinctive signal. By virtue of this fact, the regularized cycle comments on the discourse and on the linguistic interaction in which it occurs. It labels them as "dialogic," as involving the coordinated efforts of two speakers. Through iconicity with ordinary conversation, ceremonial dialogue brings the characteristics of such conversation to bear on the present case.

Importantly, performance of these dialogues requires skill and practice on the part of performers, who must pay attention to the other person and coordinate their own behavior. The skills are socially learned and transmitted across the generations. In this sense, ceremonial dialogues are part of the seizing of control by culture over the physical apparatus of the human body. The dialogues send a message to the individuals about who is in charge of their interpersonal coordination. In effect, the message reads: "tradition regulates these interpersonal relations."

But by regularizing the form-defined cycle, ceremonial dialogues not only signal that culture is in charge; they are the actual implementation of culture taking charge. The dialogues remove the timing of response from the sphere of possible actor manipulation. In ordinary conversation, interlocutors can manipulate this timing (e.g., in American English increasing the rate of response signals that one is about to take over the semantic or content-defined turn). In ceremonial dialogues, such manipulation is generally not possible; consequently a norm of "politeness" is introduced (cf. Brown and Levinson 1978, who have developed a different notion of "politeness"), albeit politeness of a peculiarly aggressive sort in the Achuar-Schuar case. This is one component of the cross-linguistic model of solidarity built into ceremonial dialogic process.

Regularization of the form-defined cycle is not the only component of this normative control. Culture also specifies what kind of form-defined response can be given. As a rule, these must be positive or affirmative responses designed to keep the dialogue going, in keeping with their back channel nature. They are not actual, content-laden responses to the lead speaker's statement. The classic case is the Waiwai ceremonial dialogue, which is literally called "yes saying" (*oho-kari*).[2] According to Fock (1963: 216), "after each sentence the opponent answers with a hardly audible 'oho,' that is, 'yes.'" Judging from two dialogues (Fock 1963:303–316), this "yes" is never a semantic response to a previously formulated yes/no question. Instead, the response indicates that the interlocutor is comprehending what the lead speaker has to say. It is a form of acknowledgment, as in the following excerpt (Fock 1963:217):

I want your hair-tube	oho
so I came	oho
you live here	oho
have lots of beads	oho
you can make another one	oho

A similar pattern is found among Trio. Rivière (1971:298–299) reports that for the least formal type of dialogue, the response is *irʌrʌ*, "that's it," and for the most formal "a low murmuring grunt," which we must presume indicates acknowledgment or comprehension. Judging from the one excerpt of a marriage negotiation dialogue (Rivière 1971:309, n. 14), the lead speaker again merely states his case.

> I have come
> I am good
> things I am wanting
> your daughter I want
> my wife, I want
> my woman, her being, I want

The desire is formulated in declarative terms, with the respondent replying affirmatively. The affirmative reply, however, only acknowledges that the lead speaker has that desire. It does not indicate that the respondent will in fact help to fulfill it by making his daughter available to the speaker.

Waiwai and Trio ceremonial dialogues suggest a delicacy in language use, in which the speaker is allowed to state a desire, but in which he does not press for an immediate yes/no response. The respondent in turn acknowledges the desire but does not thereby agree to do anything about it. Positive initiative is still left with him. Simultaneously, however, interlocutors are kept in the dialogue by the foregrounded form-defined turn-taking, which constitutes one overt social purpose of the interaction and which both interlocutors strive to maintain.

Among Kuna, response is again systematically affirmative, the lead utterance being followed by a *teki*, "indeed," or occasionally, apparently, an affirmative realized phonetically as [ayie]. Since Kuna dialogue is used for narration, the lead speaker's semantic turn is typically an actual monologue. Here the respondent's affirmation acknowledges the lead statement and simultaneously makes the content-defined monologue appear as a dialogue. This is of importance in connection with the culture-specific notion of solidarity embodied in Kuna dialogue, discussed subsequently.

The Shokleng *wãñéklèn* seems anomalous in this context, since the respondent utters exactly the same syllable he has just heard from the lead speaker. However, Shokleng repetition response is actually a signal of comprehension as well. The model for the *wãñẽklèn* style, as indicated in the preceding chapter, is the "teaching" style. The Shokleng method of teaching is to have a learner repeat verbatim, syllable by syllable, what he has just heard. If the imitation is judged incorrect, the teacher repeats the syllable until the learner has pronounced it correctly. Repetition is an affirmation and, in particular, a sign of comprehension, just as *teki* indicates affirmation and comprehension among Kuna.

In Shuar-Achuar dialogues, the respondent has available various possible responses. In one text (Gnerre 1986: 315–324), 7 distinct response types occur, including *chua*, "wow," *nekása*, "true," and even *tsaa*, "no," which occurs in 2 out of 84 turns, although here it is apparently used in an affirmative sense vis-à-vis a negative statement. There are also cases where the respondent actually repeats the line uttered by the lead speaker, something that is an echo of the Shokleng pattern. Finally, at certain points, typically at changeovers of the content-defined turn, the two interlocutors are both uttering sentences. While the Shuar-Achuar pattern is distinctive, it fits squarely into the general pattern of acknowledgment found in other South American ceremonial dialogues.

For Yanomamö, Cocco (1972: 326) indicates that the respondent "has nothing to do but repeat, even imitating, that which the other has said or asked; for this there exists a multitude of affirmative and negative synonyms." Response is again an expression of comprehension, functioning to keep the two interlocutors interacting. Moreover, the respondent can make alternative but equivalent responses, and these include repetition of the last syllable of what has just been uttered (Migliazza 1978: 574), once again echoing the Shokleng pattern.

From translated texts, it appears that Yanomamö are more overt than Waiwai and Trio in pressing their demands through dialogue, as in the following excerpt (Cocco 1972: 326), for which, unfortunately, the responses are not indicated.

> Give me, give me, nephew. Give me, give me an axe.
> They have told me that you have axes.

However, despite the pressing character of the statements, participation in the ceremonial dialogue keeps interlocutors interacting for some time, each making his case, until the entire issue has been talked out. In this regard, Yanomamö dialogues are analogous to those discussed previously. They establish a norm of linguistic interaction in which each side is heard out at length.

In all cases, ceremonial dialogues foreground dialogicality, with the response signaling comprehension, while simultaneously cuing the lead speaker to continue. It does not commit the respondent in any way to what has been semantically said. Because of its saliency, the response cycle itself simultaneously becomes a sign vehicle. While it imitates ordinary conversation, in which back channel responses play a constant part, it also becomes a "model for" how the conversation at hand ought to proceed.

If solidarity consists, on the one hand, of the coordination of one's actions with actions of another, as imaged in the form-defined cycle, it also consists, on the other hand, of a positive acknowledgment of the other, a sign that one has taken cognizance of the actions of the other and has comprehended their "meaning." Through regularization of response, ceremonial dialogues embody an icon of the general semiotic character of a solidary relationship. Simultaneously, these dialogues suggest indexically that solidarity is present in the specific linguistic interaction in which it is employed—they are also "models for" solidarity.

Because response is formally constrained—it must be a signal of comprehension—what is again a variable in ordinary conversation is fixed in ceremonial dialogue. The response may not be used to convey an opinion about the lead speaker's utterance or to take over the semantic turn, as is common in everyday conversation. The respondent may only signal his acknowledgment, and this aids in the establishment of a norm of hearing the other out.

Normative regulation of individuals by culture can be seen as well in other aspects of the discourse produced in ceremonial dialogues. There are limitations on intonation contour, stress, volume, rate of syllable metering, and use of pharyngeal and laryngeal constriction. The dialogues range between the fully musical "chanting" of Kuna, at one extreme, and the laryngealized and exploded "shouting" of Shokleng and Yanomamö, at the other.

Sherzer (1983:52) has diagrammed intonation contours for two lines of Kuna ceremonial dialogue. The lead speaker's lines descend gradually from high to low for the first part, then from mid to low for the second. All of the instances examined thus far conform to this two-part pattern. The respondent's utterance, as diagrammed by Sherzer, follows a level pitch, although pitch may taper off during the phase of overlap. In any case, the Kuna style involves musical, rather than speech, pitch, exhibiting in all cases a sustained quality. Waiwai dialogues as well are described in terms of "chanting." Fock (1963:216) notes that speakers employ a "special chant-tone" in which the short sentences exhibit a "rising in pitch at the end." Trio dialogues appear similar in this regard, though Rivière (1971) does not provide a detailed linguistic description.

In contrast to Waiwai and Kuna, Shokleng syllables are "shouted," in a voice that makes use of extreme laryngeal and pharyngeal constriction. Moreover, pitch remains level through the dialogue, each speaker uttering the syllables at the same pitch. Because syllables are metered at regular intervals, the effect would be decidedly musical in nature if pitch were varied.

The Shuar and Yanomamö dialogues are intermediate. The Shuar greeting and war dialogues clearly involve some laryngealization, and many syllables are virtually shouted. However, some are protracted, exhibiting a falling intonation contour that is marginally chantlike. Judging from the Asch and Chagnon film *The Feast*, Yanomamö ceremonial dialogues involve a voice different from ordinary speech, perhaps somewhat more constricted and exploded. Shapiro (1972:150) describes the more intense form of Yanomamö dialogue as "shouting," a characterization that may place it more in line with the Shokleng *wãñēklèn*. On the other hand, Cocco (1972:330) and Migliazza (1978:573–574) describe the dialogues in terms of musical pitch. They also indicate the regularization of stress in this special discourse style.

The different voices and intonation patterns used are probably distinct sign vehicles, with their own characteristic meanings. The Shokleng "shout," for example, sounds aggressive and, indeed, is modeled on a style of speech used in encounters between groups where manifestation of manliness is at issue, as mentioned earlier. Shuar war dialogues are certainly aggressive sounding, and this is true as well, though possibly in lesser measure, for Yanomamö. In contrast, Kuna dialogic chanting is more controlled, even serene; it would seem to suggest that a high degree of control over one's language is valuable in ordinary conversation.

Despite this diversity in voice quality, all dialogues share in common the fact that they limit the range of variation in expressive devices. They are in this sense marked speech styles, the restrictions serving to highlight the ceremonial dialogue as sign vehicle and also the associated linguistic interaction itself. The limitations thus contribute to the attention-getting function already discussed in connection with the form-defined cycle.

Significantly, variables that are here fixed form part of the resources available for accomplishing individual ends in ordinary conversation. During ceremonial dialogues, the resources are removed from individual control and made part of a culturally imposed regime, to which participants in the dialogue are subject. The purposes of linguistic interaction must be accomplished, therefore, using highly restricted means, once again constraining interlocutors to hear the other out. This is culture exercising its control over the individual and over interpersonal relations. The control is not only signaled by the discourse; it is actually present in the physical production of that discourse, in the contraints on expressive devices that may be used and on the actual physical apparatus.

We have thus far examined only one class of characteristics of ceremonial dialogues, namely, those pertaining to the actual utterances that are produced and to the physical facts of the production. However, it is not sufficient to demonstrate that we can interpret the regularities in these utterances, isolated by comparative analysis, as signaling and reflecting the normative control by culture over social relations. We must also examine the second class of characteristics—namely the contexts in which the ceremonial dialogues actually occur—and we must show that those contexts are ones in which solidarity is at issue. There is a range of possible contexts in which solidarity may be called into question, which can vary from culture to culture. From a comparative point of view, however, solidarity is always called into question when the relationship between actors is maximally distant in social terms. We wish to determine, therefore, whether ceremonial dialogues are in fact employed in the maximally distant social relationships. Empirical investigation shows that, in fact, they are. While dialogues may be employed in other, less distant relationships in a given culture, they are also employed in the more distant ones.

Rivière (1971 : 301) sums this up for Trio by saying that the "ceremonial dialogue is used between strangers or kin and acquaintances between whom the relationship has temporarily lapsed." Trio society is organized into villages, arranged in "agglomerations," which are in turn ordered in terms of "groups." According to Rivière (1971 : 304), the "ceremonial dialogue is not used within the boundaries of the agglomeration." It is used when individuals visit between villages of different agglomerations or groups—when the relationship is maximally distant.

It is difficult to obtain a clear picture of Waiwai society in this regard. *Oho-karï* can be used within the village—for example, in the chief's appeal to communal work or in connection with a death (Fock 1963 : 217–218), which echoes the Shokleng use of the *wãñẽklèn* at ceremonies surrounding death. However, it is also used between villages in negotiating trade and marriage and in making invitations to feasts. Fock (1963 : 219) argues that in general it occurs in social situations where conflicts might otherwise erupt. His ethnographic generalization is in keeping with the proposition put forth here.

Among Yanomamö, ceremonial dialogue is associated with the "feast," which occurs during visits between two villages (Chagnon 1983 : 146–169). Yanomamö society is organized into villages that are largely autonomous and are in frequent conflict with one another. Feasts are the principal mechanism for establishing intervillage alliances, which in turn ensure peace, allow for trade and marriage exchange, and furnish military allies. However, according to Chagnon's descriptions, intervillage alliances are always fragile and feasts frequently erupt in violent intervillage confrontations. Migliazza (1978:573) also notes that ceremonial dialogic style is "most practiced" and idiomatic usages are most common in "areas where warfare is more intense." It is safe to infer that ceremonial dialogues in fact occur in contexts where conflict is close to the surface.

Kuna social structure is of a different, more hierarchical, nature. Ceremonial dialogues take place within the "gathering house" located in each village and may be performed by "chiefs" exclusively for members of the village (Sherzer 1983:73–76). However, chanting also occurs during chiefly visits between villages of a given island (1983:91–95) and on the occasion of the more formal interisland visits (1983:95–98). While ceremonial dialogues operate within the village, therefore, perhaps even there helping to create solidarity—indeed, Sherzer (1983:89) himself has remarked that the purpose of Kuna gatherings is the maintenance of "social control and social cohesion"—they also function in more distant relationships where social solidarity is definitely at issue.

The same may be said for Shuar-Achuar, though here the fundamental residential unit was traditionally the "household" (Harner 1972:41, 77–80), there having been no multihousehold villages analogous to those found in the other tribes under consideration. Ceremonial dialogues took place on the occasion of interhousehold visiting (Gnerre 1986), which, as with intervillage feasting among Yanomamö, was a situation fraught with danger, owing to the general condition of feuding that prevailed. A variant form of dialogue also took place when men assembled for a war party. In addition to establishing solidarity within the war party, these dialogues, with their aggressive-sounding display, probably also functioned to key up the participants for battle.

Among Shokleng, the *wãñēklèn* is performed during the communal ceremonies associated with death. Significantly, Shokleng traditionally had no peaceful intervillage relations, villages being the highest level of social integration. Moreover, death ceremonies typically took place during reunions of different trekking groups, in the days before Shokleng were permanently settled. The relationships involved were of maximal social distance within the limits established by this tribe. Moreover, when village fissioning did occur, it typically did so along trekking group lines. The Shokleng pattern thus conforms to the general proposition, although the dialogues also occur in the course of teaching the origin myth and in connection with food taboo violation, as indicated earlier.

Ceremonial dialogues are everywhere used in interactions where the participants are maximally distant in social terms. In three of the six groups sampled here—Shuar-Achuar, Trio, and Yanomamö—ceremonial dialogues occur only in contexts of maximal social distance. In the other three, they occur in the maximally distant relationships but also in closer ones. Evidently, a linkage exists between these contexts of potential conflict and the ceremonial dialogue itself.

The semiotic arguments put forth above make sense of this linkage. Ceremonial dialogue indexes those contexts. Moreover, by virtue of its iconicity with ordinary conversation such as occurs within the household, it simultaneously suggests that these maximally distant social relations, fraught with danger, are in fact like those comfortable relations of the domestic group. It is a model of everyday social solidarity, but it is simultaneously a model for the social relations in connection with which it occurs; it signals the importation of domestic solidarity into the present context. While it functions as a signal, as a semiotic device, however, ceremonial dialogue is also the actual embodiment of a norm of sociability; it reflects the penetration of the individual body by patterns that have been socially transmitted across the generations.

Thus far nothing has been said about the semantic content of the discourse produced under ceremonial dialogue, that is, about what the dialogues are about. Is there content-defined as well as form-defined dialogicality? What is the nature of the content? In fact, there is considerable variability in this regard. I want to suggest that this variability has to do with the culture-specific models of sociability that the dialogues encode. In the previous chapter, it is shown that the Shokleng *wãñēklèn* contributes to an overall model of society as held together by cultural sharing, by the transmission of a common culture across the generations. Here I want to propose that the Shokleng model is one of a set of possible alternatives. It is possible to distinguish: (1) societies in which solidarity is seen as emerging from the sharing of a common culture and common traditions from (2) those in which solidarity is seen in terms of the exchange of material items and/or women, and (3) those in which solidarity is portrayed as the result of a "balance of power." Kuna and Shokleng, very distant from one another geographically—Kuna being located in Panama and Shokleng in southern Brazil—can be typologically grouped in the first class. Yanomamö, Waiwai, and Trio—tribes clustered in the northern South American area—fall closer to the second type. Shuar-Achuar of the western Amazonian region form the basis for the third type, which may be a variant of the second type.

Kuna and Shokleng ceremonial dialogues are, in terms of content, monologues. In other words, the dialogues are not used to exchange ideas. They are used to transmit some fixed content. Among Shokleng, as discussed previously, ceremonial dialogic form is used exclusively in connection with narration of the origin myth, which can also be told in narrative style by a single narrator. What is transmitted here is time-honored content, the content, so to speak, of culture. The situation among Kuna is more complex. As among Shokleng, dialogic form may be used to narrate myths, but it is also used to transmit histories, reports of personal experience, "metacommunicative descriptions" of the gathering itself, and counseling (Sherzer 1983 : 76–89).

From the point of view of the present hypothesis, ceremonial dialogic form functions to define these communicative situations as "dialogic," despite the underlying monologicality of the discourse content. Ceremonial dialogicality suggests that, for monologic communication to be successful, it requires a listener who is actually comprehending what has been said. Of course, in the Shokleng and Kuna cases, the respondent is only one among many listeners. His response signals comprehension to the narrator, but it simultaneously communicates to the audience the importance of comprehension. The audience hears the lead speaker, but it also hears the respondent, and the interaction between speaker and respondent comes to the fore as a model of (and for) the communicative process itself, suggesting the necessity that the audience play an active role in listening if communication is to be successful. That communicative process is one specifically of asymmetrical transmission.

This suggests that among Kuna and Shokleng the basis of solidarity is the sharing of a common culture and, especially, common linguistically transmitted traditions. The transmission process, which is at the heart of sharing, comes to the fore as the principal type of linguistic interaction for which ceremonial language is employed. What makes two individuals cohere in these societies is their shared knowledge of the world. In effect, like is seen as attracting like. The discourse produced by one individual is transmitted and copied, the copy being a replica of the original.

Among Waiwai, there is a different conception operative, one reflected in the content-defined dialogicality of ceremonial discourse. In some cases, considerable stretches of content-defined monologue appear within this overarching dialogue. In one dialogue translated by Fock (1963 : 303–312), the longest single content-defined turn is 468 lines, the line here being defined by the *oho* response. This is comparable in length to an entire myth narration. However, among Waiwai, there is always a semantic response. In the dialogue mentioned above, the first turn lasts 2 lines, fol-

lowed by the 468-line turn mentioned. This is followed by a 219-line response. The other dialogue reported by Fock (1963:312–316) consists of
two content-defined turns, the first consisting of 255 lines and the second
consisting of 52 lines. The Waiwai ceremonial dialogue is apparently used
exclusively for what are also, in terms of content, dialogues. Fock (1963:
216) reports that there is actually a cue for indicating change of content-
defined turn; the lead speaker "terminates the first phase of the *oho* by a
sentence falling in pitch or by a humming sound." Content-defined turn-
taking is built into the very structure of the Waiwai *oho*.

Implicitly, content-defined dialogue means that each participant makes
a distinctive contribution to the single totality of ongoing discourse. Neither individual alone could produce the desired effect. This stands in
sharp contrast with the Kuna and Shokleng system, in which only one individual is necessary for production of the semantic content, and in which,
if two individuals do produce semantic content, that content is the same.
Among Waiwai, the contribution of each individual must be distinct. If
there is a culture-specific model of solidarity built into the Waiwai ceremonial dialogue, it is one in which solidarity is produced through the distinctive contributions of two individuals to a single whole. In effect, difference is an attractive force. This is true not just of the discourse produced
in ceremonial dialogue. The Waiwai dialogues are also associated with
situations of actual exchange of material goods and with marriage (Fock
1963:217). Underlying the model of solidarity embodied in the notion of
content-defined dialogue, therefore, is a material counterpart. The mutual
attraction of the semantically different contents produced by each speaker,
which together form the dialogical utterance, is paralleled in the mutual
attraction through difference at the material plane in terms of the contributions each individual has to make to an exchange.

A similar pattern is found among Trio and Yanomamö. Rivière does not
describe the content-defined dialogic character of Trio ceremonial dialogues, but his discussion here leaves no doubt that they are of this nature,
each participant making a distinctive contribution. He describes the dialogue as a form of "verbal duel which is won by the man who can go on
arguing the longest" (1971:299), and also as resembling the "institutionalized haggling of the market-place" (1971:302). Simultaneously, as
among Waiwai, dialogues are used in situations of actual exchange. Indeed, in contrast with Waiwai, ceremonial dialogues function virtually exclusively in this connection. Rivière (1971:301) remarks that they have
"three main purposes: to receive visitors or announce one's arrival in a village, to trade, and to obtain a wife." He goes on to remark (1971:301) that

most visits "are made for one of two reasons, trade or marriage." The overall pattern conforms to that found among Waiwai and reflects a model of solidarity grounded in exchange.

The Yanomamö dialogues translated by Cocco (1972:328–328) are all dialogic in terms of content as well as form, with the content-defined turns being comparatively short, the equivalent of at most a few Waiwai lines. Again, the dialogues are used primarily in connection with exchange transactions. Cocco (1972:326) confirms Shapiro's observations in this regard, claiming that the dialogues are used to "effect economic exchanges, to invite to gatherings or feasts, to plan marriages, to communicate general and personal news." Evidently, as among Waiwai, these dialogues embody a model in which solidarity is produced through the distinctive contributions of two individuals, rather than through the sharing of common traditions.

Trio, Waiwai, and Yanomamö ceremonial dialogues are never used in the narration of myths and legends; Kuna and Shokleng dialogues are never used in negotiations surrounding trade and marriage. This does not mean, however, that a perfectly sharp distinction exists between these groups as regards the dialogic versus monologic character of discourse on the semantic plane. In fact, as Sherzer (1983:91) describes, when Kuna chiefs visit between villages, they take turns addressing the gathering: "first the visiting 'chief' chants and his host serves as responder . . . ; then they switch; and finally they switch once again." Moreover, the extended monologic passages in Waiwai dialogues have already been mentioned, and some of the overt purposes of these dialogues—for example, the "appeals to communal work" (Fock 1963:217)—could presumably be accomplished through an actual monologue. Nevertheless, there is an obvious distinction to be made here. Trio, Waiwai, and Yanomamö clearly tend toward content-defined dialogicality and toward a model of solidarity based upon differential contribution; dialogue is the method for integrating, for blending together, these differential contributions. Kuna and Shokleng tend toward content-defined monologicality and toward a model of solidarity based upon the sharing of common traditions; dialogue is the mechanism of transmission and sharing, of the broader circulation of discourse.

In relation to these patterns, the Shuar-Achuar dialogues are divergent. There is a reference to their use in connection with trade (Karsten 1935: 249), but it is clear that their primary use is in connection with "greetings" in the context of interhousehold visiting (Gnerre 1986). The dialogues involve content-defined turn-taking—in the dialogue presented by Gnerre, there are three turns of 18, 38, and 19 lines—but the "content-defined turn" contains largely formulaic elements, as one might expect for a greeting. There is no real totality of ongoing discourse.

The formulaic or display character of native South American ceremonial dialogues requires further research. Rivière (1971:299), for example, remarks that the "words and phrases used in [Trio] dialogues are said to be archaic," and one may wonder whether some are also formulaic. Migliazza (1978:568) reports that Yanomamö ceremonial dialogues are carried out in "an archaic form of the Yanomama language." Among Shokleng, the origin myth is something that young men learn verbatim, and in which, consequently, semantic content tends to be backgrounded relative to the performance aspects. The language as well has archaic aspects. Nevertheless, the Shuar-Achuar greetings, on the basis of present data, do seem noteworthy for their formulaic character.

Their dialogues contrast with the classic content-defined dialogue of northern Amazonia. There the turn appears as much more of a contribution to a semantic totality, with unification arising out of the different but complementary contributions of two individuals—a kind of jigsaw puzzle approach to solidarity. Among Shuar-Achuar, considerably more emphasis is placed on individual display: the dialogues "traditionally represented perhaps the most important abilities of the male speakers. . . . Achuar, and even present-day Shuar, still perceive these conversations as something worth being heard and seen by non-Jívaroan visitors" (Gnerre 1986: 311). The display is also a manifestation of aggressivity and part of a negotiation of relative status, as Gnerre's (1986:313–314) discussion of eye contact makes clear. It is as if the mutual display of power and aggressivity is what maintains solidarity, in a kind of intracultural balance of power theory of social relations.

However, the general limits, as in the other cases, are laid down by ceremonial dialogue as a model for cohesion. There is a delicate balance between aggressive display, through penetration of speaking time, and maintenance of coordination. Ever-present is the possibility that too much aggressive penetration will throw off the cycle and hence destroy the coordination that ceremonial dialogues model. The trick among Shuar-Achuar is to appear as aggressive as possible while simultaneously paying attention to how this display is affecting the other, endeavoring to achieve a balance that results in coordination. Gnerre (1986:313–314) notes that if older men and famous warriors "receive a visit from a youth who does not raise his eyes, they avoid engaging him in a ceremonial dialogue" altogether. Apparently, the interlocutor must be of relatively equal status and ability.

The model for social integration embodied in the Shuar-Achuar dialogues is one that differs in important ways from the shared culture and exchange models. There is the same underlying notion of mutual coordination and recognition. However, the shared culture model posits that there should be in addition a commonality—the tradition—while the exchange model posits that there should be complementarity—giving and getting what one needs or wants from a different other. In the balance of power model, solidarity is created through a kind of mutual respect—through the manifestation of a capability to coerce the other and through the recognition, simultaneously, of the capability of the other to coerce oneself.

It should be emphasized that these three models are ideal types and that the ceremonial dialogue complex in a given society is really a unique blend of the three. The balance of power model is clearly also present, in some measure, among Waiwai and Trio, where there is frequent reference to ceremonial dialogue as "verbal dueling." The participants there are also expressing their individual skills and capabilities. Nevertheless, a decided tendency exists for the ceremonial dialogues in a society to cluster around one of the three poles. The differing models of solidarity embodied in the dialogues seem to correlate with the broader social mechanisms by means of which cohesion is produced in each case.

It has been suggested that discourse produced in ceremonial dialogue contains in effect two signals, namely, those constituted by (1) the utterance understood in terms of linguistic segmentation, which carries semantic or conscious meaning, and (2) the utterance understood in terms of its formal dialogic properties, which carry iconic and indexical meaning. The problem of interpretability in the shared meaning model of culture and in Saussurean structuralism pertains to the former kind of meaning; the problem of solidarity pertains to the latter. Because the stylistic signal is inherently indexical, pointing to aspects of person, space, and time that are outside the utterance per se, the stylistic integration of utterances in relationship to one another is simultaneously the integration of aspects of the extradiscursive world. The Saussurean segmentations pertain only to properties internal to the discourse instances themselves. The stylistic properties face both internally—to the relationships between instances—and externally—to the relationships between instances and the world.

Some aspects of the phenomenon of ceremonial dialogue as speech style make intuitive sense. One can readily appreciate why such dialogues, which caricature or make salient the cooperative, dyadic qualities of everyday conversation, should be employed so consistently in situations of maximal social distance. By virtue of iconicity, they bring into contexts in which the cohesiveness of persons is most questionable the qualities of other contexts, such as those of the domestic group, where cohesiveness is beyond doubt. The style suggests to the participants that their interaction is a solidary one, that they are as bound to one another as they are to members of their own respective domestic spheres. And it simultaneously signals solidarity to other onlookers.

In cultures where a regularization of the form-defined cycle of alternation occurs, the contexts always include those of maximal social distance. The dialogues occur in other more intimate contexts, but, when they do, they also occur in the more distant ones. The anchor point cross-culturally for ceremonial dialogue is the situation of maximal social distance, where the cohesiveness of the participants in the dialogue is most questionable. Recent research (Bowen 1989) confirms this tendency outside South America. Participants and onlookers alike are able to sense the connections between the dialogues occurring in problematic contexts and those occurring in relatively unproblematic ones, and the resulting coherence of discourse is simultaneously the coherence of persons.

We can understand, also, why the stylistic signal operates on the relatively unconscious plane of icons and indices, rather than through overt, conscious reference by means of the semantics of the discourse. Social relations are not just, or even primarily, a matter of consciousness. They are first and foremost felt or sensed relations. To mandate solidarity through consciousness, without simultaneously embodying it, is to risk conscious rebellion against it. To effect coherence it is necessary to suggest it, to make it an aspect of the overall interpretation or feel for the meaningfulness of the event, without simultaneously exposing it to the full light of consciousness. Simultaneously, coherence is not just understood through inference; it is also felt in the actual bodily sensations of the participants.

Why do ceremonial dialogues as icons employ different models of sociability in different cultures? The argument proposed here is that there are culture-internal regularities in how discourse is put together to form a total pattern. Ceremonial dialogues reflect the overall organizing principles of the cultures of which they are part. It has been proposed that there are three basic models of solidarity operative in the South American societies studied here: (1) models based on the sharing of a common culture, on the social glue of similarity; (2) models based on the attractive forces of differences that are complementary, the jigsaw puzzle approach to social solidarity; and (3) the balance of power models, based on the display of prowess in discourse production. These different models in fact correspond to different ways of configuring a culture's discourse history.

From a social anthropological perspective, the first model is based on the idea that two individuals, A and B, cohere because they are in important respects similar to one another. From a discourse perspective, that similarity has to do with the utterances they produce. A and B are capable of producing utterances that are copies of one another; discourse can be seen to flow or circulate unidirectionally, being passed down uniformly across time as well as throughout space. From the point of view of a community, any one individual can generate the discourse necessary to replicate the total configuration. Individuals are "identified" with one another, in the psychoanalytic sense, and identification forms the basis for their mutual attraction. Ceremonial dialogues model this discourse configuration through content-defined monologicality, while simultaneously facilitating the circulation of myths, histories, reports, and so forth.

The second model is based on the idea that A and B are attracted to one another not because of their similarities, but rather because of their differences. Correspondingly, at the level of discourse, that attractiveness means that the configuration of utterances making up the culture cannot be reproduced by any one individual or part of the community in isolation. Coherence requires contributions from different individuals or parts. This is a distinct way of creating a discourse history. In ceremonial dialogues, the basis of coherence is modeled in content-defined as well as form-defined dialogicality. The actual semantic interpretation of the single utterance that is produced in this kind of dialogue presupposes an understanding that the contributions from different participants complement one another. Simultaneously, the discourse content has to do with complementary social relations, principally with trade and marriage. Indeed, the alliance models proposed by Lévi-Strauss in *The Elementary Structures of Kinship* may be seen to pertain to the content of such dialogic discourse; they are special cases of how a culture configures its discourse history. In cultures operating under the principle of similarity, rather than under the principle of difference—the central Brazilian cultures discussed in the next chapter, for instance—marriage negotiations do not figure so prominently in discourse.

From the point of view of similarity and difference, the Shuar-Achuar balance of power model is intermediate. The dialogue is not built upon similarity, that is, on the facilitation of the unidirectional transmission of an element of culture such as a myth, but, simultaneously, there is no genuine complementarity of the contributions of each individual at the level of content; the discourse is, according to Gnerre (1986), largely formulaic. Each individual displays distinctiveness, but distinctiveness is built on the foundation of shared linguistic formulae. We seem to be somewhere between the principles of similarity and difference.

It is intriguing that there is a resemblance between the principles of similarity and difference, on the one hand, and those of mechanical and organic solidarity proposed by Durkheim (1933 [1893]), on the other. The societies investigated in this chapter do not map neatly onto Durkheim's dichotomy; they are all, in his terms, mechanically solidary. However, organic solidarity, grounded in the differentiation of occupational groupings, may be understood as an extension of the principle of coherence through difference. Under the principle of similarity, the configuration of discourse instances does not presuppose distinct contributions from different parts of the community. This is mechanical solidarity, but viewed in terms of how not individuals but rather utterances are assembled. Under the principle of difference, in contrast, the configuration cannot be produced without contributions from distinct parts of the community. The issue is a cultural not a social organizational one, but it can become a social organizational one when the requisite parts are codified through social differentiation (cf. Irvine 1987), when there is a recognition, that is to say, not just that two or more contributions are required to produce a single discourse, but that the contributions must come from different parts of society.

If the distinction between mechanical and organic solidarity makes sense when viewed in terms of the discursive configuration of a culture, so do the coldness/hotness and traditional/modern distinctions discussed earlier. Under modernity, difference is projected onto the diachronic as well as the synchronic axis. Each new generation must produce new discourse and, indeed, new styles, so that coherence over time as well as throughout space depends upon the attractive properties of difference. The jigsaw puzzle model is applied diachronically as well as synchronically. In societies like Trio or Waiwai, it is applied only synchronically, diachrony being organized in terms of similarity, with each generation looking like the ones that have come before it. Under modernity or hotness, however, difference is the integrative principle of the discourse history along both axes. In contrast to the Shokleng case, the metadiscourse is here one of discontinuity not continuity. At the same time, discontinuity is viewed as a configuring principle, a positive mode of relationship, the basis of coherence among utterances within a larger formation.

CHAPTER 7

Style and the Meaning of Emotion

What the preceding account leaves out are the emotional facets of social life, such as Feld (1982) has so convincingly argued are central to the interpretation of sound among the Kaluli of New Guinea. One may appreciate that marriage alliance is first of all a discourse process, a form of dialogicality in which there are distinct semantic contributions from the participants, and in which the discourse produced depends for its existence upon complementary difference. One may appreciate that the signaling of attraction through difference proceeds on a relatively unconscious plane, being phenomenal and sensible without becoming the object of reflection. But there is a difference between the phenomenal and sensible interpretation of signaling, on the one hand, and the emotions that erupt in certain contexts, on the other. The question here is whether the discourse-centered approach—which casts some new light on the nature of thought, on the normative regulation of conduct, on the process of cultural continuity, and on the classical distinctions pertaining to social solidarity—can also be of use in investigating the role of emotions in social life.

In his discussion of ritual in *The Elementary Forms of the Religious Life*, Durkheim acknowledges the centrality of emotion. The argument goes two ways: either (1) emotions are individual or biological, and ritual serves to summon them up from their slumber within their Leibnitzian monadic underworld; or (2) emotions are social, felt by the group, and their expression is imposed upon the individual by the group as a duty or obligation. There is a problem here, in the first place, with the individual versus collective character of emotion.[1] In the second place, there is the problem of how to study the emotions within their social matrix, a problem that Victor Turner (1967) addresses in a discussion of the role of depth psychology in anthropology. Can the study be conducted only by the empathic interpretation of the subjectivity of another? What is the relationship between the emotion and its empirical manifestation?

With its basic proposition that culture resides in concrete utterances, the discourse-centered approach suggests that we look to the actual sign vehicles in which emotion is manifested. This does not mean the discourse by means of which people talk to one another or to anthropologists *about* emotion, since the latter approach leads to an anthropology of consciousness as discussed earlier, as can be found, for example, in Lutz's (1988) work on the Ifaluk of Micronesia or M. Rosaldo's (1980) study of Ilongot of the Philippines—their method probes the consciousness of emotion as reflected in the semantic meaning of words, but cannot address unconscious, publicly signaled emotion; their method is ultimately the shared meaning approach to culture applied to feelings. Nor does the idea that emotion is publicly encoded in discourse mean looking at the lexical items through which emotion is encoded in language, although that study may be relevant for certain purposes. It means rather investigating the discourse or nondiscursive sign vehicles in which the emotion of the moment is lodged, through which it is expressed, and by means of which it is communicated to others.

For this purpose, discourse encoding sadness and grief is particularly well suited. Grief and sadness seem, on the one hand, essentially individual, since they so typically focus on situations involving loss, abandonment, and isolation. On the other hand, from an anthropological perspective, such expressions are known to be stereotyped in many cultures, pressed into a prescribed mold in another salient speech style known variously as "ritual wailing," "tuneful weeping," or "lament." Indeed, in Feld's (1982) justly celebrated study of the Kaluli of New Guinea, the emotions of sadness and grief within the context of ritual wailing form a key object of investigation.[2]

Durkheim (1965 [1915]: 443) himself notes the existence of stereotyped aspects of mourning among the Australian Arunta, Kurnai, and Warramunga: "mourning is not a natural movement of private feelings wounded by a cruel loss; it is a duty imposed by the group." He adds (1965 [1915]: 447), with his characteristic emphasis on the collectivity as an active entity, that "the foundation of mourning is the impression of a loss which the group feels when it loses one of its members." Radcliffe-Brown (1964: 239–240) similarly observes that "weeping" in the Andaman Islands is of two sorts: a spontaneous expression of "sorrow," as when a child is scolded, and a ceremonial form in which "men and women are required by custom to embrace one another and weep." He proposes that the purpose of the latter is "to affirm the existence of a social bond between two or more persons." However, neither author analyzes the form of the mourning expression or delves into detail regarding the relationship between that form and others within the culture, although they both suggest the role of mourning with respect to the maintenance of solidary social relations.

If the language of solidarity can profitably be recast in the language of discourse in the study of ceremonial dialogue, is it possible to do the same in regard to ritual wailing? After all, the phenomena are arguably related, if inversely. Whereas ceremonial dialogue occurs in the most distant social relations, ritual wailing focuses on the disruptions of the domestic sphere itself. Where ceremonial dialogue transports into the arena of potential boundary conflict the characteristics of solidary relations within the domestic sphere, ritual wailing transports collective reassurance of the group into the domestic sphere that has been disrupted.

However, there is more than a theoretical relationship between the two. They are also empirically complementary within South America. In a portion of South America (namely, the region of central and eastern Brazil south of the Amazon basin), ritual wailing assumes a unique form. There it is used as a greeting, which was observed by sixteenth-century Europeans who visited the Tupinamba and has since become known as the "welcome of tears." What is noteworthy is that both ceremonial dialogue and ritual wailing can be used as forms of greeting, but that the principal locus of dialogue as greeting is geographically complementary to the locus of lament as greeting. Whereas the former occurs primarily to the north and west of the Amazon basin, ritual wailing as greeting occurs primarily to the south. This geographical complementarity was first noticed by Fock (1963:228), who compares his distributional study of the dialogic complex with the earlier study of the welcome of tears by Métraux (1947). Why should this complementarity occur?

To answer this question, I have analyzed taped instances of ritual wailing for which there are available reasonably well-documented ethnographic contextualizations: (1) Shokleng, for whom I have drawn on my own tape recordings and field data, as well as the information supplied by Henry (1964), some of which has been discussed earlier; (2) Shavante of central Brazil, who like Shokleng speak a language belonging to the Jê family, for whom I use the work of Laura Graham (1984, 1986, and personal communications), which includes tape recordings and ethnographic descriptions; and (3) Bororo of west-central Brazil, for whom I use the tape recordings supplied by the Brazilian anthropologist and Bororo specialist Sylvia Caiuby Novaes (see also 1990:208 ff.), who has also provided me with ethnographic information. The latter has been supplemented by

the ethnographic materials in the *Enciclopédia Bororo* (Albisetti and Venturelli 1962).

It is regrettable that the data on Amerindian Brazilian ritual wailing are
so few and fragmentary. The reasons for this are complex, some having to
do in part with the "observer's paradox": that ethnographic situations are
affected by the presence of an observer. On the one hand, the people with
whom one lives and works may not wish to express strong feelings in the
presence of an anthropologist, especially if recording equipment is being
used. On the other hand, anthropologists may feel conflict about treating
situations of strong emotion as objective, investigable by ethnographic
techniques. A considerable amount of the intellectualization of culture
may stem from these interactive effects.

This problem is especially acute at the core of ritual wailing, where the
expression of grief at death or loss seems perfectly reasonable or "natural"
to the anthropologist. There is a common humanness here. Consequently,
the situation becomes *transparently* understandable, not in need of detailed
ethnographic description. Ethnographies tend to pass over the details with
such cover descriptions as: "immediately a man is dead, and the women
have raised their great wail"; "his mother and sister cried for a long time."

Where the formal wailing sign vehicle is removed from the core of "crying," and the functional motivation seems less "natural," ritual wailing
becomes *opaque,* signaling a different and unintelligible relationship to sociability. Consequently, the details more readily become the focus of ethnographic description. So the welcome of tears employed by the sixteenth-
and seventeenth-century coastal Tupinamba startled the European visitors
into reasonably careful descriptions (Métraux 1928, 1947; Léry 1972
[1578]; d'Abbeville 1975 [1614]; Cardim 1978 [1665]).

It is curious that there are almost no good descriptions of the welcome
of tears among the contemporary Tupian populations. Despite its title,
Wagley's ethnography *Welcome of Tears* in fact discusses the phenomenon
only cursorily in one brief passage (1977:238). Conceivably, the processes
discussed here have rendered the formal wailing style of the welcome of
tears susceptible to contact effects and thus to early demise in many of the
postcontact cultures. It is conceivable as well that for recent ethnographers
ritual wailing has become transparent even in its marked contexts just because there exists an anthropological category of "ritual wailing" that renders it intelligible and understandable. This is part of a more general tendency in twentieth-century ethnographies—the tendency discussed earlier
to treat discourse as a window through which culture can be glimpsed,
rather than as the locus of culture.

A key aspect of the formal sign vehicle of ritual wailing is its cultural specificity, the fact that each culture defines a unique form for the expression of grief. At the same time, from a comparative vantage point, it is relevant that there are certain commonalities in the sign vehicles that can be grouped under the term "ritual wailing." These provide clues to the functioning of ritual wailing as a semiotic mechanism. The three commonalities isolated here are: (1) the existence of a musical line, marked by a characteristic intonational contour and rhythmical structure; (2) the use of various icons of crying; and (3) the absence of an actual addressee in the here-and-now, which renders the ritual wailing an overtly monologic or expressive device, despite the importance that may accrue to its status as public, with the desired presence of someone to "overhear" it.

The sound emitted during ritual wailing shows a musical regularity, which may be described in terms of "lines." The line is essentially a pulse unit, corresponding to the sound that is produced through exhalation from one inhalation. Lines are thus demarcated by breath pauses. The actual length of lines varies within a given instance of ritual wailing by a particular individual. Table 2 illustrates this. Shown here are the lengths in seconds of the first five lines of tape-recorded instances of wailing from Bororo, Shokleng, and Shavante. The table also gives the average length in seconds of these lines, as well as an average from a 20-line sample. In these samples, lines may differ in length from the average by a maximum of 1.5 seconds for Bororo, 5.2 seconds for Shokleng, and 3.4 seconds for Shavante.

In some cases, the large variation is due to the use of the breath pause, rather than some other criterion, as the basis for line segmentation. Thus, in the Shokleng case, line 4 of the sample, representing the extreme in length, could have been analyzed into two lines, using intonational parallelism as the means of segmentation. Nevertheless, even employing other criteria, variation in length still occurs and seems, indeed, to be fundamental to ritual wailing as an expressive device.

The issue of variability is fundamental because it has to do with ritual wailing as an *expressive* sign vehicle, designed to communicate affect. Regularity in length, as well as in other aspects of ritual wailing, appears to signal standardization and hence sociability or compliance with a norm. Such standardization and repetition is the best evidence of mastery by the individual over the cultural ideals for sensori-motor coordinations. But mastery by the individual over culturally specified sensori-motor coordinations is, simultaneously, mastery by culture over the individual body. Irregularity, or variability, as the other pole of the continuum, however, seems to be essential for signaling the individual or unique aspects of the emotion. Indeed, there is arguably in ritual wailing a necessary dynamic

Table 2. Data on Line Length

	1	2	3	4	5	Av.[a]	Av.[b]
Total length of lines							
Bororo	17.1	16.8	14.1	14.1	15.7	15.6	15.9
Shokleng	8.6	9.9	7.6	14.7	6.5	9.5	9.2
Shavante	3.4	6.2	8.2	7.8	8.4	6.8	6.6
Pause length							
Bororo	6.4	4.2	4.6	3.3	3.4	4.4	4.3
Shokleng	1.8	2.2	1.6	3.5	0.7	2.0	2.0
Shavante	0.5	0.8	1.3	1.1	1.7	1.1	1.0

[a]Average for the 5 lines shown here.
[b]Average for a 20-line sample.

tension manifested in the formal sign vehicle between regularity and ir-regularity, uniformity and uniqueness, standardization and individuation.

At the same time, there is the tendency within a culture toward a general norm for line length. The standardization of line length, together with the range of variation, cannot be established with certainty at the present time, owing to the small sample size. Nevertheless, two well-analyzed instances of Shokleng ritual wailing from two different occasions show striking uniformity. This uniformity is confirmed by three separate tape-recorded and analyzed instances of Bororo ritual wailing.

Given this intracultural regularity, it is of special interest that there are marked differences in the standardized line lengths between cultures. This points to the fact that ritual wailing is a culturally specific sign vehicle. The longest Shokleng line (14.7 seconds), for example, is still below the average Bororo line length (15.9 seconds), and the shortest Shokleng line (6.5 seconds) almost coincides with the average Shavante line length (6.6 seconds). While there is overlap in the extremes, the norms for line length in these three cultures are distinct.

While each of the three cultures has a distinct line length, it is also important, at a still higher level of abstraction, that in each case there *is* a regular line. Ritual wailing, like ceremonial dialogue and other marked speech styles, makes use of a pattern of parallelism, wherein a given line strikes the hearers as in certain respects similar to other lines they have heard, just as it is felt to be similar by the producer—through the actual bodily sensations and muscle contractions. In this case, one aspect of similarity between lines is actual length.

Such parallel structures can be understood in terms of the Jakobsonian attention-getting function discussed earlier. At their most basic level they are perceptually salient, serving to kindle interest in the discourse of which they form a part. This poetic or musical function is an extremely important aspect of ritual wailing in all three cultures considered here and is detectable as well in the ethnographic descriptions of other cultures. For a sign vehicle that is overtly "expressive" of emotion, the attention-getting character is of special interest. Precisely whose interest is being gotten? The signal is getting the attention not only of its producer, but of other members of the community as well. It is thereby pointing to the other aspects of the signal that are expressive. This is one of the ways in which the ritual wailing signal functions as a metasignal.

Like line length, intonation contour tends to be fixed within a given instance of ritual wailing, has a circumscribed range of variation, and tends toward uniformity within a given culture, while exhibiting considerable variation between cultures. The voice used in these cases also at least in some measure approximates a musical, as opposed to speech, voice, with the vowels capable of being protracted and carrying a musical pitch.

Shavante represent an extreme in this regard. The instances recorded and analyzed by Graham (1986) appear to be almost fully musical. Shavante ritual wailing makes exclusive use of vowels, there being no full syllables, words, or higher levels of language involved. It is also characterized by a musical intonational contour that may readily be diagramed using musical staff notation (Graham 1984). In general, each line shows a rise to a single peak, which may be articulated in a falsetto voice, and then a decline to a pitch level near that where it began.

Graham's (1986) analysis shows two kinds of phrase, which she labels A and B, with different motifs based upon the number of vowel articulations after the peak. While there are some regularities in how these phrase types and motifs are arrayed, however, the actual composition of the wailing is an individual matter. Graham (1986:114, n. 10), for example, refers to an A motif, which "appears irregularly." She also (1986:90) indicates variability in the number of A phrases intervening between occurrences of B phrases. This allowance for individual creativity is arguably associated with the issue of expressivity and irregularity discussed above in connection with line length. Still, Shavante ritual wailing represents an extreme in being the most musical and most standardized of the ritual wailing forms considered here.

Shokleng wailing involves spoken words and is thus more speechlike, less perfectly regular in musical terms. Yet it makes use of a distinctive singsong intonation, involving a number of tonal peaks. Typically, pitch rises immediately to the highest tone from an initial glide, then drops back down, then up again, with the second tone being slightly lower than the first, and so forth, in gradual descent to the end of the line. In many of the lines, there are two major peaks, from which descent occurs. The second tonal peak is invariably lower than the first. The overall effect of each line is a gradual downward tonal slope, with singsong movements in between. However, each instance has a unique intonation contour, dependent upon the specific words that are being uttered. Thus, in the question of regularity versus irregularity, Shavante is closer to the extreme of standardization, Shokleng to that of individuation.

As regards irregularity, the Bororo line is similar to the Shokleng line: both make use of spoken words. However, the Bororo intonational contour type itself is wholly distinct. The Bororo line begins with a perfectly flat intonation contour. It then tapers slightly, prior to rising to one of several "spiked" peaks. Each peak involves a single protracted vowel, and the voice immediately tapers off in volume while it falls tonally. The length of the level onset and the number of such protracted vowel peaks vary considerably from one line to the next. In one sample studied, the level onset lasted anywhere from 1.3 to 6.8 seconds, with an average of 3.9 seconds. The number of protracted vowel peaks ranged from 2 to 7, with an average of 4.6.

Entering into this irregularization of the typical line in both Shokleng and Bororo is the presence of other signals, particularly the cry break, discussed in more detail below. In Shokleng, the cry break is the only added factor, and it may or may not appear in a given line. If it does, the exact location of the break is nevertheless variable. Among Bororo, there are actually two distinct kinds of cry break, one of which occurs during the level onset, and the other just at the end of the line, prior to the breath. The latter is a more regular feature, though it is omitted in a few of the lines sampled and in some of them is so faint that the precise number is difficult to determine. Generally, there appear to be between 1 and 3 such soft cry breaks. The level onset break is much sharper or harder and is an irregular feature, appearing in some lines and not others, and in variable numbers and locations.

The Bororo line also has an occasional extra feature not found in the Shokleng line, namely, a falsetto cry involving a single protracted nondistinct [i] sound in a pitch range far above that of normal voice. In its high-pitched falsetto character, it is reminiscent of the Shavante tonal peak. However, it is much more protracted and involves a gradual tapering in volume and decline in pitch. This is a highly irregular feature, found in only a few of the Bororo lines sampled.

If there is an intonational contour "type" within each of these instances of wailing, that type is also socially shared. Within Shokleng, the different instances of wailing analyzed showed the same general pattern. In addition, an imitation of wailing that occurs in the course of one myth narration also captures the essential features of the intonationally defined ritual wailing line discussed here. The Shavante and Bororo types as well are confirmed in numerous instances. In addition, there is a careful description of the typical Bororo line from Albisetti's and Venturelli's (1962) *Enciclopédia Bororo*.

While the intonational type is standardized within a given culture, it is equally remarkable how divergent the types are between cultures. The Shavante line has a single rise to and fall from a tonal peak; the Shokleng line is singsong, with the peaks gradually descending; the Bororo line is flat at the onset, followed by a variable number of protracted vowel peaks. One can readily distinguish these types with minimal experience. The implication is that the ritual wailing sign vehicle, while simultaneously signaling grief, is signaling something about sociability, about the conformance of the individual to collective norms.

If ritual wailing is a highly culture-specific form, there is also the question of whether it taps into any cross-culturally isolable devices for the expression of affect. Listening to the tapes, Americans will guess, with greater or lesser difficulty, that the sounds they hear have something to do with sadness or grief. In order to isolate precisely what about the wailing signal communicates this affect cross-culturally, I have collected a number of examples of Americans imitating crying and one instance of "actual" crying. A great deal of variability is found among Americans in this regard, but some striking similarities with the Amerindian Brazilian cases emerge. The four common crying signal types to be discussed here are: (1) the cry break, (2) the voiced inhalation, (3) the creaky voice, and (4) the falsetto vowel.

The cry break is found in Bororo and Shokleng, but not Shavante, ritual wailing, as well as in imitations of crying and actual crying by Americans. This is evidently one of the cross-cultural signals that can be drawn on to communicate sadness or grief. From an articulatory point of view, the cry break involves a pulse of air initiated by a push from the diaphragm. Pressure from the pulse is built up behind the closed glottis, which is then released with the vocal cords vibrating to produce any of various nondistinct vowels. This vibration is often accompanied by friction noise, as the air is forced out the mouth and/or nose. In addition, the sound is typically produced with a falling tone. The pulse is then checked through a second closure of the glottis, the entire process lasting a fraction of a second. Two variants of the cry break involve the absence of glottal closure at either the beginning or the end of the sound.

Cry breaks can be chained to form a sobbing action. The extended sob was not found on the tape selections from Shokleng, where the isolated cry break only occasionally interrupts the ritual wailing line. However, such cry breaks in sequence do occur in Bororo ritual wailing, invariably at the end of a given line, where from one to three breaks may occur in succession.

For Bororo, as well, two types of cry break may be distinguished on the basis of pitch. High-pitched breaks occur during the period of level onset, or between the protracted vowels, in keeping with the generally high pitch of the voice at this time. These also typically have only the final glottal closure. The cry breaks occurring at the end of a line have a much lower pitch and volume and are glottal-stopped at each end.

The cry break is arguably the most transparent index of "crying" and deserves more careful semiotic study of the actual physiological mechanism. Among other things, it is closely related in articulatory terms to the "laugh," which may also prove cross-culturally isolable. The pulsing of the air flow in each case provides a signal that stands out in sharp relief against the relative calm of the airflow during normal speech and even during much singing. It may be accompanied by the actual visual signal of the chest heaving, often accompanied by other movements of the body. The agitation of the sound and body may be an important part of the signal communicating the presence of strong emotion.

Another characteristic of some of the Amerindian Brazilian wailing that is also found in American imitations of crying is the presence of voicing while inhaling. This is found consistently in Shokleng and Bororo examples, but not in the Shavante examples studied thus far. The voiced inhalation typically involves a falling intonation. It can be compared with a signal associated in American culture, and perhaps elsewhere, with fright or being startled. However, the intonation contour in this latter case is distinct, and the inhalation is sudden. In both cases, however, the voicing seems to signal something about the individual's intense involvement in the emotional state, which in effect interrupts the ordinary procedure of relaxing the vocal cords during inhalation. It may be this heightened emotional involvement that is signaled by use of the voiced inhalation at the line junctures in the Brazilian cases.

Another characteristic of all of the Brazilian Amerindian instances and parts of the American examples is the use of the creaky voice, which in articulatory terms involves the production of sounds with the vocal cords vibrating at a lower than normal rate. There is variation again as regards (1) just how much lower than normal the rate is, and (2) how frequently the creaky voice is used.

Among Shokleng, the vocal cords vibrate quite slowly, and the creak occurs throughout the entire line. In the Shavante examples, the creak is very light throughout, becoming more noticeable at some points than at others, for example, around the falsetto vowels. However, the voice is clearly distinct from a normal speaking voice. Among Bororo, there is light creaking during the level onset, which, as among Shavante, becomes heavier with the protracted vowels. Similar creaking—both the light and heavy varieties—can be found in portions of the American imitations of crying. Children often make this sound in the course of complaining.

If sadness and grief are in fact cross-linguistically associated with this signal, it would be of interest to study its semiotic functioning more closely. As in the case of the cry break and voiced inhalation, there is the question of distinctiveness from normal voice, which serves an indexically differentiating function. However, it remains to be understood precisely why creakiness gets used for this purpose. It may be related to its association with various abnormal states of the organism, particularly sickness or physical exhaustion, where the organism lacks the energy to produce a normal robust sound. Under this hypothesis, creakiness would be related to showing that the person engaged in ritual wailing or crying is afflicted by the situation that occasioned it, much as an organism is afflicted by external disease or injury. This is an instance of the phenomenon, discussed in chapter 5, wherein the indexical value (affliction) of a feature (creakiness) in another context is drawn into the present context by iconicity.

A further component of some instances of Amerindian Brazilian wailing that is also found in American imitations of crying is the articulation of a vowel with a pitch well beyond that of the normal voice range. This falsetto vowel is typically accompanied by a slight creaking of the voice and falling intonation over a protracted articulation. This occurs in its purest form among Bororo, but only highly irregularly (approximately 1 in 10 of the lines sampled). The vowel used in this case is an [i]. It is possible that the protracted or "spiked" vowels mentioned earlier are actually modeled on this falsetto vowel. Among Shavante, the point of highest pitch in the wailing line is also an [i], very frequently also articulated as a falsetto vowel. The vowel also has the most pronounced creaking of any vowel in the line. However, the protraction and falling intonation of the Bororo falsetto vowel are not encountered here. None of the Shokleng instances shows the falsetto vowel, though its presence is not entirely ruled out.

We know as yet little about the semiotic functioning of this signal, though, as in the case of creaky voice, it is possible that it obtains some of its efficacy through iconicity with other sounds produced by the organism. In particular, falsetto may be associated with shrieks or cries produced through startling, which can occur as reflex acts. If so, the falsetto vowel may be a signal of heightened emotional response.

The purported communicative function of ritual wailing varies from one cultural complex to the next. Among Shavante, the wailing consists only of vowels, together with the glottal stop. There are no full syllables, let alone words, used here. The communicative device portrays itself as nonreferential. In this it differs from Shokleng and Bororo, where full words and even sentences are used. Here the signal portrays itself as referential at least in part, with the words occurring alongside the cry breaks, voiced inhalations, falsetto vowels, and so forth.

No complete transcriptions of the Bororo wailing are currently available. Albisetti and Venturelli (1962:971) mention only that "the expressions of grief vary considerably from one individual to another." However, they also note that the words used in wailing are of a special ritual sort, distinct from the everyday lexicon. Moreover, they give a vocabulary of these words (1962:985–987). These specifically pertain to the wailing that occurs in connection with death, but give some idea of the content here. Some examples are: "your body," "your fine lip," "your head," "tear," "your beautiful hands," "my brother," "my maternal grandmother," "their ancestors," and "numerous relatives."

Among Shokleng, where full transcriptions are available, it is clear that the wailing consists of a set of statements, which may be about the current plight of the person wailing or about the person whose absence has caused the grief. An extended example collected in 1975 is given in chapter 5. This example may be compared with those published by Henry (1964:188–191). Although Henry gives only English translations and the wailing he reports was elicited rather than transcribed from recordings, it is evident that his materials collected in the early 1930s are closely similar in content to those collected in context in 1975.

I am remembering my mother.
I want to call her mother.
I am remembering my mother.
I am the one who called her mother, but now it is all over.
I am remembering my mother.

When my mother would look at me she would remember that my father
    had seen me and she would weep—now that is all over.
I am remembering my mother.
I and my children used to call my mother mother—that is all over.
I am remembering my mother.
I want to see my mother.
When my father would return after leaving me he would think of how I
    suffered, and he would weep.
Grandmother, whose name I bear, would think of my sickness and
    suffering.

The important point as regards the type of communication involved is
that all of the statements are descriptive-expressive. There are no questions to a real interlocutor who might respond, no commands to action,
and, indeed, no endeavor to communicate any information that is not already known. There may be praise for the dead person, as in the Bororo
case, or for someone who has returned after a long absence. There may be
comments on what the other person has had to endure. However, these are
of a purely expressive or empathic type, indicating the feelings of the person wailing, high regard for the other, and ability to feel the pain the other
has endured.

It is unclear whether this conclusion can be generalized to Amerindian
Brazilian wailing as a whole. The Bororo data suggest this, but we need
complete transcriptions. There are also remarks of ethnographers about
other groups that would tend to confirm this. Notable is Métraux's (1947:
40) summary of the evidence on Tupinamba: "although our sources do not
agree about the content of their speeches [during wailing], they say that
the women alluded to the death of close relatives and to the fatigue of the
traveller."

Tentatively, therefore, it can be proposed that Amerindian Brazilian ritual wailing ranges from fully expressive (among Shavante) to expressive-
descriptive (among Shokleng). Linguistically, we do not find evidence of
the attempt by the ritual wailer to communicate information or to elicit a
direct response from some other through questions or commands. Wailing
is rather a process of making public the feelings of the person who is wailing. It is intended not to be heard, in the ordinary linguistic sense, but
rather to be *overheard*. This is a key to its semiotic functioning. By its very
design, ritual wailing purports not overtly to engage an addressee, but to
allow anyone within earshot access to something that would otherwise
be private.

This overt or represented function of ritual wailing, however, must be
differentiated from its actual function for the person who engages in the

wailing. The purpose of the individual's action is undoubtedly communicative—to let other members of the community know that the individual has the proper orientation to the dead person, visitor, or whatever life situation occasions the wailing—whether or not it is expressive. In other words, there is a disjuncture between how the ritual wailing represents itself and how it is actually being used. It is a kind of calculated accident, an action designed to appear spontaneous.

One can imagine that the ritual wailer might engage in some other kind of communicative act as a way of accomplishing the same end, that is, letting others know that the individual has an appropriate emotional response. The individual could say, for instance, "I want you all to know that I am grief stricken." Such communications are familiar in American culture, but completely foreign to the Amerindian Brazilian cultures considered here. There is no necessary difference in the formality or genuineness of the sentiment in the two cases. However, the communicative types are wholly distinct.

It may also be said that ritual wailing can motivate others to action, by kindling in them either the emotion of grief or the desire to display that they also have the socially appropriate sentiment. Graham (personal communication) mentions that one person wailing may stimulate others to do so, resulting in a veritable chorus, something hinted at by Albisetti and Venturelli (1962 : 971) for the Bororo: "the crying, when it is performed by various persons, men and women, frequently has the character of true duets." In recent and equally fascinating papers, Briggs (1989) and Feld (1989) have shown for Warao of Venezuela and for Kaluli of New Guinea, respectively, that the content of the wailing produced by multiple wailers is related. Despite the appearance of a monological discourse, there is in fact complex intertextuality and polyphony. The wailing becomes functionally dialogical, even though it marks itself overtly as monological.

The cases reported by Briggs and Feld are inversely related to those discussed in the previous chapter. Whereas Shokleng and Kuna were able to make what was in fact monological discourse appear to be dialogical, through the use of the ceremonial dialogue speech style, Warao and Kaluli are able to make what is functionally dialogical interaction appear to be wholly monological, through use of the ritual wailing speech style. Ceremonial dialogue plays up its character as interactive when it in fact may be a monologue; ritual wailing denies its character as interactive when it in fact may be a kind of dialogue.

The situations in which ritual wailing occurs are by no means well documented, but it is clear that the principal situation throughout Native South America is death. This is so among Shokleng, where the immediate relatives of a dead person may wail at any time they happen to be thinking of him/her. Similarly, Graham (1986:88) states that among Shavante "individuals may wail at any time when reminded of the deceased, such as when seeing a photograph or visiting the grave." Albisetti and Venturelli (1962) indicate that death is the principal motivation for wailing among Bororo as well.

Ritual wailing is also used in other situations, for example, among Shokleng, when thinking about someone who has been away for some time. However, the theme that unites all of these situations would seem to be the feeling of separation and loss that is canonically associated with death. Graham (1986:87) writes that "Shavante express intensely felt emotions associated with profound feelings of loss, separation, abandonment, and death through wailing." Wailing is an index not of the situation directly, but of the feeling associated with it. It is to that feeling that we must look if we are to understand the semiotic functions of wailing, especially its use in cases, such as greetings, that seem maximally distant from death.

It has already been shown that wailing is a socially communicative stylized expression. This means that it does not merely index a feeling of loss. It is an attempt to communicate to others that one has that feeling. Why should it be the case with regard to death specifically that individuals wish to signal their feelings to others? Death is perhaps the prototypical situation in which social relations are disrupted, solidary bonds broken. It is appropriate that it be accompanied by profound feelings of loss. However, the feeling of loss need not be signaled to others. It may be proposed that ritual wailing represents not simply the feeling of loss, but, in a more complex way, the desire for sociability that is the inverse side of loss. Loss occasions the wish to overcome loss through sociability, which is signaled through adherence to a culturally specific form of expressing grief. One wishes to signal to others that one has the socially correct feelings at the socially prescribed times.

This is not to deny that ritual wailing may in some measure index feelings of loss, but rather to note that this function stands in a dynamic relationship with the function of indexing a desire for sociability. These are two poles of a continuum, and every instance of ritual wailing probably involves some admixture of each. We can imagine situations in which the feeling of loss is the more immediate trigger for wailing, and the desire for sociability plays a smaller role. Alternatively, the desire for sociability may be preeminent, any actual feeling of loss being secondary.

The general model proposed here makes sense of the gamut of situations reported in the literature. The welcome of tears puzzled early travelers in part because of the seeming absence of "genuine" emotion after the ritual greeting. The wailer, whose face is often covered during the actual performance, may suddenly upon its completion reveal a smiling and seemingly untroubled countenance, a phenomenon remarked by Durkheim (1965 [1915]:443) for the Australian case: "if, at the very moment when the weepers seem the most overcome by their grief, some one speaks to them of some temporal interest, it frequently happens that they change their features and tone at once, take on a laughing air and converse in the gayest fashion imaginable."

The welcome of tears form in particular is very near the extreme of a pure expression of sociability. The situation is related to the canonical separation surrounding death. Baldus (1970) makes it clear that ritual wailing was generally not performed for complete strangers, but for those who have been away for some time. The ritual wailing is designed to communicate to visitors a desire for sociability by signaling the grief caused by their absence. However, it may achieve its communicative purpose even in the absence of a profound prior sense of loss.

If the sociability function of ritual wailing can be distinguished from its function of indexing feelings of loss, it is nevertheless impossible for this function to free itself entirely from emotional indexation. In fact, the ability of ritual wailing to signal a desire for sociability is directly predicated upon its ability to index emotion. What signals sociability is (1) the use of the socially proper means of expression of emotion, (2) under the socially appropriate circumstances for its expression. For the signal to communicate, the ritual wailer must wail under circumstances in which other members of the community would find it appropriate for that individual to be experiencing a feeling of grief or loss, and the actual wailing itself must suggest that feeling, at least in some measure.

There is a sense in which the use of any collective signal (e.g., body ornamentation, posture, language) is a sign of sociability. However, there is something more involved in the case of signs of emotions, especially such powerful emotions as grief. Because emotions can be the cause of social breakdowns, it is all the more significant when they are socialized. Potentially an individualized and idiosyncratically differentiated response to a situation, the emotion, when regimented, becomes an especially salient signal of sociability.

To make this argument more forcefully, it is necessary to consider the ways in which the actual wailing signal differs across contexts. The general argument I wish to develop is that wailing becomes less regular in parallel structure, and less socially standardized, the closer the signal is to being a pure expression of emotion. Unfortunately, ample studies of the comprehensive sort needed to verify this hypothesis are not available for Amerindian Brazil. I will have to draw upon two sources: (1) my own ethnographic observations of the Shokleng case; and (2) consideration of how ritual wailing is construed within the lexical classification scheme, along with some evidence from native commentary.

I heard but was unable to record the wailing that occurred immediately upon the announcement of a death. It was different than the type I did record and involved much more in the way of high-pitched shrieks and falsetto vowels. It seemed to lack the metrical structure of the recorded wailing, which is the sort that occurs days and even months after a death, in greetings, and so forth.

This style of wailing is called *plāl*, which means "crying." The same term is used for the crying done by children, which is not of the specialized sort discussed here, the Shokleng term for which is *zō*. Superficial observations suggest that *plāl* is less regular in its line structure and more exclusively based upon the kind of cross-linguistically isolable crying signals discussed earlier: cry breaks, voiced inhalation, falsetto vowels, and so forth. But there is a continuum between *plāl* and *zō*: a given expression of grief or sadness can fall at different points along it. One particularly striking example of this occurred in 1981, when I returned to the field after six years' absence. I had brought back tapes from my previous visit, including tapes of myth narrations by one man who had died in the interim. His wife and family asked to hear the tapes. The entire situation was emotion-laden for me as well as for the family. Even as the voice was only just beginning to come through the speaker, the widow began crying (*plāl*), at first with tears and some intermittent cry breaks, but then gradually moving into the metrical *zō* form, the lines becoming regular, albeit still interrupted by cry breaks.

In any case, in Shokleng there are definite differences in the sign vehicles associated with the expression of grief, but these seem to have to do with the two poles of crying (*plāl*) and wailing (*zō*). In particular, while it is possible that there could be formally distinct wailing styles in a culture, marking different kinds of grief, different contexts, or the different social statuses of the wailer (especially male versus female), this does not seem to be the case for Shokleng.

Nor does it seem to be the case for Shavante. Graham (personal communication) indicates that the *dawawa* is actually the generic term "to cry," coming from *da*, "of the people," and *wawa*, "crying." There is a specialized term meaning "to wail ritually," but this is in fact a marked form used only to differentiate wailing from crying. The markedness relationship also holds for Shokleng, where *plāl* can be used generically to mean "crying" or "wailing," while *zō* can only refer to wailing. Nevertheless, the term *zō* is regularly used for the wailing form.

The Bororo data, as contained in the Albisetti and Venturelli (1962) *Enciclopédia Bororo*, are somewhat more complex. It is clear from their description that there is only one ritual wailing form, the description of which matches the example analyzed above: "the one who cries uses many expressions and forms articulated hurriedly with a level tone with periodic acute or grave inflections of the voice." However, their Portuguese-English dictionary entry for "wailing" (*pranto*, Port.) is organized into three subcategories: (1) wailing, (2) ritual wailing, and (3) wailing due to missing someone. There are two or three Bororo terms given under each subcategory, with some overlap between them. Under the general term for wailing is given *ōku.ˊdu.* ("crying out," literally, "showing the teeth," from *ō* = "tooth" and *ku.ˊdu.* = "shout"). The emphasis is on "crying out" as a voice quality. The other two Bororo terms listed in connection with the generic term for wailing are variants of this: *ōragu.ˊdu.* has an apparently identical translation, differing only in the plural form *ōra*, "teeth," versus *ō*; the other term, *ōragu.du.ˊdō*, "to make cry," apparently involves only the addition of a causative suffix to the previous term. Judging from the sentential examples ("don't make your little brother cry," "my son is about to cry"), *ō ku.ˊdu.* and its variants may be a generic term for crying in Bororo, analogous to Shokleng *plāl* and Shavante *dawawa*.

It is not clear whether the other two subcategories, "ritual wailing" and "wailing due to missing someone," are actually distinguished in Bororo, since the Bororo terms given here overlap: *aˊkō ōtaigōˊdu.* ("song of anxiety," from *aˊkō* = "song" and *ōtaigōˊdu.* = "anxiety") is given under both subcategories.[3] It apparently refers specifically to the musiclike attributes of ritual wailing, and we may think of it as the term that distinguishes ritual wailing from crying. Both subcategories also contain a variant of the term *kurōrōˊdu.* ("crying," literally, "liquid flowing," from *kuˊro* = "liquid" and *ōrōˊdu.* = "flowing"). Evidently, this term refers specifically to the production of tears. It apparently does not distinguish a form of "ritual wailing" from a form of "wailing due to missing someone."

Despite the complexity of presentation in the *Enciclopédia Bororo*, it would seem that Bororo, like Shokleng and Shavante, have only one type of ritual wailing, which is also distinguished from crying. Furthermore, it would seem that generic term for "crying" (*ku.ˊdu.*), as in Shokleng and Shavante, can also be used to describe wailing, since this term is given under the subcategory "ritual wailing." For all of these societies, there-fore, there is a linguistically encoded recognition of (1) the distinctiveness of crying and ritual wailing, and (2) a relationship between the two.

The early descriptions of the welcome of tears found among the coastal Tupian populations indicated that wailing was primarily a female activity. Métraux (1947:40), summarizing this evidence, states that "men rarely joined in these demonstrations of grief." This does not seem to be the case among the interior Brazilian tribes today, where ritual wailing is both a male and female phenomenon. Graham (1986:87), for example, writes of Shavante that "as a form of expressive communication that is equally avail-able to both sexes, [wailing] cannot be considered a predominantly female genre . . ." Similarly, Albisetti and Venturelli (1962:971) suggest the in-volvement of both sexes: "the wailing when it is done by various persons, *men and women* [emphasis added], frequently has the character of a true duet." Research among Shokleng confirms that wailing is both a male and female vocal style there as well.

There may be a difference between Jê and Tupian groups in this regard. Métraux's (1947:40) conclusion is based on sources dealing with the coastal Tupi. Baldus's (1970:455) discussion of an instance of Tapirapé (also Tupi) wailing also only mentions performance by a woman. In contrast, Shokleng and Shavante are Jê languages, and Bororo, still considered an isolate, may be related to Macro-Jê.

In any case, the comparative evidence suggests that in cultures where men wail women also wail, but not vice versa. Graham (1986:87) origi-nally formulates this as a possible implicational universal: "in societies where ceremonial keening is a male form of expression, it is also a mode of expression available to women." If such a universal does in fact obtain—and, in any event, it does seem to obtain for Amerindian Brazil—it still is possible to view wailing as a more typically female activity (cf. Sherzer 1987b). This is of special interest because ceremonial dialogue is most typically a male activity, and the opposite implicational universal would seem to apply—in cultures where women engage in ceremonial dialogue, men do also. In South America, therefore, insofar as highly formalized styles are concerned, there is a tendency to connect conversational dia-logicality with men, expressive monologicality with women.

In theory, ritual wailing and ceremonial dialogue could co-occur in a given culture in connection with the same "greeting" function. Men could greet a visitor through dialogue, women through wailing. Indeed, it would be possible to imagine different forms of greeting arranged serially, say, first a ritual weeping, then a ceremonial conversation. It would even be possible for the two forms to be used in connection with different types of visitors—wailing for a returning kinsman, dialogue for a more distantly related or unrelated visitor. It is difficult to find clear instances of the simultaneous occurrence of these different forms of greeting.[4] Among Shokleng, ceremonial dialogue is not properly speaking a form of greeting, although it is used in the course of ritual interactions between different trekking groups. Ritual wailing is the proper form of greeting, once someone has entered the village per se.

However, there was apparently traditionally a different form of greeting when the presence of another person or group was detected far in the distance. This is the "aggressive" greeting described in various ethnographic accounts. It occurs as reported speech in one historical narrative of an encounter between different trekking groups, where the separation had been prolonged, and there was doubt about the good intentions of the other group. Here, the greeting is accomplished through very aggressive sounding (with extreme laryngeal and pharyngeal constriction) shouts. The purpose of the greeting would seem to be mutual identification and the assessment of intentions. Métraux (1928:186–188), basing himself on the description by F. Cardim, indicates that the "aggressive greeting" (*salutation aggressive*) actually occurred among the Tupinamba, for whom the welcome of tears was first described. It is unclear, however, to what extent speech forms part of this greeting. An unspoken aggressive greeting can be seen in the Asch and Chagnon film *The Feast*, showing the visiting Yanomamö taking the hammocks of their hosts, whereupon the hosts menace them with bows and arrows.

Despite these partial overlaps between the welcome of tears and dialogic greeting, there is nevertheless an interesting geographical complementarity between them. In central Brazil, the ritual wailing greeting has attracted most ethnographic attention and appears to be most salient. Ceremonial dialogue is nowhere used for greeting, and, indeed, generally does not occur at all. To the north and west of the Amazon River, however, ceremonial dialogue is typically found as a form of greeting, and ritual wailing rarely so. Why should this be the case?

In the previous chapter a distinction is proposed between societies that are glued together, discursively, through sameness or sharing, on the one hand, and through difference or complementarity, on the other. In the former societies (Kuna and Shokleng), dialogicality is in the service of monologicality, that is, it represents transmission or sharing between individuals. Dialogicality of this sort seems to be much less widespread than dialogicality of the other sort, wherein complementarity involves the distinctive contributions of different individuals or parts of society. In South America, where the latter sort of dialogicality occurs, ceremonial dialogues are used as a form of greeting and ritual wailing is not typically used for that purpose. Correspondingly, in central Brazil, where ritual wailing occurs as a greeting, ceremonial dialogue does not occur in this complementarity-based variety. Indeed, Shokleng have the only reported occurrence of ceremonial dialogue of any sort for this region.

Distributional evidence, therefore, suggests that ritual wailing as greeting—the welcome of tears—tends to occur in societies that do not represent their internal cohesiveness as based on complementary difference. This negative conclusion, in other words, suggests that the ritual wailing greeting may be positively associated with the similarity or sharing model of sociability. Certainly this is true in the Shokleng case, which is located within the broader region of the welcome of tears complex. But is there a basis in the sign vehicle itself for supposing this?

It has already been shown that ritual wailing more generally is predicated upon "overhearing" rather than upon "hearing." The speech style purports to give to the overhearer privileged access to the subjectivity of the ritual wailer. This is the specific meaning of the style as a metasignal, which points to and classifies the discourse of which it forms a part. By drawing on "natural" or cross-culturally interpretable signs of crying—cry breaks, creaky voice, falsetto vowels, and so forth—it suggests that the discourse encodes those feelings. Simultaneously, the discourse is never overtly addressed to a real potential interlocutor. Hence, the style as metasignal defines the utterance as expressive of private, natural emotions.

At the same time, however, the form of the sign vehicle is socially prescribed, culturally standardized—and not only is the form standardized, but the contexts in which it may appropriately be used are regimented as well. Where the ritually wailed utterance encodes semantic content, there are as well prescribed characteristics of that content. This is shown by the consistency in Shokleng ritual wailing over a forty-year period. The wailing, in short, reveals its public and shared character, while simultaneously marking itself as an expression of private feelings.

But the sharing in this case is distinct from that found, for example, in the Shokleng origin myth. There it is the semantic details of the discourse, as well as its concrete, sensible form, that must be faithfully reproduced and circulated throughout society. In ritual wailing, it is important for the individuals to be, in some measure, individuals, to create room for their own individuality within the prescribed form. But, contrary to the difference represented in complementarity-based ceremonial dialogue, where the individual contribution is marked as a part of the whole, as a piece of jigsaw puzzle, here the individuality is unconnected in a positive way to anything else, even though it may be in real terms synchronized, as Feld

(1989) and Briggs (1989) have shown. The individuality is a characteristic of the discourse as a whole, which is tagged or overtly marked with the traces of the specific individual who produced it.

It is curious that such an overtly individualistic model of discourse should be found in societies where the self-representation of sociability is in terms of sharing or transmission. Apparently, the discourse marked as purely individual, like that marked as purely social, can be a signal of sociability grounded in similarity. Both stand in opposition to the discourse marked as the joint product of a cooperative endeavor, involving distinct contributions from different individuals or parts of society.

If one probes further, the curious relationship between the two makes sense. The different models of sociability involve distinct conceptualizations of the self and its relationship to others. In the complementarity-based dialogical model, sociability is seen as involving the relationship between different selves, which are acknowledged to be different. This acknowledgment is made overtly, in the form of the sign vehicle and in the norm of hearing the other out. The other is explicitly addressed as an interlocutor, who can simultaneously address one's self. Sociability is a matter of bringing these distinct, acknowledged selves together.

In the similarity-based dialogical model, when there are two interlocutors, they nevertheless engage in producing a single stretch of speech, which could also be produced by either of them separately. Emphasis is not on the distinctiveness of the two individuals, but rather on their similarity. They both participate in the process of transmitting a single thing. The notion of the individual involved here is not predicated upon the idea of different selves, each making a contribution to a joint endeavor; this is a model in which the different selves are the same. There is no uniqueness.

In the case of ritual wailing, the discourse does not have an overt addressee. Hence, it is not a question of two selves being the same or different, but rather of allowing the overhearer a privileged access to the self. Sociability involves getting inside the self of the other, but what one finds when one gets there is that it is in all essentials like one's own self. To make the ritual wailing sign vehicle appear to be expressive of the self, it must encode some of the irregularities that are the hallmark of individuality or natural expression. At the same time, because that expression is so socially standardized, the unique individuality of the ritual wailer is revealed to be like the unique individuality of the overhearer. Overhearers recognize themselves in the ritual wailer. Like the similarity-based dialogical model, the ritual wailing model is grounded in the demonstration of the fundamental similarity between individuals. Whereas similarity-based dialogicality begins with two individuals, highlighting the dyadic character of the interaction, but ends with the demonstration that those two individuals share a single thing, ritual wailing begins with a single individual, suggesting that the overhearer has privileged access to a unique subjective experience, but ends up showing that that subjective experience is essentially like that of one's own self.

So the curious difference between ritual wailing and ceremonial dialogue as manifestations of sociability through sharing makes sense. As a salient speech style, dialogicality foregrounds the idea of contributions of distinct selves. In the complementarity-based model, this is taken in the direction of genuine distinctiveness. Here sociability is modeled as organic solidarity, as involving trade and exchange, as based on the attractive forces of difference. In the similarity-based model, it is taken in the direction of showing that the distinct selves are the same. They share a single thing, namely, the discourse that circulates by means of their interaction. The starting point of ritual wailing is different. It begins with monologicality, foregrounding the idea of the individual and the private. But it ends with a demonstration that what is private does not vary from one individual to the next.

It is undoubtedly the case that many, if not all, societies contain within themselves both representations of sociability. As has been shown, the sociability based upon overhearing and upon incorporating the other into one's self is, from a cross-cultural perspective, more regularly female and more typical of domestic relations. However, by means of the ritual wailing speech style, this female and domestic version of sociability can be extended progressively outward to the limits of the community, as in central Brazil, where it is both a male and female form and where it occurs at the boundaries of the community as a form of greeting. In contrast, the sociability based upon hearing the other out and upon cooperative interrelationship is, from a cross-cultural perspective, more regularly male and more typically associated with the maximally distant political relations. It can be extended inward, so to speak, becoming female as well as male, as among Trio, and functioning within the community and even in relationship to death, as among Waiwai.

The contrast between similarity- and difference-based societies is therefore one of degree, of the relative mixture of the models of sociability and of the self. The distinctiveness of central Brazil emerges because these cultures have extended the overhearing model so far. To be a member of these communities is to participate in the lives of other members in a thoroughgoing manner. The boundaries of the self are extended to encompass others—and they do not encompass just one or a few others but the entire community. The self is co-extensive with the community, beyond whose boundaries lies the dangerous other, the enemy, nature, death. Within the community is the warmth of co-participation in the lives of others.[5]

The uniqueness of a culture can be seen to arise out of the differing possibilities for configuring the discourse history. Salient speech styles are modeled on the widespread or universal characteristics of discourse, which are related by virtue of contiguity to canonical contexts. Salient speech styles reshape those characteristics, turning them into culturally unique artifacts. Correspondingly, they transport the contextual features with which they are canonically associated into new contexts. Ritual wailing becomes male as well as female. It occurs in connection with greetings as well as death. In this way, a unique order of discourse is created.

That order is not just intellectual and phenomenal; it is also emotional. And the discourse that carries emotions is always simultaneously individual and collective—individual because it is produced by the physical organism, but collective because it is immediately inserted into the discourse history making up a culture; it faces toward its producer, but also toward the broader collection of utterances into which it is inserted and in relationship to which it becomes interpretable. The intensely emotional utterance is empirical and public, investigable in the same way as other utterances. It is, in short, a part of culture. But this is not culture in the sense of shared, abstract meanings; rather it is culture in the discursive sense of a set of discourse instances to which new ones can be added, and from which old ones fade out.

CHAPTER 8

Style and Grammar

Social cohesion produced by the attractive forces of difference, as modeled in salient speech styles and, in particular, the complementarity-based ceremonial dialogue, is a notable feature of northern Amazonian societies. It is intriguing that this is the same region in which we find remarkable cases of institutionalized multilingualism. Among the Tukanoan groups of the Vaupés, there is an entrenched pattern of linguistic exogamy (Sorensen 1967, 1985; Jackson 1974, 1983; Chernela 1983; Grimes 1985). A spouse must be selected from a patrilineal grouping whose language is distinct from one's own. While the result is multilingualism, it is important that the father language of each partner continues to act as a badge or index of distinctiveness: "individuals identify with and are loyal to only one language, their father language" (Jackson 1983:164). The notion of marriage alliance is grounded in the concept of difference not just as regards the production of discourse, but also as regards the abstract grammatical patterns by means of which it is produced.

Taylor and Hoff (1980) have investigated a different but equally fascinating case, that of the seventeenth-century Island-Carib men's language. The men's language evidently developed out of the Carib language known as Kariña through a curious pattern of "linguistic exogamy," namely, the conquest of the Arawaks by Carib groups, who then took the women as wives. If the hypothesis put forth by Taylor and Hoff is correct, the men's language originated as a pidgin, spoken on the northern fringe of South America and in the islands. As it expanded into the islands, it gradually adopted Arawakan morphology, retaining only the Kariña lexicon. This hybrid language did not evolve into a mother tongue, but it did function stylistically to set men apart from women.

Central Brazil, in contrast—which, as we have seen, tends to model solidarity on the ideas of sharing and similarity—simultaneously hews more closely to the classical model of a society knit together by a single language, a single grammar. Historically, Tupinamba was used along the Brazilian coast as a trade language, which evolved into the *lingua geral* of the eighteenth and nineteenth centuries. But it was spread primarily by mestizos, especially by the bands known as *bandeirantes* that settled Brazil's interior, and also by missionaries. Within the Indian communities themselves, especially those belonging to the Jê linguistic family, one language typically corresponded to one culture. Bilingualism in these communities is a recent phenomenon and usually involves Portuguese plus the Amerindian language.

This suggests that societies in which solidarity is based on similarity and sharing, as modeled in the salient speech styles, tend to be monolingual, having what might be termed "linguistic endogamy." Correspondingly, societies in which solidarity is based on difference, as modeled in the salient speech styles, are more likely to be multilingual and to practice some form of linguistic exogamy. The correlation is by no means a necessary one, but it is suggested by the South American facts.

In the case of the similarity-based cohesion, as modeled in the salient speech styles, the configuration of discourse making up the culture is seen as homogeneous with respect to the community; the whole may be reproduced by any part of society, without the help of other parts. For this to be the case, every individual must share the same grammatical code for linguistic segmentation. This tends to foster the prevalence of a single shared language. However, the requirements of a similarity-based cohesion model could also be fulfilled if every member of the community were equally multilingual—that is, if there were more than one grammatical code, but those codes, rather than being identified with distinct subgroups within the community, were themselves shared. Hence, while providing the conditions for monolingualism, similarity-based cohesion is also compatible with certain types of multilingualism.

Attraction through difference, in contrast, as modeled in ceremonial dialogue, rests upon the idea that a single instance of discourse requires for its production contributions from different individuals. The instance cannot be produced by one of them in isolation. At the level of the community, the idea is that the total configuration of discourse depends upon contributions from different parts. Linguistic exogamy is compatible with such a model. If the configuration requires utterances producible and segmentable through more than one grammar, and if each grammar is in turn identified with a part of the community, then a pattern of multilingualism

would establish the principle of attraction through complementary difference. However, since the differences can be produced within a single
grammar, multilingualism is not a prerequisite for this type of solidarity.

Despite the only partial correlation between linguistic exogamy versus
endogamy, on the one side, and cohesion through difference versus through
similarity, on the other, the cases considered here point to an intriguing
fact. When it comes to supplying the basis of social cohesion, "sameness"
or "difference" involves judgments about discourse regarded in terms of
grammatical segmentations, not just in terms of stylistic characteristics.
Two utterances are the "same" insofar as their grammatical segmentations, and hence conscious or semantic meanings, are the same. This is so
in spite of possible stylistic differences.

The differential role of grammar and style is demonstrated with unusual
clarity in the Shokleng case, where, as discussed in chapter 5, the origin
myth can be told in two different styles: ordinary narrative style and the
dyadic *wãñēklèn* style. The utterances produced in these different styles
are regarded as the "same," despite the fact that, from the point of view of
their concrete sensuous characteristics, they are so remarkably different.
Correspondingly, two utterances are "different" when they give rise to different grammatical segmentations, that is, different conscious or semantic
meanings, despite the fact that they may be remarkably similar from a stylistic point of view. Sameness, in other words, insofar as cohesion is concerned, has to do first and foremost with consciousness. Sharing means the
sharing of conscious content, even though there may be stylistic differentiation and complementarity.

The case of ritual wailing is distinct. Sameness here is not a question
of grammatical segmentation, although where the wailing discourse does
contain semantic meaning, as among Shokleng and Bororo, there is an
overall similarity. Wailing accomplishes its trick in part through the meta-
signaling process discussed earlier, whereby the signal is marked as individual, private, spontaneous, and unique at the metalevel, but turns out to
be collective, public, tightly controlled, and shared in its actual form. The
semantic content also contributes to this disparity, since the utterances are
not marked as addressed to any actual individuals in the immediate context. Nevertheless, similarity and communality here are meant to be felt,
not stated explicitly. It is a matter of sensibility, not of consciousness.

In societies based on the attractive power of difference, grammatical segmentation is also at issue. But it is evident that difference can be achieved
through the same grammar as well through different grammars. In addition to the prominence of cooperatively produced utterances, complementary difference can be achieved when there is an understood connection

between certain parts of society and certain classes of utterances. For example, different clans or sibs may have distinct mythological traditions, as in the Vaupés region, where origin myths differ from one sib to the next. The difference here is based upon the grammatical segmentation or semantic meanings of the discourse instances in question, regardless of the stylistic uniformities that unite them. But such differences become truly complementary only when it is recognized that the discourse configuration of a culture depends for its existence on the continuation of these different traditions. Cohesion in the Vaupés region may operate in this way, but the recognition of complementarity through distinct mythological traditions—through the association between social groupings and certain subclasses of utterances—is at best tenuous. The social groupings threaten to become isolated units, based upon similarity and sharing.

For this reason, the notion of complementary difference depends first and foremost on the concept of a single jointly produced utterance requiring contributions from distinct parts of society for its completion. These include the discourse of trade and negotiation, especially, in the case of the northwest Amazon, negotiation in regard to marriage exchanges. While from a materialist point of view it appears that cohesion arises from the exchange of actual human beings in the case of marriage or material items in the case of trade, from the perspective of discourse what is critical is that the configuration of utterances making up a culture in this type of society is reproducible only through such jointly produced utterances. Similarly, in the development in the West of what Durkheim called organic solidarity, the "contract" loomed large. Like the dialogical discourse of negotiation and trade, the contract is a type of discourse that depends for its completion on the joint contributions of two or more parties, two or more parts of society. If Western societies emerged as organically solidary, from the point of view of culture as actually occurring discourse, they were able to do so in part because of the centrality of these cooperatively produced instances.

The issue of grammar is like that of the distinct mythological traditions. If different grammars become associated with distinct parts of society, they can contribute to complementarity-based cohesion. This is so, however, only insofar as it is explicitly recognized that the presence of distinct utterances, produced by different grammars, is central to the configuration of the discourse history. In the northwest Amazon, this seems to be the case. The rule of linguistic exogamy presupposes that distinct grammars are essential to the maintenance of culture. Grammars are in this way more important to complementarity-based cohesion than are distinct mythological traditions. At the same time, because they are identified with local groups, there is an implicit threat that they may revert to being simply different, and that each local group may become isolated, basing itself upon an internally shared discourse and grammar. The perpetuation of the system is finally possible only through the existence of jointly produced utterances that are related to negotiation and trade.

It is interesting that trade is so little developed among the Jê tribes of central Brazil, who simultaneously operate in accord with the shared culture model, grounded in the attraction made possible by virtue of similarity. It is not that giving is unimportant, but rather that the circulation of goods is not accompanied by the back-and-forth dialogical processes of bartering and negotiation in which utterances are cooperatively manufactured. Such utterances do not seem to play an important role in the discourse formations in these societies, if, indeed, they are present at all. Sociability depends upon sharing and upon the circulation of common traditions. Even in the case of collective singing, where utterance production involves the participation of various individuals, each individual is producing the same thing. The contributions of the different individuals are not distinctive and not complementary, but rather, in effect, interchangeable.

If sameness is grammatically segmentable sameness, and difference is grammatically segmentable difference, what are we to make of the existence of stylistic differentiation, such as that discussed in chapter 5? Even among the Jê tribes, where emphasis is on cohesion through similarity and sharing, there is internal stylistic diversity within the community. That diversity establishes a differentiated order of space, time, and person, even as the circulation of grammatically segmentable discourse presents to consciousness an image of homogeneity. Of course, styles do not only establish difference, contrary to the tenets of structuralism. They also establish similarities through their iconic relations. One style reaches out to another style, drawing its associations into the present context. But this positive, linkage-establishing iconicity is found in the northern Amazonian region as well, where cohesion is based instead upon difference. Like ritual wailing in central Brazil, ceremonial dialogues in northern Amazonia look to other contexts, namely, to the conversations of the domestic sphere, to more intimate social relations. They purport to draw the solidary qualities of those relations into the more distant, more fragile relations in connection with which they are used.

What this suggests is that sameness and difference, as bases of cohesion, operate at two planes: the plane of consciousness, grounded in the semantic meanings and grammatical segmentations of utterances, and the plane of relative unconsciousness, grounded in the phenomenal and sensible characteristics and contiguities of utterances. Sameness or difference is a matter of conscious content, but it is also a matter of perception and of feeling. Moreover, the two planes are not always in accord. Indeed, Jackson (1983: 101) observes for the Vaupés region of northwestern Amazonia that, while there is a remarkable flowering of linguistic difference, through linguistic exogamy, "the similarity of observable phenomena throughout the region is indisputable." "Cultural homogeneity is readily apparent even to a nonanthropologist, regardless of how one defines 'culture'" (1983: 101). The multiplicity of grammars presents to consciousness a picture of difference, which, however, stylistic uniformity tends to belie.

One may conclude from this that the attractive forces of similarity and difference are not typologically differentiating characteristics of societies. They are rather forces present in every society. The empirical question concerns their precise manifestation and distribution with respect to consciousness and unconsciousness in a given case. If the previous chapters propose that we could think of social organization from the point of view of how a discourse configuration characterizing a culture is pegged to people, space, and time, it is now apparent that social organization is also a matter of the degrees of conscious and unconscious encoding of the principles of similarity and difference or complementarity as bases of cohesion. The key difference between northern Amazonia and central Brazil is that, while the former presents to consciousness a picture of cohesion grounded in difference, the latter presents a picture grounded in sameness.

Without endeavoring to elaborate the point, it is worth noting that these principles have correlates in the psychoanalytic understanding of the self and its developmental phases. Ernest Wolf (1989:21) distinguishes four kinds of experiences a developing child needs to have, if "a healthy, whole cohesive self" is to develop. Among these are that "the child needs to feel its essential likeness to another person, the so-called *alter-ego* selfobject experience" and that "the child needs to feel it can assert itself against another person's benevolently opposing intent, the so-called *adversarial* selfobject experience" (Wolf 1989:21). At the level of discourse, the "alter-ego selfobject experience" is the production of discourse instances that are replicas or copies of one another. Each individual or part of society is like every other in being able to reproduce the overall configuration. Alternatively, the "adversarial selfobject experience" has its analogue in the cooperatively produced discourse of negotiation, barter, and haggling, wherein a single utterance requires for its production the distinct but complementary contributions of two or more participants.

There is also an analogue to the distinction between conscious, semantic, grammatically segmentable meaning, on the one side, and unconscious, indexical/iconic, sensible meaning, on the other. This is not just the abstract distinction of "conscious" and "unconscious" from classical Freudian theory. It is also the clinically accessible distinction between "verbalizing" and "acting out," the latter akin to Mauss's (1979) *techniques du corps*. Certain patterns that patients may not be able to verbalize, they nevertheless may be able to experience through their actions. Patterns, for example, having to do with the loss of a parent in childhood may be re-enacted in the course of psychotherapeutic treatment through the patient's effecting various kinds of separation from the therapist. In the course of treatment, such acting out may be "a first step on the way to remembering and talking about the loss" (Kent 1989:27).

In any case, from the perspective of discourse, it is possible that the relations between similarity and difference, on the one hand, and consciousness and unconsciousness, on the other, configure themselves differently from one society to the next. For this reason, the classical models of mechanical versus organic solidarity, tradition versus modernity, and hotness versus coldness are inadequate. Not only do the principles of sameness and difference that underlie these distinctions not map onto an evolutionary sequence in any simple way, but there is a constant tension between their conscious, grammatical encoding, on the one side, and their unconscious, sensible encoding, on the other. The order of social life is to be found not just in consciousness or only in the phenomenal and sensible. It is to be found in the interplay between the two. If the northwest Amazon exhibits grammatical diversity, it also exhibits stylistic homogeneity. If central Brazil displays grammatical homogeneity within the community, it also exhibits stylistic heterogeneity.

The early chapters of this book, which focus on parallelism within myth, suggest that consciousness and unconsciousness are not mutually exclusive categories. They are rather poles of a continuum. Parallel patterning can force patterns and conclusions to hover just beneath the surface of awareness, preventing them from sinking into the inaccessible realm of transcience and ephemerality, but simultaneously keeping them out of the realm of explicit semantic encoding in discourse. If style and grammar are related to the respectively unconscious and conscious encoding of principles of sameness or difference, one may wonder whether the two are sharply opposed or, alternatively, whether they are also poles of a continuum.

As formulated earlier, a style is a cluster of features that characterizes utterances relatively independently of their semantic content or grammatical segmentation. The characteristics may include voice quality, pitch contour, rhythm, and the presence of nongrammatical sounds, such as cry breaks.

Style understood in this way may be regarded as *grammar-independent*. It gives rise to a model of the relationship between grammar and style, as well as between grammar and a community of speakers, that is widely assumed by practicing field linguists and anthropologists and that is associated with the classical understandings of language and culture as abstract systems. This model can be opposed to another, which can be called the *grammar-dependent* model of style.

In the grammar-independent model, there is an array of distinct styles within the community, each style characterizing a large and potentially infinite class of utterances. But each of these is segmentable by means of the same set of grammatical patterns, which exist at the level of types. The actually occurring utterances do not so much carry the grammatical patterns—contra the discourse-centered model—as undergo interpretation by means of the patterns, which form a kind of canopy. Style is accessible through the concrete and sensuous characteristics of discourse; grammar is accessible through reflection and awareness, through phonemic judgments about sameness and difference of meaning, as in the minimal pairs test, and through judgments about grammaticality. Also assumed in this model is the idea that grammar is a single consistent system, in which, in the celebrated Saussurean dictum, "everything hangs together." The system is acquired and transmitted en masse.

If styles involve nongrammatical features, it is an empirical question whether and to what extent they also involve grammatical features. Insofar as they do, they may be referred to as *grammar-dependent* styles, the limiting case being the fully distinct language. The continuum between unconscious and conscious, or enacted and verbalized, articulations of sameness and difference suggests an analogous continuum between grammar-dependence and grammar-independent of style. A speech style, like the dyadic Shokleng origin myth telling, is made up of sensible sound qualities, which occur together with the embodied characteristics already discussed. The style differs in its sound qualities and sensori-motor patterns from the ordinary narrative style. From the point of view of consciousness, however, if the grammatical segmentations of the two utterances are identical, then the stylistic difference does not correlate with a difference in consciousness. It remains phenomenal and sensible, but not, so to speak, intelligible.

But the stylistic difference can be made a matter of conscious difference as well, insofar as the grammar, in accord with which utterances are segmented in one style, is distinct from the grammar in accord with which they are segmented in the other. Under the view of grammar as a complete and consistent whole, in which all of the parts "hang together," this would mean substituting one language for another. But the difference can be a matter of degree. It is possible for two styles to differ in terms of the lexical items they use. There may be alternative lexical items in only a few cases or, as in the Island-Carib men's language, in virtually all cases. The two styles could also differ morphologically or in terms of the syntactic patterns they employ. By modulating the differentiation of styles grammatically, the conscious encoding of difference can be effected in virtually any degree.

In this latter grammar-dependent model, there may be no unified grammatical system overarching the distinct styles. The patterns within one style may be distinct from those within another style. In some styles, grammatical relations and conscious meanings may assume a large role in the interpretation of utterances. This is true in the ordinary narrative style of myth telling in Shokleng, where the most complex grammatical patterns found anywhere in Shokleng culture occur. In other styles, for example, the ritual wailing of Shavante, there may be very little evidence of grammatical patterning at all. In the latter case, there is no morphology or syntax, and there are, indeed, few full syllables, the major portion of the utterance consisting of vowels that are juxtaposed and given musical pitch. A grammar-dependent model of style sees grammatical structure itself not as a coherent, abstract system—a canopy uniting the diverse styles—but as a local phenomenon, differing from one style to the next, with parts that are not so much bound to one another by virtue of necessity as loosely cohering and subject to reconfiguration. Global grammatical structure, under this interpretation, has only a virtual existence, as a hypothesis or interpretive attempt to unite discrete patterns into a single system.

The question of grammar-independence versus grammar-dependence of styles, and, correspondingly, of the systematic canopy versus locally patterned and hypothetically global model of grammar, is sometimes solved on the theoretical plane in a priori fashion. This is done by arguing that, if there is to be mutual intelligibility, then there must be shared grammar— the point of view of structural linguistics, which enabled researchers to work with a single informant and subsequently to produce a grammar of the language. The view is taken to an extreme within transformational generative grammar, where the argument is that the only valid data regarding language structure are the intuitions of native speakers.

The argument assumes (1) that the function of language is to convey semantic meanings, and (2) that speakers will share a common grammar if they do in fact interact with one another by means of language long enough. Correspondingly, grammatical variation is thought of in terms of the lack of sharing due to the relative isolation of subgroups, whether defined geographically, in which case one speaks of *dialects*, or in terms of social class or occupation or other aspects of differentiations within a complex social order, in which case one speaks of *registers*.

But the discourse-centered approach places emphasis on the "if" in the phrase "if there is to be mutual intelligibility." Intelligibility is not necessarily the function of language use, at least not in all and perhaps not in most cases. Many examples from South America and elsewhere indicate that a style may be used to conceal or shroud in mystery, as in the Suyá curing chants examined by Seeger (1986), or to stimulate aesthetic interest, as in the poetic function of parallelism noted by Jakobson (1960, 1966, 1968, 1980), or to index social categories and/or aspects of space and time, as discussed earlier. As in northern Amazonia, difference may be part of the mechanism of cohesion itself. If styles function in relationship to the processes of social order, only one of these functions is the communication of semantic meanings, that is, of referential contents that are not already known.

There is an irony in this. Intelligibility and the communication of new semantic meanings may be more important in large-scale societies than in small face-to-face communities. When people are in daily contact in small-scale communities, functions other than semantic communication may take precedence, especially where experiential commonality can be presupposed. Far from being the case that constant interaction by means of language produces a uniformly shared grammar, with relative isolation giving rise to variability, such interaction may give rise not only to stylistic difference, but also to grammatical difference. Small-scale societies, in other words, may foster grammar-dependent variation as well as grammar-independent stylistic diversity, and the variation may include entirely different grammatical apparatuses.

While the evidence is far from adequate to assess the extent of grammar-dependent variation, there can be no doubt that it is present in some measure even in those societies characterized by the principle of similarity and sharing, that is, societies that are most compatible with the shared grammar model. Inspection of Shokleng ritual wailing in fact reveals at least one instance of lexical variation. The term used in everyday speech for "sibling" is *nũgñẽn*, but in ritual wailing the variant *nũgñẽl* is also used. There is a difference here of only a single phoneme, but in fact the difference is noticeable from a phonetic perspective, since the change from /n/ to /l/ in final position results in the addition of an unstressed "echo vowel." Whereas the everyday word is phonetically [nũŋñẽn´], the ritual wailing term is [nũŋñẽl´ lẽ]. Regardless of its perceptual or phonetic saliency, however, the point is that the difference is salient to consciousness.

Shokleng are aware of the difference and can direct the researcher's attention to it. Its existence was even noted by Henry (1964: 190, n. 32).

Examination of the origin myth reveals greater lexical variation with respect to everyday speech. A small but substantial lexical subset—a sample of these is shown in table 3—distinguishes this style. The variation here is complex. In some cases, there is an exclusive difference between origin myth telling and all other speech; the everyday term never occurs in the origin myth and the origin myth item never occurs in everyday usage, at least insofar as has been possible to determine through observations and through questioning. This type of variation is indicated by the letter A in table 3. If one were to attach a felt sensibility to the variation, it would be that the everyday items are too vulgar, too colloquial, to be used in the lofty, solemn rhetoric of origin myth telling, whose discourse comes as close as any in Shokleng culture to being "sacred." The lexical items are incomprehensible and mysterious to young people who have not been initiated into the exegetical tradition surrounding the myth.

A second set of items, indicated by the letter B in table 3, shows a different type of variation. The special origin myth words are never used in everyday speech, but the everyday words do occur as lexical variants within the origin myth. The variation is like that reported above in connection with ritual wailing. The ritual wailing item never occurs in ordinary speech, but the everyday item does occur as a variant within ritual wailing. In these cases, while the special origin myth terms, like those discussed earlier, are lofty and solemn, the everyday terms are not regarded as colloquial or vulgar. They are suitable but less impressive, less mysterious. Indeed, as noted in chapter 4, there is actually variation in this regard between tellings. B.2.1 (1975) and B.2.1 (1981) both use the special origin myth term *wãgyò*, "relative," but B.2.1 (1982), which was produced by a younger speaker, makes use of the everyday word *kòñka hà*, "relative," although in everyday speech, the morpheme /hà/, "good, whole," is rarely used.

In at least one case, there is yet a third type of variation, labeled C in table 3. In this type, both lexical items are used in the origin myth, and both terms are used outside the origin myth. However, the special origin myth term is used in everyday speech only by elders, and, indeed, even for them it indicates their special status. They use the everyday term as well, but when they use the special term, everyone around them is aware that they are indexing elderhood. It is remarkable how salient this particular item is to consciousness. One thinks of it as an ancient term, but in fact there is no evidence that it is. The everyday term for "fire" /pẽ/ is cognate with the Kaingang term /pĩ/, and both are related to the proto-Jê word *pĩ

Table 3. Lexical Differences between the Shokleng Origin Myth and Everyday Speech

	Origin Myth	Everyday Speech	Translation	Type
1.	kũnõ	tà tag	"young girl"	A
2.	wãmõhà	kake	"friend"	A
3.	yògwañ	pa'i	"chief"	A
4.	zuwàgzàl	kul	"blanket used as skirt"	B
5.	zòklãl	kute	"forest"	B
6.	wãgyò	kòñka	"relative"	B
7.	zãñkò	pē	"fire"	C

(Davis 1966:22). Indeed, there is no reconstructive evidence that any special origin myth terms pertain to an earlier history of the language, contrary to what one might suppose. They appear to be lexical alternates that have been created for this purpose, not simply maintained from some prior stage.

It is curious that these lexical variations should be so salient to consciousness. One senses that they are indirect designators of the styles in question. Without the styles, however, which are defined as well through characteristics of morphology and syntax, not to mention nongrammatical features, lexical variation in itself might not be so important. In the Shokleng research, one case of lexical variation with no apparent stylistic basis surfaced somewhat fortuitously. When eliciting the word for "hair," I was repeatedly given the lexeme /kïki/. One day, however, a woman used the word /kàgci/. When asked about this, she indicated that it was the word for "hair." Presented with the suggestion that the word /kïki/ also meant "hair," she categorically denied this, claiming that the latter word did not even exist in the Shokleng language. When the individual from whom the original form /kïki/ had been elicited was presented with the form /kàgci/, he claimed to be wholly unfamiliar with it. Pursuing the matter, I brought the two together, and they were astonished regarding one another's usage. Despite the fact that the two were cousins and talked to one another on an almost daily basis, they had never noticed this lexical difference that separated them. While I subsequently observed the use of each of these terms in the speech of different individuals, no systematic association emerged. An individual who used one word did not use the other, but the individuals using a given term apparently did not form a socially significant group.

It is possible that the social groupings do exist, but are emergent ones, resulting from contact with Brazilians. The form /kïki/ is evidently the older form, having an exact cognate in Kaingang and reflecting the proto-Jê word for "hair." /Kàgci/ appears to be the innovative form. It may be used to set apart the nontraditionalists, who identify with Brazilians, from the traditionalists, who identify with the Shokleng elders. There are other emerging stylistic variations that do this. The phoneme /z/ in standard Shokleng is pronounced as an ungrooved dental fricative /ð/, as in the *th* sound of "these" in English. The sound is not distinctive in Brazilian Portuguese; when Brazilians endeavor to pronounce Shokleng names, they substitute a grooved alveolar fricative /z/. For example, the name that is phonemically /kuzug/ and phonetically [kʰuðugⁿ´] is pronounced [kuzu´] by Brazilians. Young Shokleng imitate this kind of pronunciation in what is effectively a slang style. /Kàgci/, however, does not co-occur with these other slang features. Although /kàgci/ was never observed in the speech of elders, it is used by some people who would never engage in the slang pronunciations. If it does mark an emerging group of nontraditionalists or modernists, it nevertheless is not co-occurrent with other emerging stylistic features.

From this evidence, it appears that an isolated lexical difference, unbolstered by a recognizable style, is not necessarily salient to consciousness. When even small grammatical differences have stylistic associations, however, such as the single phoneme that differentiates the ritual wailing term *nũgñēl* from the everyday term *nũgñēn*, the difference looms large in consciousness. It is as if the segmentable differences enabled the reflective faculty to grasp the broader contrast, which might otherwise only be perceived or felt.

While lexical variation is by no means well studied in central Brazil, it should be noted that the Shokleng case is not anomalous. In an unpublished paper, Laura Graham (n.d.) has documented the existence of what she refers to as a special "language" among Shavante, who are otherwise thoroughly within the shared culture, shared grammar model of social cohesion. The language is used by a ritual specialist known as the *'a'ama*, and Graham calls it accordingly the *'a'ama* language. It is apparently not given any other explicit name by Shavante, who refer to it as the way *'a'ama* speaks. The basic syntax and morphology are those of Shavante more generally, but, as in the Island-Carib men's language, the lexicon is distinct. Not every lexical item is different from that found in ordinary Shavante, but the variation is extensive. Interestingly, the language is not associated with a distinctive style, as marked by intonation, voice quality, rhythm, or other nongrammatical features. Without commanding Shavante grammar, one cannot distinguish *'a'ama* speech from ordinary Shavante.

If we are to call this a style, then it is evidently an entirely grammar-dependent style. There is no trace of grammar-independent recognizability. The alternative lexical forms characterizing *'a'ama* speech are constructed in accord with the principles of Shavante phonology, and they are embedded in discourse that makes use of Shavante morphology and syntax. The style is not perceptually salient, in contrast to ceremonial dialogue and ritual wailing. However, it is salient to consciousness. For any Shavante speaker, *'a'ama* speech is distinctive, unique, something that cannot be confused with ordinary Shavante. Yet there is clearly a continuum from the Shokleng dyadic origin myth telling, which is first and foremost salient perceptually, involving only some lexical and grammatical variation, to the *'a'ama* language of Shavante, which is not perceptually salient but is grammatically salient, even though it is distinctive only in its lexicon, to the complete contrasts between grammars found in northwest Amazonia. Conscious differentiation is downplayed in central Brazil, in favor of an emphasis on the sharing of grammatically segmentable discourse, despite the flourishing of unconscious differentiation through sensible encoding. Nevertheless, even here unconsciousness is a matter of degree. Some differences do present themselves to consciousness through grammar in some measure. From the point of view of the overall organization of Shavante social life, however, it is intriguing that the most consciously salient or grammar-dependent style is associated with a social category that has, apparently, so little overall significance with respect to the cohesion of society more generally. It is almost as if the consciously encoded difference were designed to distract attention from the solidarity-threatening differences, which, in turn, are relatively concealed from consciousness, even though they are phenomenally displayed.

It is important to note that stylistic contrast involves more than lexical variation. In the case of Shokleng elder versus younger speech, there are lexical differences, such as the word for "fire" discussed earlier. But there are also important grammatical differences. One feature of the presence of elder speech—at least during the period from 1974 to 1982—is the existence of shape categories, coded lexically in certain verbs, and position-shape categories, coded grammatically in the continuative aspect and locative markers. The verb "to give [singular]" has two distinct forms, *zi* and *ném*, which can be glossed as "to give a longish object" and "to give a roundish [i.e., nonlongish] object." In this language, it is the shape of the transitive object rather than the transitive subject that determines the choice of verb forms, just as it is the number of the transitive object rather than the transitive subject that determines the singular or plural marking of the verb. In any case, elder speech also makes use of four forms of the continuative/locative particle: *ñã, nē, nõ,* and *cò,* which pertain to the shape-positions of "standing," "sitting," "lying," and "hanging." In a sentence such as "the man was sleeping," for example, the continuous nature of the action is indicated by one of the continuative markers. One would normally use the particle *nõ,* "lying," indicating that the object in question, the man, was stretched out and longish. To choose the particle *nē,* "sitting," would indicate specifically that he was bunched up into a roundish shape.

What is interesting is that younger people do not make use of these distinctions. They do not even have grammatical intuitions about how the forms should be used. This is despite the fact that their grandparents use these forms consistently in conversations with them. When asked to make a grammaticality judgment about the continuative/locative particles, one young man gave instead a sociological judgment about the style: "it's the elders who talk that way." This may be a case in which the stylistic difference is associated with language shift. Alternatively, as the younger generation gradually matures, it may adopt the patterns of elder speech. We will know more about this forty years from now. But it is of interest that such an important grammatical difference can exist within a community of only 300 or so native speakers.

Nor is this difference an isolated one. There is also in Shokleng elder speech a form of focused noun phrase, which emphasizes the pronoun or noun in question. This is used only for nominative case noun phrases, that is, for noun phrases that are subjects of transitive or intransitive sentences. The examples in (1) and (2) were elicited from one elder, and subsequently confirmed by observation of the speech of other elders.

(1) ã   hã   mã   ti   pɛnũ   mũ
     you   focus   2p   he   shoot   active

   "You shot him" or "It is you who shot him."

(2) ti   hã   wũ   ti   pɛnũ   mũ
     he   focus   3p   he   shoot   active

   "He shot him" or "It is he who shot him."

The noun phrase here consists of the pronoun followed by the focus marker /hã/ followed by the person marker. The person marker in effect functions

Table 4. Shokleng Pronouns and Person Markers

	Pronoun	Person Marker
First person singular	ēñ	nū
First person plural	åg	nã
Second person	ã	mã
Third person singular masculine	ti	wū
Third person singular feminine	zi	
Third person plural	òg	

as a postposition, making the noun phrase a postpositional phrase, analogous to other such phrases. A list of the pronouns and person markers is given in table 4.

Two other forms are relevant here: *ē* and *tã*. The former has a purely co-referential function and is used in embedded clauses to refer to the appropriate noun phrase in the main clause with which it is co-referent. The form *tã* may be derived from the contraction of *ti* and *hã*, but it is in any case now distinct from them. While in elder speech it shows some alignment with the person marker series, it is also definitely aligned with the pronouns and can be used together with the third person marker *wū*, as in example (3).

(3)   tã   wū   ti   pɛnū   mū
        he   3p   he   shoot   active

"He shot him."

What is striking in the speech of younger people is that they lack the focused noun phrase involving third person of the type shown in example (2). Simultaneously, they have interpreted the form *tã* as more closely aligned with the person marker series than with the pronoun series, reversing the pattern in elder speech. Consequently, instead of the example in (2), the sentence in (4) was elicited and subsequently confirmed through observation of actual speech.

(4)   ē   hã   tã   ti   pɛnū   mū
        coref.   focus   3p   he   shoot   active

"*He* shot him" or "He, who is he, shot him."

What this means, in effect, is that the postpositional noun phrase has been reinterpreted as a relative clause, as "he, who is he . . ."

We do not know, again, whether this is an indication of historical change in the language or whether the younger people will modify their speech patterns when they themselves become elders. Forty years from now we will know more. But the important point for present purposes is that the grammar of Shokleng, even in this community of 300, is not uniformly shared. Stylistic differences result in distinct grammatical parsings for the sentences in question.

The model of a uniformly shared abstract grammatical system, learned and transmitted en masse, in which "everything hangs together," is not applicable to this small community. If it is true that grammatical patterns must be shared in order for there to be mutual intelligibility, then one must conclude that in this small community intelligibility in some measure is secondary to other functions of language use, in particular, those pertaining to the social differentiation of elders from young people. It is more important, in other words, to etch in consciousness by means of grammatical usages the distinction between old and young than it is to ensure total intelligibility at the plane of semantic meaning.

The elder/younger distinction is indeed crucial, as befits a society so thoroughly immersed in the self-representation of continuity. The young people are on their way to becoming elders who are in turn on their way to becoming ancestors.[1] But the important point for present purposes is that the processes of representation of cultural continuity, which form part of the problematic of producing a cohesive social order, take precedence, in some measure, over the necessities of being able to communicate referentially. It is more important to represent to consciousness the disjunctions along the temporal path from childhood to elderhood than it is to ensure the felicitous and precise communication of new information.

The existence of grammatical differences in small-scale societies has been known for some time, especially in the area of men's and women's speech (Sherzer 1987b). Sapir (1949) and Haas (1964) describe such differences for the North American Indian Yana and Koasati, respectively, and male and female differences are found in the South American data as well. David and Gretchen Fortune (1975) have described an interesting set of phonological contrasts for the Karajá language of central Brazil, which is itself distantly related to Shokleng, Shavante, and other central Brazilian languages of the Jê family. They demonstrate the existence of phonological rules, differentially applied by men and women, that generate the surface forms of lexical items from "base forms," which are generally identical to the female usages. There is, for example, a "k-dropping rule" that men apply to a base form to yield actual lexical items that are distinct from those employed by women: for example, "fish" = *kətora*, f. and *ətora*, m.; "turtle" = *kətu*, f. and *ətu*, m.; "wind" = *kihi*, f. and *ihi*, m. The Fortunes posit eight gender-distinguishing phonological rules, which include rules that change /č/ to /ǰ/ in some cases and drop it in others, that drop /n/ when it occurs between /ã/ and /õ/, and so forth.

Since one can imagine that men and women have control over the grammatical patterns employed by the other, it has been possible to dismiss these kinds of grammatical differences within the community. Women could use the rules utilized by men in producing sentences and presumably do so in interpreting such sentences. This is a phenomenon that could be studied empirically. The Fortunes (1975 : 124, n. 3) in fact employed both male and female informants in their study, but they could have endeavored to test female intuitions about the male forms and vice versa to see whether the intuitions were shared. Even so, one would need to posit social correlates to grammatical rules.

In any case, it is apparent that stylistic differences, even in these small-scale societies, are a matter of grammar as well as of sound; they are intelligible as well as perceptible; and they pertain to consciousness as well as to sensibility. At the same time, there is a continuum from minimal grammar-dependent variation, with an emphasis on the phenomenal display of difference, to maximal grammar-dependent variation, with no otherwise perceptible or sensible difference. In the limiting case, which is found in South America in the Vaupés region, stylistic differentiation may involve the substitution of entire grammars. Far from being a uniform medium of communication, homogeneously spread throughout a community, therefore, grammar turns out to function at the behest of social relations. The sharing and nonsharing of grammar make salient to consciousness the similarities and differences that are socially significant.

This has implications for an understanding of language and grammar. It means first of all that the grammar derived from studying utterances elicited from a single informant, as in standard structural field linguistics, cannot exhaust the grammatical patternings within a community of speakers. The selection of just one informant will not do, if there are differences between speakers. Much less is it possible exhaustively to explore the grammatical patternings within a community by means of the intuitionist methods propounded by Noam Chomsky and his followers. The central Brazilian data indicate that there may be important differences in the intuitions of different speakers, even, for example, as regards the interpretation of a given constituent as a noun phrase or a relative clause. In some cases, indeed, what is for some speakers a part of standard grammar is for others a relatively opaque marker of stylistic difference.

Intuitionism, however, has a much deeper, and perhaps ultimately fatal, flaw. It depends entirely upon a conscious, reflective understanding of grammatical patternings. If there is a continuum between style and grammar, between grammar-independent and grammar-dependent style, between unconscious and conscious signaling, and between the sensible and the intelligible, then intuitionism probes at best one end of the continuum, the protruding tip of a much larger iceberg that is the total configuration of discourse patterns within a community. The iceberg consists, moreover, in the crystallization, within the memories of members of the community, of actually occurring discourse. Since different individuals have access to different parts of that total collection, there is no guarantee that the fragment of patterning that has surfaced into consciousness will be the same for any two individuals, or even for the same individual at different points in time. Intuitionist grammar is a virtual construct, a hypothesis of the moment, not a reflection of underlying structure.

It is possible to expand the limits of such a grammar, as has been tried on occasion, by expanding the scope of intuitions. Instead of asking whether a given utterance is "grammatical," one could pose to consciousness some other question: for example, "is there any context in which this utterance might occur?" Attention is directed to the indexical dimensions of discourse, to utterance-world contiguities. In theory, if one individual could achieve a totalized awareness of the discourse history within a community, an intuitionist grammar—nearly co-extensive with a total consciousness of culture and society—might be possible.

In fact, there are reasons to suspect that such a consciousness cannot be achieved without the help of empirical investigation, if it can be achieved at all. It has been stressed throughout this book that consciousness and unconsciousness, or intelligibility and sensibility, are in a dynamic tension within society. Evidently, the functioning of discourse within a community depends in part upon the capacity of that discourse, as well as nonverbal signs, to communicate phenomenally in ways that may actually elude conscious awareness. In the case of Shokleng mythological discourse, for example, it has been shown that the norms of language use encoded there are suggested through parallelism without being explicitly stated. This enables them to slip past the beacon of public consciousness, which acts as a censor. If the rules were explicitly stated, then they could be explicitly rejected. While empirical study reveals the regularities by means of which relatively unconscious communication takes place, it is important to the proper social functioning of this message that it not be directly accessible to consciousness. Similarly, in the case of style, processes of differentiation within the social group may depend upon using grammatical patternings as a way of creating consciously articulated differences. If the patterns responsible for distinguishing some part of a community were not directly accessible to consciousness, the social purpose of the differentiation might be circumvented. That is, in some cases *it is in the interests of social order that grammar not be uniformly distributed*. This is in keeping with Sorensen's (1967:676) speculation regarding the existence, in the Vaupés region, of "a force that makes a speaker want to render closely-related languages further apart."

If a complete understanding of the relationships between grammar and community cannot be achieved through intuitionism or informant work, but rather only with the help of empirical investigation of actually occurring discourse, one should not conclude that the study of discourse instances alone is sufficient to produce that understanding: the phenomenal must be studied in conjunction with an exploration of consciousness. Discourse faces in two directions: on the one hand, toward the sensible, through its concrete characteristics and through the this-world contexts in which it occurs; on the other, toward the faculty of reflection, being interpretable in part only through a feel for grammatical patterning. It may not be possible to achieve an understanding of this fact without the aid of intuitionist methods.

Indeed, the problematic of publicness turns out to be a problematic simultaneously of sensibility and intelligibility: the discourse instance as, on the one hand, phenomenal, perceptible sound or writing—"the boy got up to the nest"—and, on the other, consciousness or awareness of a physical world outside the discourse, a world filled with boys and nests and climbing. We cannot have a public, construed in its broadest sense as a society or culture, without the public circulation of discourse, and discourse has both these facets: how could we think of understanding the one without understanding the other? At the same time, it is too easy to assume that sensibility and intelligibility go together, exhibit a transparency that allows us to read through from one to the other. If this book has one overriding purpose, it is to break down that assumption, to open it up to empirical investigation, in the course of which a more complex problematic of publicness emerges. Society depends upon the interaction between consciousness and perception, awareness and feeling, and the two are sometimes at odds, exhibiting a mutual tension in which feeling tricks consciousness and vice versa, in which similarity in one area goes along with diversity in another, in which metadiscursive awareness of mutual understanding covers over misunderstandings, often the product of discourse entropy—part of the broader entropy of the universe—and in which, finally, discourse configures and reconfigures, producing the shifting visage of culture, an ephemeral sand painting that can be drawn and redrawn, but also easily dispersed by the winds of time.

Notes

1. An Approach to Culture and Language

1. The term "discourse-centered approach" took shape through discussions at the University of Texas at Austin, especially among Joel Sherzer, Steve Feld, Anthony Woodbury, Richard Bauman, and myself. Joel Sherzer may have coined the term and was, in any case, the first to use it in print as the title of a work (Sherzer 1987a).

2. From an interaction among children observed while walking down a Chicago street in the late 1970s.

3. An alternative approach in which emotion is the subject of ethnographically studiable metadiscourses about emotion—the intellectual culturalization of affect—is the theme of Rosaldo's (1980) study of the Ilongot of the Philippines and Lutz's (1988) of the Micronesian Ifaluk.

4. Chomsky (1984:19) notes that this example "is not idiomatic English, but [that] we may assume this to be an accidental gap reflecting properties that are not part of core grammar."

5. This subject has evoked much interest in linguistic anthropology, thanks to the work of Jakobson (1960, 1966, 1968), Hymes (1981), and Tedlock (1983), each in different ways; see also Fox (1977, 1988), Sherzer (1982), and Woodbury (1985).

2. Grammatical Parallelism and Thought

1. For the linguistic concepts of "agent" and "patient," see Fillmore (1968). For an alternative structural account of agency and patiency in narrative, see Bremond (1973).

2. It is possible for a myth in theory to be "dual-centered" or "multicentered," that is, to have two or more centers, which consecutively dominate it. It is useful to distinguish such consecutive domination from situations in which two or more personages or entities vie for the center in a given stretch of discourse.

3. At the annual meeting of the American Anthropological Association in 1980.

4. Phonemic representation in Shokleng, as in Kaingang (Wiesemann 1972 and

1978) and many languages of the Jê family of central Brazil, is remote from the phonetic representation, /g/, for example, being realized as [ŋ] before a nasal vowel, [ⁿg] before an oral vowel, and [gⁿ] after an oral vowel. There are nine oral and four nasal vowels, configured and represented orthographically as follows:

i ï u   ū
e à o   ē   ō
è a ò   ā

There are twelve consonants, configured and represented as follows:

p t c k
m n ñ g
   z
w   l y

5. This and other birds mentioned here are kinds of falcon.
6. For a related discussion, see E. Basso (1985).
7. This may be a typical property of hyperanimate entities generally; they become, so to speak, too lofty to be of interest to humans.

3. Consciousness, Norm, and Metadiscourse Parallelism

1. The history of research on reported speech can be traced back to Bakhtin (1973) and Voloshinov (1986) through Matejka and Pomorska (1971) or, in the Americanist tradition, to Sapir (1949), Hymes (1979), Bauman (1983), and Silverstein (1985). A book dealing with issues of reported speech and metalanguage that has grown out of work at the Center for Psychosocial Studies in Chicago is currently being prepared under the editorship of John Lucy. The planned title is *Reflexive Language*.

2. This is possible even in the case of a single myth. Hymes (1985), for example, shows that two tellings, regarded as variants of the same myth, can have different parallel structures, associated with distinct functions.

3. The telling was produced in 1975 by Wãñêkï Tèy, who died a few years later. He was a remarkably intelligent, philosophically inclined person, as evidenced in the particular shape of the discourse, which shows a greater abstract propositional grasp of the issues than other tellings I have examined.

4. For a related view of myth as normative or prescriptive, see Hymes (1968).

5. In 1975b, this process is described as resembling the "shattering of glass."

4. Time, Continuity, and Macroparallelism

1. In chapter 3 the term "parallelism" is used to encompass similarities based on hierarchical embedding, where the relationship of simple succession ceases to be fundamental.

2. Henry's (1964) orthography attempts to capture the phonetic characteristics of Shokleng words through a partial match with English orthography and pronunciation habits. The transcriptions given in the present work are phonemicized, as indicated in chapter 2, note 4.

5. Style and Social Order

1. There are precedents for this usage. Hymes (1974b:435–439), for example, distinguishes "referential" from "stylistic" functions. The term is widely used to distinguish "formal" from "colloquial" varieties of speech (Ervin-Tripp 1972: 235ff.). In the literature, there are good descriptions of the linguistic characteristics of a range of styles, although these are rarely contextualized in social anthropological terms (see Bauman and Sherzer [1974], especially the articles by Fox and Sherzer, and Sherzer [1983]; see also the close description of Kuna chanting by Sherzer [1982]).

2. The problem of totemic representations as indexical, grounded in spatial-temporal contiguities between sign vehicle and meaning, is formulated in Urban (1981b).

3. An example of this from a different culture can be seen in the Asch and Chagnon film *A Man Called Bee,* when the camera shows Chagnon working with one of the Yanomamö on transcription.

4. One autodesignation of the Shokleng is *āglēl,* "human being," which means literally, "we live" or "we the living."

6. Stylized Dialogicality and Interpretability

1. The "model" terminology is from Geertz (1973:93–94). However, his distinction between the "of" and "for" aspects of modeling remains cryptic without some conception, such as that developed here, of a source for the "model of" relationship that is removed in space or time from the present but is, so to speak, brought into the present by virtue of iconicity as a "model for" it.

2. The "what-sayer" reported by E. Basso (1985) for the Kalapalo, who, like the Waiwai, are Carib-speaking, is probably related to this dialogic complex. The Kalapalo, however, long ago left the Carib homeland and penetrated into central Brazil, where the dialogic complex washes out in favor of a different model of sociability, grounded in ritual wailing, as discussed in the next chapter.

7. Style and the Meaning of Emotion

1. For a summary of recent literature on the subject of the social versus individual character of emotions, see Lutz and White (1986).

2. A conference on ritual lament, organized by Steven Feld, was held at the University of Texas at Austin in the spring of 1989. The papers included discussions of the phenomenon in cultures ranging from ancient Egypt, the contempo-

rary Middle East, Greece, Eastern Europe, Finland, and the United States through New Guinea, Polynesia, and South America. The proceedings are currently being assembled for publication.

3. It is an intriguing fact that in Bororo the term for wailing actually aligns this form with music. There is no corresponding alignment in Shokleng or Shavante, where in fact it is explicitly denied that wailing is a form of music.

4. However, Janet Chernela (personal communication) reports that among the Uanano Tukano of the Vaupés region in the extreme northwest of Brazil—an area within the broad belt of complementarity-based ceremonial dialogue—both forms of greeting do in fact occur. The Tukanoan area is noted for its grounding of sociability in difference through linguistic exogamy and large-scale multilingualism (Sorensen 1967, 1985; Jackson 1974, 1983). It will, therefore, be extremely interesting to examine in greater detail the form and context of Uanano ritual wailing and ceremonial dialogue as greetings.

5. It is for this reason that I have elsewhere referred to these societies as having "impermeable membranes" (Urban 1988), in contrast with the northern Amazonian "permeable membrane" societies.

8. Style and Grammar

1. I owe this formulation to Laura Graham, who originally proposed it for Shavante. It seems equally apt for Shokleng, however. Both societies have built their discourse around the principles of sharing and sameness, on the one hand, and continuity over time, on the other.

References

d'Abbeville, Claude
  1975 [1614] *História da missão dos Padres Capuchinos na Ilha do Maranhão e terras circunvizinhas.* São Paulo: Itatiaia/EDUSP.
Albisetti, César, and Angelo Jayme Venturelli
  1962 *Enciclopédia Bororo.* 3 vols. Vol. I. Campo Grande, Brazil: Museu Regional Dom Bosco.
Asch, Timothy, and Napoleon Chagnon
  1970 *The Feast.* 40-minute film. Watertown, Mass.: Documentary Educational Resources.
  1974 *A Man Called Bee.* 29-minute film. Watertown, Mass.: Documentary Educational Resources.
Bach, Emmon
  1974 *Syntactic Theory.* New York: Holt, Rinehart and Winston.
Bakhtin, M. M.
  1973 *Problems of Dostoevsky's Poetics.* Trans. F. W. Rotsel. Ann Arbor: Ardis.
  1986 *Speech Genres and Other Late Essays.* Trans. V. W. McGee. Austin: University of Texas Press.
Baldus, Herbert
  1970 *Tapirapé: Tribo Tupi no Brasil central.* Brasiliana, série Grande Formato, vol. 17. São Paulo: Nacional/EDUSP.
Basso, Ellen
  1985 *A Musical View of the Universe: Kalapalo Myth and Ritual Performance.* Philadelphia: University of Pennsylvania Press.
Basso, Keith
  1988 "Speaking with Names": Language and Landscape among the Western Apache. *Cultural Anthropology* 3(2):99–130.
Bauman, Richard
  1983 Reported Speech as Esthetic Focus in Narratives. Paper delivered at the University of Texas at Austin, March 1983.
  1986 *Story, Performance, and Event: Contextual Studies of Oral Narrative.* New York: Cambridge University Press.

Bauman, Richard, Judith T. Irvine, and Susan U. Philips.
    1987 Performance, Speech Community, and Genre. *Working Papers and Pro-
          ceedings of the Center for Psychosocial Studies.* Chicago: Center for Psycho-
          social Studies.
Bauman, Richard, and Joel Sherzer (eds.)
    1974 *Explorations in the Ethnography of Speaking.* New York: Cambridge Uni-
          versity Press.
Boas, Franz
    1898 *The Mythology of the Bella Coola Indians.* Memoirs of the American Mu-
          seum of Natural History 2. New York: American Museum of Natural
          History.
Bowen, John
    1989 Poetic Duels and Political Change in the Gayo Highlands of Sumatra.
          American Anthropologist 91(1):25–40.
Bremond, Claude
    1973 *Logique du récit.* Paris: Editions du Seuil.
Briggs, Charles
    1989 Personal Expression and Social Criticism in Warao Ritual Wailing. Paper
          given at the Austin Lament Conference, Austin, Texas, March 1989.
Brown, Penelope, and Stephen Levinson
    1978 Universals in Language Usage: Politeness Phenomena. In *Questions and
          Politeness: Strategies in Social Interaction,* ed. E. N Goody, 56–289. Cam-
          bridge: Cambridge University Press.
Caiuby Novaes, Sylvia
    1990 Jogo de espelhos: Imagens da representação de si através dos outros.
          Ph.D. thesis, Department of Anthropology. São Paulo, Universidade de
          São Paulo.
Cardim, Fernão
    1978 [1665] *Tratados da terra e gente do Brasil.* Brasiliana, vol. 168. São Paulo:
          Nacional/MEC.
Chagnon, Napoleon A.
    1983 *Yãnomamö: The Fierce People.* New York: Holt, Rinehart and Winston.
Chernela, Janet M.
    1983 Hierarchy and Economy of the Uanano (Kotira) Speaking Peoples of the
          Middle Uaupes Basin (Brazil). Ph.D. thesis, Department of Anthropol-
          ogy. New York, Columbia University.
Chomsky, Noam
    1984 *Lectures on Government and Binding: The Pisa Lectures.* Dordrecht, Hol-
          land: Foris Publications.
Cocco, P. Luis
    1972 *Iyëwei-teri: Quince años entre los Yanomamos.* Caracas, Venezuela: Edición
          de la Escuela Técnica Popular Don Bosco Boleíta.
Curtiss, Susan
    1977 *Genie: Psycholinguistic Study of a Modern-Day "Wild Child."* New York:
          Academic Press.

Davis, Irvine
   1966 Comparative Jê Phonology. *Estudos Lingüisticos* 1(2):10–24.
Dixon, R. M. W.
   1979 Ergativity. *Language* 55:59–138.
Durkheim, Emile
   1933 [1893]   *The Division of Labor.* Trans. George Simpson. New York: Macmillan.
   1960 [1914]   The Dualism of Human Nature and Its Social Conditions. In *Essays on Sociology and Philosophy*, ed. Kurt H. Wolff, 325–340. New York: Harper and Row, Publishers.
   1965 [1915]   *The Elementary Forms of the Religious Life.* New York: Free Press.
Ervin-Tripp, Susan
   1972 On Sociolinguistic Rules: Alternation and Co-occurrence. In *Directions in Sociolinguistics: The Ethnography of Communication*, ed. J. J. Gumperz and D. Hymes, 213–250. New York: Holt, Rinehart and Winston.
Feld, Steven
   1982 *Sound and Sentiment: Birds, Weeping, Poetics, and Song in Kaluli Expression.* Philadelphia: University of Pennsylvania Press.
   1988 Aesthetics of Iconicity of Style, or 'Lift-up-over-sound': Getting into the Kaluli Groove. *Yearbook for Traditional Music* 20:74–113.
   1989 Wept Thoughts: The Voicing of Kaluli Memories. Paper given at the Austin Lament Conference, Austin, Texas, March 1989.
Fillmore, Charles
   1968 The Case for Case. In *Universals in Linguistic Theory*, ed. E. Bach and R. T. Harms, 1–88. New York: Holt, Rinehart and Winston.
Fish, Stanley
   1980 *Is There a Text in This Class? The Authority of Interpretive Communities.* Cambridge, Mass.: Harvard University Press.
Fock, Niels
   1963 *Waiwai: Religion and Society of an Amazonian Tribe.* Ethnographic Series, no. 8. Copenhagen: Danish National Museum.
Fortune, David, and Gretchen Fortune
   1975 Karajá Men's-Women's Speech Differences with Social Correlates. *Arquivos de Anatomia e Antropologia*, vol. 1, ano 1: 110–124. Rio de Janeiro.
Foucault, Michel
   1980 *Power/Knowledge: Selected Interviews and Other Writings, 1972–1977.* Ed. and trans. C. Gordon. New York: Pantheon.
Fox, James J.
   1977 Roman Jakobson and the Comparative Study of Parallelism. In *Roman Jakobson: Echoes of His Scholarship*, ed. D. Armstrong and C. H. van Schooneveld, 59–90. Lisse: Peter de Ridder.
   1988 (ed.) *To Speak in Pairs: Essays on the Ritual Languages of Eastern Indonesia.* New York: Cambridge University Press.
Frazer, J. G.
   1911 *The Magic Art and the Evolution of Kings.* London: Macmillan.

Geertz, Clifford
   1973   *The Interpretation of Cultures*. New York: Basic Books.
Gnerre, Maurizio
   1986   The Decline of Dialogue: Ceremonial and Mythological Discourse among
          the Shuar and Achuar. In *Native South American Discourse*, ed. J. Sherzer
          and G. Urban, 307–341. Berlin: Mouton de Gruyter.
Graham, Laura
   1984   Semanticity and Melody: Parameters of Contrast in Shavante Vocal Ex-
          pression. *Latin American Music Review* 5: 161–185.
   1986   Three Modes of Shavante Vocal Expression: Wailing, Collective Singing,
          and Political Oratory. In *Native South American Discourse*, ed. J. Sherzer
          and G. Urban, 83–118. Berlin: Mouton de Gruyter.
   n.d.   Putting the '*a'ama* in Context. Unpublished paper. Department of An-
          thropology. Austin, University of Texas at Austin.
Grimes, B. F.
   1985   Language Attitudes: Identity, Distinctiveness, Survival in the Vaupes.
          Journal of Multilingual and Multicultural Development 6: 389–401.
Haas, Mary
   1964   Men's and Women's Speech in Koasati. In *Language in Culture and So-
          ciety*, ed. D. Hymes, 228–233. Berkeley: University of California Press.
Halliday, M. A. K.
   1971   Linguistic Function and Literary Style. In *Literary Style: A Symposium*,
          ed. S. Chatman, 330–365. New York: Oxford University Press.
Halliday, M. A. K., Ruqaiya Hasan
   1976   *Cohesion in English*. London: Longman.
Harner, Michael
   1972   *The Jívaro: People of the Sacred Waterfalls*. Garden City, N.Y.: Doubleday.
Henry, Jules
   1935   A Kaingang Text. *International Journal of American Linguistics* 8: 172–
          218.
   1964   *Jungle People: A Kaingáng Tribe of the Highlands of Brazil*. New York:
          Vintage Books.
Hill, Jonathan D.
   1988   Myth and History. In *Rethinking History and Myth*, ed. J. D. Hill, 1–17.
          Urbana: University of Illinois Press.
Holmer, Nils M.
   1951   *Cuna Chrestomathy*. Etnologiska studier series, no. 18. Göteborg: Göte-
          borgs Etnografiska Museum.
Hulkrantz, Åke
   1957   *The North American Orpheus Tradition*. Monograph Series, no. 2. Stock-
          holm: Ethnographical Museum of Sweden.
Hymes, D.
   1968   The "Wife" Who "Goes Out" Like a Man: Reinterpretation of a Clacka-
          mas Chinook Myth. *Studies in Semiotics* 7(3): 173–199.
   1974a *Foundations in Sociolinguistics: An Ethnographic Approach*. Philadelphia:
          University of Pennsylvania Press.

1974b Ways of Speaking. In *Explorations in the Ethnography of Speaking*, ed. R. Bauman and J. Sherzer, 433–451. New York: Cambridge University Press.

1979 How to Talk like a Bear in Takelma. *International Journal of American Linguistics* 45:101–106.

1981 *"In vain I tried to tell you": Essays in Native American Ethnopoetics*. Philadelphia: University of Pennsylvania Press.

1985 Language, Memory, and Selective Performance: Cultee's "Salmon's Myth" as Twice Told to Boas. *Journal of American Folklore* 98(390): 391–434.

Irvine, Judith

1987 *The Division of Labor in Language and Society*. Working Papers and Proceedings of the Center for Psychosocial Studies, no. 7. Chicago: Center for Psychosocial Studies.

Itard, Jean-Marc

1932 *The Wild Boy of Aveyron*. Trans. G. Humphrey and M. Humphrey. New York: Century.

Jackson, Jean

1974 Language Identity of the Colombian Vaupés Indians. In *Explorations in the Ethnography of Speaking*, ed. D. Bauman and J. Sherzer, 50–64. New York: Cambridge University Press.

1983 *The Fish People: Linguistic Exogamy and Tukanoan Identity in Northwest Amazonia*. Cambridge: Cambridge University Press.

Jakobson, Roman

1960 Concluding Statement: Linguistics and Poetics. In *Style in Language*, ed. T. A. Sebeok, 350–377. Cambridge: MIT Press.

1966 Grammatical Parallelism and Its Russian Facet. *Language* 42:399–429.

1968 Poetry of Grammar and Grammar of Poetry. *Lingua* 21:597–609.

1980 *The Framework of Language*. Michigan Studies in the Humanities, no. 1. Ann Arbor: University of Michigan.

Karsten, R.

1935 *The Head Hunters of the Western Amazon*. Commentationes humanarum litterarum, Societas Scientiearum Fennica, VII, i. Helsingfors: n.p.

Kent, Patricia

1989 Enactment in the Treatment of Two Patients with Early Parent Loss. Unpublished residency qualifying paper, Department of Psychiatry. Chicago, Michael Reese Hospital.

Lane, Harlan

1976 *The Wild Boy of Aveyron*. Cambridge, Mass.: Harvard University Press.

Léry, Jean de

1972 [1578] *Viagem a terra do Brasil*. São Paulo: Martins/EDUSP.

Lévi-Strauss, Claude

1963 *Totemism*. Trans. R. Needham. Boston: Beacon Press.

1966 *The Savage Mind*. Chicago: University of Chicago Press.

1967 Social Structure. In *Structural Anthropology*, trans. C. Jacobson and B. G. Schoepf, 277–323. Garden City, N.Y.: Anchor.

1969a [1949]   *The Elementary Structures of Kinship.* Trans. J. H. Bell, J. R. von Sturmer, and R. Needham. Boston: Beacon Press.

1969b *The Raw and the Cooked.* (Mythologiques I). Trans. J. Weightman and D. Weightman. New York: Harper and Row, Publishers.

1973   *From Honey to Ashes.* (Mythologiques II). Trans. J. Weightman and D. Weightman. London: Jonathan Cape.

Lutz, Catherine A.

1988   *Unnatural Emotions: Everyday Sentiments on a Micronesian Atoll and Their Challenge to Western Theory.* Chicago: University of Chicago Press.

Lutz, Catherine, and Geoffrey M. White

1986   The Anthropology of Emotions. *Annual Review of Anthropology* 15: 405–436.

Malinowski, Bronislaw

1954   Myth in Primitive Psychology. In *Magic, Science, and Religion,* 93–148. Garden City, N.Y.: Doubleday Anchor Books.

1965   *Coral Gardens and Their Magic.* 2 vols. Vol. 2. Bloomington: Indiana University Press.

Matejka, L., and K. Pomorska

1971   *Readings in Russian Poetics: Formalist and Structuralist Views.* Cambridge, Mass.: MIT Press.

Mauss, Marcel

1979   Body Techniques. In *Sociology and Psychology,* trans. B. Brewster, 97–123. Boston: Routledge and Kegan Paul.

Mertz, Elizabeth, and Richard Parmentier (eds.)

1985   *Semiotic Mediation: Sociocultural and Psychological Perspectives.* New York: Academic Press.

Métraux, Alfred

1928   *La religion des Tupinambá et ses rapports avec celles des autres tribus Tupi-Guaraní.* Paris: Libraire Ernest Lerou.

1947   Mourning Rites and Burial Forms of the South American Indians. *América Indígena* 7(1):7–44.

Migliazza, Ernst C.

1978   Yanomama Diglossia. In *Approaches to Language,* ed. W. C. McCormack and S. A. Wurm, 561–580. The Hague: Mouton.

Mooney, James

1892–1893   *The Ghost-Dance Religion and the Sioux Outbreak of 1890.* 14th Annual Report of the Bureau of Ethnology, part II. Washington, D.C.: U.S. Government Printing Office.

Osgood, Charles E.

1960   Some Effects of Motivation on Style of Encoding. In *Style in Language,* ed. T. A. Sebeok, 293–306. Cambridge: MIT Press.

Propp, Vladimir

1968   *Morphology of the Folktale.* Trans. L. Scott. Austin: University of Texas Press.

1976   Study of the Folktale: Structure and History. *Dispositio: Revista Hispánica de Semiótica Literaria* 1(3):277–292.

Radcliffe-Brown, A. R.

1964 *The Andaman Islanders.* New York: Free Press.

Radin, Paul

1949 *The Culture of the Winnebago: As Described by Themselves.* Indiana University Publications in Anthropology and Linguistics, memoir 2. Baltimore: Waverly Press.

1965 [1933] *The Method and Theory of Ethnology: An Essay in Criticism.* New York: Basic Books.

Ramsey, Jarold

1977 The Wife Who Goes Out Like a Man, Comes Back as a Hero: The Art of Two Oregon Indian narratives. *Modern Language Association Publications* 92:9–18.

1983 *Reading the Fire: Essays in the Traditional Indian Literatures of the Far West.* Lincoln: University of Nebraska Press.

Rivière, Peter

1969 *Marriage among the Trio: A Principle of Social Organization.* Oxford: Clarendon Press.

1971 The Political Structure of the Trio Indians as Manifested in a System of Ceremonial Dialogue. In *The Translation of Culture,* ed. T. O. Beidelman, 293–311. London: Tavistock Publications.

Rosaldo, Michelle Z.

1980 *Knowledge and Passion: Ilongot Notions of Self and Social Life.* New York: Cambridge University Press.

Sacks, Harvey, Emmanuel A. Schegloff, and Gail Jefferson

1974 A Simplest Systematics for the Organization of Turn-taking for Conversation. *Language* 50(4):696–735.

Sapir, Edward

1949 Male and Female Forms of Speech in Yana. In *Selected Writings of Edward Sapir,* ed. D. G. Mandelbaum, 206–212. Berkeley: University of California Press.

Saussure, Ferdinand de

1966 [1915] *Course in General Linguistics.* Ed. C. Bally and A. Sechehaye. Trans. W. Baskin. New York: McGraw-Hill.

Scott, James

1985 *Weapons of the Weak: Everyday Forms of Peasant Resistance.* New Haven: Yale University Press.

Seeger, Anthony

1986 Oratory Is Spoken, Myth Is Told, and Song Is Sung, But They Are All Music to My Ears. In *Native South American Discourse,* ed. J. Sherzer and G. Urban, 59–82. Berlin: Mouton de Gruyter.

1987 *Why Suyá Sing: A Musical Anthropology of an Amazonian People.* Cambridge: Cambridge University Press.

Shapiro, Judith

1972 Sex Roles and Social Structure among the Yanomama Indians of northern Brazil. Ph.D. thesis, Faculty of Political Science, Columbia University. Ann Arbor, University Microfilms.

Sherzer, Joel
    1982 Poetic Structuring of Kuna Discourse: The Line. *Language in Society*
          11:371–390.
    1983 *Kuna Ways of Speaking: An Ethnographic Perspective.* Austin: University
          of Texas Press.
    1987a A Discourse-Centered Approach to Language and Culture. *American An-
          thropologist* 89:295–309.
    1987b A Diversity of Voices: Men's and Women's Speech in Ethnographic Per-
          spective. In *Language, Gender, and Sex in Comparative Perspective,* ed. S.
          Philips, S. Steele, and C. Tanz, 95–120. New York: Cambridge Univer-
          sity Press.
Silverstein, Michael
    1976a Hierarchy of Features and Ergativity. In *Grammatical Categories in Aus-
          tralian Languages,* ed. R. M. W. Dixon, 112–171. Canberra: Australian
          Institute for Aboriginal Studies.
    1976b Shifters, Linguistic Categories, and Cultural Description. In *Meaning in
          Anthropology,* ed. K. Basso and H. Selby, 11–55. Albuquerque: Univer-
          sity of New Mexico Press.
    1985 The Culture of Language in Chinookan Narrative Texts; or, On Saying
          That . . . in Chinook. In *Grammar inside and outside the Clause: Some Ap-
          proaches to Theory from the Field,* ed. J. Nichols and A. C. Woodbury,
          132–171. London: Cambridge University Press.
Singer, Milton
    1984 *Man's Glassy Essence: Explorations in Semiotic Anthropology.* Blooming-
          ton: Indiana University Press.
Singh, J. A. L., and Robert M. Zingg
    1942 *Wolf-children and Feral Man.* New York: Harper and Brothers, Publishers.
Smith, Barbara Herrnstein
    1978 *On the Margins of Discourse: The Relation of Literature to Language.* Chi-
          cago: University of Chicago Press.
Sorensen, Arthur P.
    1967 Multilingualism in the Northwest Amazon. *American Anthropologist* 69:
          670–684.
    1985 An Emerging Tukanoan Linguistic Regionality: Policy Pressures. In
          South American Indian Languages: Retrospect and Prospect, ed. H. E. M.
          Klein and L. Stark, 140–156. Austin: University of Texas Press.
Taussig, Michael
    1980 *The Devil and Commodity Fetishism in South America.* Chapel Hill: Uni-
          versity of North Carolina Press.
    1987 *Shamanism, Colonialism and the Wild Man: A Study in Terror and Healing.*
          Chicago: University of Chicago Press.
Taylor, Douglas R., and Berend J. Hoff
    1980 The Linguistic Repertory of the Island-Carib in the Seventeenth Cen-
          tury: The Men's Language—A Carib Pidgin? *International Journal of
          American Linguistics* 46(4):301–312.

Tedlock, Dennis
1983 *The Spoken Word and the Work of Interpretation.* Philadelphia: University of Pennsylvania Press.
Turner, Terence
1988 Ethno-ethnohistory: Myth and History in Native South American Representations of Contact with Western Society. In *Rethinking History and Myth*, ed. J. D. Hill, 235–281. Urbana: University of Illinois Press.
Turner, Victor
1967 *The Forest of Symbols: Aspects of Ndembu Ritual.* Ithaca: Cornell University Press.
1969 *The Ritual Process: Structure and Anti-Structure.* Chicago: Aldine Publishing.
Urban, Greg
1981a Agent- and Patient-Centricity in Myth. *Journal of American Folklore* 94(373): 323–344.
1981b The Semiotics of Tabooed Food: The Shokleng Case. *Social Science Information* 20(3): 475–507.
1984 Speech about Speech in Speech about Action. *Journal of American Folklore* 97(385): 310–328.
1985 The Semiotics of Two Speech Styles in Shokleng. In *Semiotic Mediation*, ed. E. Mertz and R. Parmentier, 311–329. New York: Academic Press.
1986 Ceremonial Dialogues in South America. *American Anthropologist* 88(2): 371–386.
1988 Ritual Wailing in Amerindian Brazil. *American Anthropologist* 90(2): 385–400.
1989 The "I" of Discourse. In *Semiotics, Self, and Society*, ed. B. Lee and G. Urban, 27–51. Berlin: Mouton de Gruyter.
n.d. The Represented Functions of Speech. In *Reflexive Language*, ed. J. Lucy. Forthcoming.
van Gennep, Arnold
1960 *The Rites of Passage.* Trans. M. B. Vizedom and G. L. Caffee. Chicago: University of Chicago Press.
Voloshinov, V. N.
1986 *Marxism and the Philosophy of Language.* Cambridge: Harvard University Press.
Wagley, Charles
1977 *Welcome of Tears: The Tapirapé Indians of Central Brazil.* New York: Oxford University Press.
Wassén, Henry S.
1949 *Contributions to Cuna Ethnography.* Etnologiska studier series, no. 16. Göteborg: Göteborgs Etnografiska Museum.
Wiesemann, Ursula
1972 *Die phonologische und grammatische Struktur der Kaingáng-Sprache.* Janua linguarum, serie practica, no. 90. The Hague: Mouton.
1978 Os dialetos da língua Kaingang e o Xokleng. *Arquivos de Anatomia e Antropologia*, vol. 3: 199–217. Rio de Janeiro.

Wolf, Ernest S.
  1989 The Self in Psychoanalytic Self Psychology. In *Semiotics, Self, and So-
        ciety*, ed. B. Lee and G. Urban, 15–25. Berlin: Mouton de Gruyter.
Woodbury, Anthony C.
  1985 The Functions of Rhetorical Structure: A Study of Central Alaskan
        Yupik Eskimo Discourse. *Language in Society* 14:153–190.

Index